Neurobehavioral Toxicology

STUDIES ON NEUROPSYCHOLOGY, NEUROLOGY, AND COGNITION

Series Editor:

Linas Bieliauskas, Ph.D.
University of Michigan, Ann Arbor, MI, USA

Other titles in this series:

Fundamentals of Functional Brain Imaging: A Guide to the Methods and their Applications to Psychology and Behavioral Neuroscience. Andrew C. Papanicolaou

Forensic Neuropsychology: Fundamentals and Practice. Edited by Jerry J. Sweet

Neuropsychological Differential Diagnosis. Konstantine K. Zakzanis, Larry Leach and Edith Kaplan

Minority and Cross-Cultural Aspects of Neuropsychological Assessment. Edited by F. Richard Ferraro

Ethical Issues in Clinical Neuropsychology. Edited by Shane S. Bush and Michael L. Drexler

Practice of Child-Clinical Neuropsychology: An Introduction. Byron P. Rourke, Harry van der Vlugt, and Sean B. Rourke

The Practice of Clinical Neuropsychology. A Survey of Practice and Settings. Edited by Greg J. Lamberty, John C. Courtney, and Robert L. Heilbronner

Neuropsychological Rehabilitation: Theory and Practice. Edited by Barbara E. Wilson

Traumatic Brain Injury in Sports. An International Neuropsychological Perspective. Edited by Mark R. Lovell, Ruben J. Echemendia, Jeffrey T. Barth, and Michael W. Collins

Methodological and Biostatistical Foundations of Clinical Neuropsychology and Medical and Health Disciplines. Edited by Domenic V. Cicchetti and Byron P. Rourke

A Casebook of Ethical Challenges in Neuropsychology. Edited by Shane S. Bush

Neurobehavioral Toxicology: Neurological and Neuropsychological Perspectives. Volume I Foundations and Methods. Stanley Berent and James W. Albers

Neurobehavioral Toxicology: Neurological and Neuropsychological Perspectives. Volume II Peripheral Nervous System. James W. Albers and Stanley Berent

Neurobehavioral Toxicology: Neurological and Neuropsychological Perspectives. Volume III Central Nervous System. Stanley Berent and James W. Albers (2006)

Neurobehavioral Toxicology

Neurological and neuropsychological perspectives

Volume I
Foundations and methods

Stanley Berent and James W. Albers

Neurobehavioral Toxicology Program,
Division of Neuropsychology,
Departments of Psychiatry and Neurology,
University of Michigan Medical School,
Ann Arbor, Michigan

Taylor & Francis
Taylor & Francis Group

LONDON AND NEW YORK

First published 2005 by Taylor & Francis,
27 Church Road, Hove, East Sussex BN3 2FA

Simultaneously published in the USA and Canada
by Taylor & Francis
270 Madison Avenue, New York, NY 10016

Taylor & Francis is an imprint of the Taylor & Francis Group

Copyright © 2005 Taylor & Francis

Typeset in Times by RefineCatch Limited, Bungay, Suffolk
Printed and bound in Great Britain by
TJ International Ltd, Padstow, Cornwall
Cover design by Jim Wilkie

British Library Cataloguing in Publication Data
A catalogue record for this book is available from the British Library

Library of Congress Cataloging-in-Publication Data
Berent, Stanley.
  Neurobehavioral toxicology : neuropsychological and neurological
perspectives / Stanley Berent and James W. Albers.
    p. cm.
  Includes bibliographical references and index.
  ISBN 1–84169–564–5 (hard cover)
  1. Behavioral toxicology. 2. Neurotoxicology. I. Albers, James W.
  (James Wilson) II. Title.
  RA1224.B47 2005
  616.8′0471–dc22

                                                    2004025284

ISBN 1-84169-564-5

Contents

Contents of Volume II

Contents of Volume III

From the Series Editor

I am particularly proud to introduce the first of our three volume series *Neurobehavioral Toxicology, Neurological and Neuropsychological Perspectives*. Previous texts regarding the behavioral effects of exposure to neurotoxins have generally been written from somewhat narrowed perspectives, either purely from a medical and neurological standpoint or from a psychological and neuropsychological focus. In either case, either the importance of psychological measurement has been de-emphasized or the accurate identification of underlying neurophysiological mechanisms has been neglected. It was the purpose of this series to produce a collaborative, state-of-the-art product addressing the impact of neurotoxic exposure on behavior.

Both Dr. Berent and Dr. Albers are professors at the University of Michigan and are board certified respectively in Clinical Neuropsychology and in Neurology. Both have published extensively in the area of neurotoxicology, among others, and they approach their subject with a refined expertise based on extensive clinical and research experience. They have collaborated extensively over the years and the fruits of their labors are evident in this series.

Volume I, *Foundations and Methods*, serves as an introduction to the field. Quite often clinicians may approach the subject of neurobehavioral toxicology in a manner which does not do justice to the methods of classification and appreciation of toxin-related information, appropriate interpretation and integration of clinical and research findings, and a genuine appreciation for the contributions of neuropsychology and neurology to the formulation of case impressions. This volume approaches each of these areas in detail, ending with an extensive treatment of how to establish whether causality exists between neurotoxic exposure and apparent behavioral consequences. Too often, both clinicians and researchers have fallen prey to making causal inferences from toxic exposure to behavior without appreciating neurological underpinnings of their subject, the power and limitations of behavioral measures, or even the logic of the process of inference. Volume I serves to provide the background from which the clinical and thought process regarding neurobehavioral toxicology can be rationally engendered, either in appreciating research reports or appraising and interpreting individual clinical data. Volume II, which will follow shortly, will specifically address the impact of neurotoxic exposure on the Peripheral Nervous System, while Volume III will cover the effects of exposure on the Central Nervous System.

This series of volumes is a milestone in the field of neurobehavioral toxicology and is one of the highlights of our series. I strongly commend it to the attention of practicing clinicians, postdoctoral residents and fellows, and all students who wish to seriously approach the subject of the effects of neurotoxins on behavior. The authors are to be applauded on providing what will certainly be a most needed foundation for neurobehavioral understanding of toxic exposure.

Linas A. Bieliauskas
Ann Arbor
October, 2004

Acknowledgments

The authors owe a debt of gratitude to many individuals for their support, encouragement and patience during the long periods of effort required to bring this work to completion. We wish especially to acknowledge our students and colleagues who motivated us to obtain and remain current in the knowledge needed for this work. A special thank you to our families, who made sacrifices along with us while we completed this project (Joy, Melissa, Alison, and Rachel [SB]; Janet, Jeffrey, Matthew, Katherine, and Elizabeth [JWA])

Stanley Berent
James W. Albers

Disclosures

The authors have at times been retained as consulting experts by companies concerned with the manufacture or use of solvents, pesticides, pharmaceuticals or other substances with the potential for toxicity; or by firms representing those companies in litigation. Also, the authors have at times received funding support for research from government agencies, foundations, and private industry.

1 Introduction to neurobehavioral toxicology

Introduction

Volume I of this three-volume book introduces an emerging field, Clinical Neurobehavioral Toxicology, one which we believe will become a primary vehicle when addressing important questions related to the effects of toxins on the nervous system and behavior. There is at present no single, recognized field that encompasses all relevant aspects of this problem area, but there is general recognition that a multidisciplinary response is indicated. Our writings will reflect a multidisciplinary approach to Neurobehavioral Toxicology, with an emphasis on the independent and collaborative contributions of Neurology and Neuropsychology to this endeavor. The present chapter begins with a brief historical perspective and some conceptual considerations. It then focuses on one important biological aspect of the nervous system – neurotransmission – as a way of discussing biological vulnerability and, more specifically, neurotoxicology. Case-related material at times is presented to illustrate the complexity of this area of human understanding.[1] Finally, and since almost nothing occurs in isolation, we conclude the chapter with a discussion of the importance of individual and contextual factors in determining the impact of toxicant-induced damage to the individual.

Many substances affect the human nervous system and its various functions, both positively and negatively. Some are seen as beneficial, while others are considered detrimental or toxic. Interestingly, the amount of a specified substance often determines its characterization as one or the other. Some substances, endogenous (i.e., intrinsic to the organism) as well as exogenous (i.e., extrinsic to the organism), have been hypothesized to play a causative role in a host of specific as well as non-specific disorders. These disorders include progressive neurodegenerative conditions such as Alzheimer disease, Parkinson disease, and motor neuron disease, as well as depression, anxiety, and other neurobehavioral disorders (Grunhaus, Dilsaver, Greden, & Carroll, 1983; Forno, 1992). To complicate matters or, depending on one's viewpoint, to make them more interesting, compounds that are potentially pathogenic exist naturally in the environment. The popular view is often one that considers toxic materials limited to the careless waste of an industrial society or the agents of individual or of mass destruction. In actuality, toxicity is a relative concept that earns its precise definition by consequence. The same agent that is toxic in one circumstance might be non-toxic in another (Cooper, Bloom, & Roth, 1996). Even when toxic, these substances play important roles in nature, e.g., as naturally occurring pesticides and herbicides that aid in plant survival, as animal defenses, and as aids in human and animal neurogenesis and neurotransmission (Goetz, 1985; Cooper, Bloom, & Roth, 1996; Siegel, Agranoff, Albers, Fisher, & Uhler, 1999).

Toxicity is a complex topic. For most of history it has been dealt with intellectually through anecdote and subjective reasoning and, emotionally, with fear and anxiety. While to some extent these tendencies continue, a number of fields have directed scientific attention to the problems associated with toxicity. These include the scientifically based disciplines of Medicine, Psychology, Toxicology, Chemistry, Physiology, Neuroscience, and others. Some of the specialties within these disciplines that have an interest in toxicity include Developmental Psychology, Neuropsychology, Epidemiology, Internal Medicine, Neurology, Nuclear Medicine, Occupational Medicine, Pediatrics, Psychiatry, and the various subspecialties of Toxicology. The approaches to the study of toxicants have become sophisticated, and the knowledge base has become substantial. At the same time, considerable misunderstanding persists, especially amongst the lay population, but also among scientists and other professionals. Also, there is some fragmentation in scientific understanding that appears to result from the fact that there is no one field that encompasses the various discipline- and specialty-specific methodologies applied to the study of toxicants. The multidisciplinary effort represented by Neurobehavioral Toxicology is an attempt to enhance collaboration between these various specialties. Through didactic and case-related material, we will describe in the present volume concepts and methods that we view as particularly relevant to the field. While, as mentioned above, Neurobehavioral Toxicology is a multidisciplinary topic, emphasis will be on two professions, Neuropsychology and Neurology, and how these disciplines interact and complement one another in their approach to this topic. The present work will emphasize methodology, with the inclusion of specific toxicants and clinical entities that relate to the nervous system as needed for illustration.

The approach taken in this work is largely, although not entirely, empirical in nature. That is, the approach is based on observation. However, to the extent possible, we attempt to make our observations verifiable through citation or experiment. We will at times refer to 'science' and the 'scientific method,' and we claim that the fields of Neurology, Neuropsychology, Neurobehavioral Toxicology, and related disciplines are empirical and based on a scientific foundation. While science is empirical, scientific method refers to a specific approach to problem-solving, as discussed further below. We recognize that limits of our knowledge will also limit what can be concluded in a given case. Diagnosis of a medical or neuropsychological condition frequently can be specified even when etiology cannot. For instance, we do not yet know what causes Alzheimer disease, but there are criteria for its diagnosis. While theory plays an important role in the development of such criteria, our developing knowledge requires that adjustments to these criteria be made periodically. Rather than focusing on specific substances, we have chosen to emphasize a science-based, problem-solving approach that will be applied to a variety of neurotoxicological problems. We view such an approach as the best way to address the various clinical and scientific challenges that the professional must meet in order to determine the adverse effects a substance might have, or might have had, on human behavior and the nervous system. When specific compounds are mentioned, we focus primarily on those agents that adversely effect the nervous system, directly or indirectly, with some regularity. The effects of toxic substances must be determined within a framework of differentiation from potentially competing contributions to the clinical picture or scientific problem (i.e., in the form of the differential diagnosis in clinical practice and by control of nuisance variables, or confounders, in research). Because of this, we will also discuss some of the factors that serve to obscure accurate conclusions.

The neurobehavioral approach strives for an objective and scientific analysis of the topic. By scientific, we mean more than the application of the experimental method. Mounting concerns for the environment have led to diverse opinions and sometimes conflicting methodologies about how best to address the issue – from legal and regulatory branches of government, industry, and science to vested interest groups and the lay public. We see these problems as calling for objective and multidisciplinary solutions. To be effective, however, the knowledge base upon which decisions are to be made must be accurate. There is need for a common language and, where possible, consensus in decision-making. Science, it seems to us, represents the best model upon which to base the methods of neurobehavioral toxicology. While the science may not appear to be manifest in all of the clinical approaches and examples described in the various sections that follow, we attempt to remain objective and maintain an empirical approach that relies on scientifically derived information in reaching our conclusions.

Some conceptual considerations

The word 'toxin' has crept into common parlance and is often used to mean something that is poisonous. Strictly speaking, the word 'toxicant' is more correct since toxin has a more technically restricted definition, often referring to substances produced by living organisms and which are injurious to bodily tissue (Merriam-Webster, 1993). Both terms, toxin and toxicant, derive from the ancient Greek word for bow and, later, for the poison in which the arrow was dipped (Merriam-Webster, 1993; Shipley, 1995). The word 'poison' itself has very interesting origins. From Old French and originally Latin (*potare*, to drink), the word was used until medieval times to refer only to an alcoholic drink. With the practice of adding lethal substances to a person's drink for purposes of assassination, the word took on its more sinister meaning (Shipley, 1995). Vestiges of the earlier meaning are still found in everyday English (e.g., 'Name your poison').

Theoretically, anything in sufficient dose can be toxic, including seemingly benign substances such as water and oxygen. The word 'toxicant' in its various forms, however, is generally reserved for substances that have adverse effects in relatively small amounts. From a lay perspective, the concept of what is poisonous and what is not has been largely derived from historical experience. There are a variety of substances that are not included in the concept of toxicity at a given time, even though, in fact, they may later be seen as toxic. They were not included initially, perhaps because their adverse effects may have been too subtle, or because the effects may have occurred too rarely to be noted in historical experience. Sunlight is a fairly recent example of something that for many years was thought to be benign, even desirable, and which now is recognized as toxic, in sufficient doses. Agents that produced a dramatic effect, on the other hand, were more likely to be quickly labeled as 'poisons.' Also, the specific dose required to produce a toxic effect may change in response to new information. Lead is an example of a substance that over time has come to be seen as harmful at lower levels than was originally thought (Harte, Holdren, Schneider, & Shirley, 1991).

A lay understanding of toxicity rests on a historical knowledge base that has been derived, at least in part, serendipitously and, almost certainly, vicariously. Two people go into the forest to find mushrooms. One finds and eats a mushroom, becomes ill and dies. The other witnesses the event, avoids the same fate and brings the knowledge back to the community. Of course, the example just given is a gross oversimplification and almost certainly fails to give proper credit to the ingenuity and cleverness of people to derive increasingly sophisticated methodologies that involve more than simple observation and deductive logic for acquiring knowledge. Before the metal thallium found wide use as a rodenticide, for instance, it was used in the treatment of a variety of illnesses that included syphilis, gonorrhoea, and tuberculosis. The metal never found wide acceptance as a therapeutic agent, however, because of its adverse side-effects (Reed, Crawley, Faro, Pieper, & Kurland, 1963). Thallium was discovered in 1861 by Sir William Crooks and was suspected of being toxic by his contemporary, Claude August Lamy. Lamy tested his hypothesis that thallium was poisonous by feeding it to various animals, which all died within days of ingesting the metal (Reed *et al.*, 1963). Despite such instances of prospective testing to confirm a 'hypothesis,' there is likely to be some element of accuracy in the earlier description of the hypothetical scenario that employed deductive reasoning following a chance experience, a method that is clearly not sufficient for an objective, scientific study of toxicants.

Although a cliché, it is true that when some of us were children, life seemed simpler than today. To us at that time the world contained things that were positive and some that were toxic or otherwise dangerous. We were taught, or learned, to avoid the dangers. There is no doubt that since that time, the world has experienced an increasingly expanding explosion of knowledge. Our previous, perhaps naive, notions of a manageable world, one in which the rules could be learned and dangers avoided by the 'correct' applications of these rules, has been challenged. The word 'challenged' is used purposely. An alternative word would be 'lost.' Since as individuals, and as a society, we can not afford to accept this loss, we continue to believe that we can discover the 'correct' rules by which to live safely.

An objective approach to understanding the effects of toxicants on the nervous system requires some knowledge of normal biological functions. Such knowledge provides a basis for understanding the vulnerabilities of these systems and the mechanisms involved in the impairment of those functions by the introduction of intrinsic or extrinsic substances. While there are a number of ways in which damage can occur in the nervous system (e.g., metabolic disturbance, damage to neuronal membrane, axonal degeneration, and apoptosis), the following section describes some basic aspects of one biological system that is particularly susceptible to toxicant damage: neurotransmission. This system represents, therefore, a convenient model for discussing some basic issues regarding toxicant-induced damage.

Neurotransmission

Intact neurotransmission is a complex process that is necessary to the continued normal functioning of the nervous system. Although some specialized cells communicate to one another by way of direct electrical connections, chemical transmission is the primary mode of communication between cells in the nervous system (Siegel *et al.*, 1999). Siegel *et al.* list five basic steps that occur in chemical transmission of nerve signals, which include the following:

- Synthesis.
- Storage of the neurotransmitter substance.
- Regulated release of the neurotransmitter in the synaptic cleft between the pre- and postsynaptic neurons.
- Presence of specialized receptors that will recognize the specific neurotransmitter on the postsynaptic membrane.
- Capacity to terminate the action of the neurotransmitter following its release.

In its simplest aspects, transmission of signals between cells begins with the release at the presynaptic nerve terminal of a chemical neurotransmitter into the synaptic cleft between the communicating cell and its postsynaptic target cell (Figure 1.1). The neurotransmitter is usually stored in vesicles within the presynaptic cell. In addition, these vesicles play an important role in packaging, transporting, releasing, and recycling the neurotransmitter substance

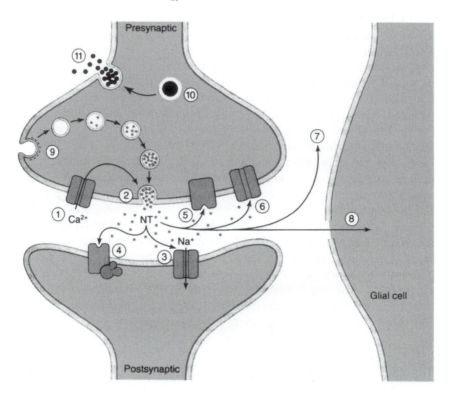

Figure 1.1 Schematic drawing of a cholinergic synapse. ① Depolarization opens volt-
age-sensitive Ca^{2+} channels in the presynaptic nerve terminal. The influx
of Ca^{2+} and the resulting high Ca^{2+} concentrations at active zones on the
plasma membrane trigger ② the exocytosis of small synaptic vesicles that
store neurotransmitter (NT) involved in fast neurotransmission. Released
neurotransmitter interacts with ③ receptors in the postsynaptic membrane,
which couple directly with ion channels and with receptors that act
through second messengers, such as ④ G-protein-coupled receptors.
⑤ Neurotransmitter receptors, also in the presynaptic nerve terminal
membrane, either inhibit or enhance exocytosis upon subsequent depolarization. Released neurotransmitter is inactivated by reuptake into the
nerve terminal by ⑥ a transport protein coupled to the Na^+ gradient, e.g.,
dopamine, norepinephrine, glutamate, and GABA, by ⑦ degradation
(acetylcholine, peptides); or by ⑧ uptake and metabolism by glial
cells (glutamate). The synaptic vesicle membrane is recycled by ⑨ clathrin-
mediated endocysosis. Neuropeptides and proteins are stored in ⑩
larger, dense core granules within the nerve terminal that are released from
⑪ sites distinct from active zones after repetitive stimulation. Reproduced
with permission from Siegel *et al.* (1999).

(Siegel *et al.*, 1999). Once released and its communication function completed, the neurotransmitter is inactivated by one of several mechanisms.
These might include reuptake of the neurotransmitter by the presynaptic cell
through glial absorption or by chemical inactivation by a specific enzyme.

Normally, this process is repeated throughout the nervous system, leading ultimately to the various physiological manifestations needed for survival of the organism.

There are a number of neurotransmitter systems in the nervous system, each with specific and sometimes overlapping anatomical distribution and function. More than 20 individual substances, and more when subtypes are included, have been purported to act as neurotransmitters (Cooper *et al.*, 1996). The best known of these substances includes acetylcholine (ACh), monoamines and enkephalins, peptides, and amino acids (Gilman & Newman, 1996). Specific monoamines include serotonin, epinephrine and norepinephrine, and dopamine. Other specific and probable neurotransmitters include substance P, gamma-aminobutyric acid (GABA), aspartate, and glutamate. Some neurotransmitters are found primarily at inhibitory synapses (e.g., GABA), whereas others are believed to be primarily excitatory (e.g., glutamate) (Gilman & Newman, 1996). Obviously, any antagonistic substance that finds its way to these receptor sites may perturb the usual actions of these chemicals by interfering with one or more of the steps in the process of transmission, disrupting the balance between excitation and inhibition, thus resulting in dysfunction of the nervous system.

Neurotransmission and disease

Because normal functioning depends on the intactness of these neural systems, substances, endogenous as well as exogenous, that have the potential to interfere with their usual actions have been extensively studied with regard to the role they might play in neurodegenerative and other diseases involving the nervous system. Similar to the story of Achilles, these biological systems reflect aspects of vulnerability despite the existence of mechanisms for their protection, e.g., blood–brain, nerve–blood barriers. When the defenses are breached, the result can be disease. The symptoms seen in these diseases almost certainly reflect the functional neuroanatomical regions that have been adversely effected. For instance, the major motor symptoms in Parkinson disease, e.g., akinesia, rigidity and tremor, reflect degenerative changes in the substantia nigra and locus ceruleus and consequential depletion of dopamine in the caudate nucleus and putamen (Forno, 1992; Gilman & Newman, 1996). In Huntington disease, abnormalities of neurotransmission are found in both cortical as well as subcortical levels of the brain, and the clinical manifestations usually reflect a combination of motor, cognitive, and psychiatric symptoms. While, as in Parkinson disease, the caudate and putamen are sites of major damage, in Huntington disease, unlike Parkinson disease, dopaminergic cells remain relatively unperturbed (Forno, 1992). With regard to psychiatric disturbances more specifically, physostigmine has been shown to reduce manic symptoms and worsen depression (Cooper *et al.*, 1996). Other cholinergic drugs have been shown to affect mood, cognition, and additional behaviors as well (Davis, Hollister, Overall, Johnson, & Train,

1976; Risch, Cohen, Janowsky, Kalin, & Murphy, 1980; Greenwald & Davis, 1983).

The cholinergic system has also been implicated in Alzheimer disease, where major damage occurs in the cortex of the brain (Figure 1.2). Impairments of cognitive function are characteristic in Alzheimer disease, especially memory for recently learned material early in the course of this disease (Berent, Giordani, Foster, Minoshima, Lajiness-O'Neill, Koeppe, & Kuhl, 1999). To date, however, research has failed to produce definitive findings with regard to the specific role played by the cholinergic system in Alzheimer disease, and it is likely that multiple systems are involved (Cooper *et al.*, 1996). Also, disease progression represents a major challenge

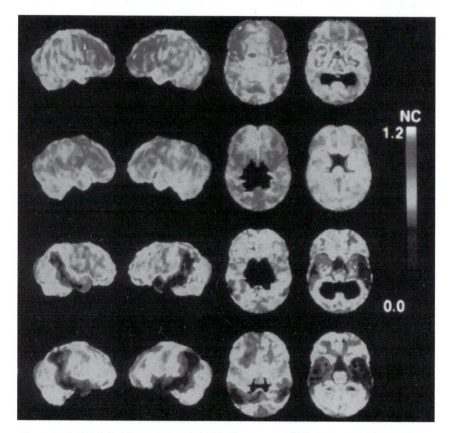

Figure 1.2 Three-dimensional stereotactic surface projections of [¹⁸F]flurodeoxy-glucose position emission tomography (PET) normalized to the thalamus of four subjects of equivalent age comparing results in Alzheimer disease (top row) with isolated memory impairment (middle two rows) and normal metabolic function (bottom row). The relatively lighter regions represent areas of higher metabolism, while relatively darker areas reflect hypometabolism. The authors thank Drs Bruno Giordani and Satoshi Minoshima for help in the construction of these images.

in the study and understanding of any neurodegenerative disease such as Alzheimer disease. There is ample evidence to conclude that the symptoms of memory impairment begin long before an individual meets the clinical diagnostic criteria for Alzheimer disease (Berent *et al.*, 1999). At the same time, there is presently no definitive way to determine the exact point in the progress of this disease when that functional decline begins. The cholinergic system could be of primary importance in one phase of the disease but less so in another. Nevertheless, and because ACh is known to be involved at some point in the degenerative process of the disease, a variety of medications have been tested in Alzheimer disease, based upon their ACh-enhancing or ace-tylcholinesterase (AChE)-inhibiting effects (Krall, Sramek, & Cutler 1999). From a neurotoxicological viewpoint, it is interesting to note the use of these compounds in medicine. This use reflects the notion we presented at the beginning of this chapter, i.e., that a toxicant earns its definition at times by its consequences. The same, or a similar, compound that might be viewed as an insecticide in one circumstance can act as a therapeutic agent in another. This seeming paradox emphasizes the complexities involved in attempting to determine the harmfulness of a particular substance in any given instance.

As mentioned above, the symptoms that accompany neurodegenerative disorders are expected to reflect dysfunction in the affected neuroanatomical region, 'region' being defined by the interaction between a cytoarchitectural location as well as the neurochemical system. This observation has import-ant implications for the practicing clinician, who must differentiate between several competing, potential diagnostic explanations for presenting symp-toms and signs. Since some of the possible explanations will refer to neuro-logical dysfunction and others to experiential or other non-neurological considerations, a knowledge of the expected functional neuroanatomical relationships will allow for a statement about what is, and what is not, biologically sensible.

Aside from consideration of sensible functional anatomic relationships, there are other aspects to a clinical presentation that may leave it appearing more or less congruent with our knowledge about pathology. Clinical course, for instance, has well-recognized characteristics in many disorders. In general, and at the risk of oversimplifying, we expect the symptoms of some disorders (e.g., toxic exposure or physical trauma) to improve over time, often with an expected time course, while the clinical manifestations of other (e.g., neuro-degenerative) diseases are expected to worsen. These and other clinical expectations will be mentioned and discussed in the remainder of this work.

From a clinical perspective, the clinician must consider a host of factors in attempting to understand a given case. Symptoms are most often non-specific, and many disorders share a common clinical presentation. The clin-ician must differentiate between a variety of possibilities (the differential diagnosis) to determine the most likely explanation. Importantly, establishing the correct clinical diagnosis is independent from determining the cause of the problem. Even when exposure to a substance has been documented, or someone else has diagnosed a toxicant-induced disorder, the clinician must remain objective and open to alternative explanations for the patient's condition. Alternatives will include conditions that can be termed 'para- or extra-toxic' since they reflect conditions that may be either unrelated to a suspected toxicant-induced disorder or in addition to that disorder. Some regularly occurring alternatives include degenerative neurological conditions, systemic illnesses, reactive or pre-existing emotional or other psychiatric illness, base-line low ability, and situational considerations (e.g., presence in litigation). To arrive at a correct conclusion requires a combination of scientific and clinical knowledge and an objective approach to problem-solving that considers both.

Neurotoxicity

To have a direct neurotoxic effect (e.g., to cause neuronal loss), an agent must be able to access the nervous system by having the capacity to penetrate the blood–brain or blood–nerve barriers or through some other mechanism, e.g., retrograde transport via nerve terminals. Chemicals also can affect the nervous system secondarily, e.g., through their metabolites or via indirect consequences from action on other organs such as heart, liver, or lung. Once in the nervous system, a neurotoxin may cause reversible effects or irreversible damage. Neurotoxicant-induced damage may be reversible, for instance, if neurons or glial cells become dysfunctional through a mechanism such as distal axonal degeneration or demyelination. However, such damage may be irreversible if the nerve cells die as a result of apoptosis (intrinsic or extrinsic activation of the cell's encoded death program) or oncosis (abrupt fragmentation and cell death because of loss of energy, e.g., oxygen or glucose deprivation). In both situations, recovery of function is possible if the toxicity is removed in time. Depending on the type of damage, recovery will be based upon either a direct process of cellular recovery or by a process of compensation in which other cells take over the functions of the lost cells (McDonald & Windebank, 2000).

Of course, dysfunction in the nervous system can result from substances that are intrinsic to the organism as well as from those that originate in the external environment. The release of toxic substances internally might be the result of disease, or the direct or secondary effects of extrinsic substances that trigger their release. There is evidence as well that experience can interact with biological systems and lead to such release (Cameron, Starkman, & Schteingart, 1995; Starkman, Giordani, Gebarski, Berent, Schork, & Schteingart, 1999). A number of medical conditions can lead to cognitive dysfunction and other impairments. Usually secondary to the primary condition, these symptoms are often reversed with amelioration of the primary problem, even though they may become intractable when the primary condition persists over time. These include the reversible cognitive impairments that are associated directly with the endogenous neurotoxicity of some medical disorders, those that result from conditions of intense or prolonged psychological stress, and impairments that can be viewed as the residuals of prolonged stress (Starkman *et al.*, 1999). We are excluding for the moment the transient changes in neurobehavioral functioning that can occur as a result of side-effects from medications, another example of toxicity. As will be discussed in this volume, toxicity does not occur in isolation, and the complexity of the human organism needs to be considered in arriving at a final conclusion that a specific toxicant is responsible for the patient's condition.

Common clinical neurobehavioral toxicology issues

Clinical neurobehavioral toxicology differs from basic science neurotoxicology in several ways. Whereas the research-oriented toxicologist traditionally studies the dose–response effects and the pathology of a known substance on the experimental organism, the clinician involved in problems related to clinical neurobehavioral toxicology is asked to evaluate an individual patient (or group of individual patients) to establish the explanation for their symptoms and signs. This process involves two separate and distinct questions. First, what is the patient's clinical diagnosis and, second, what is the cause of the problem. The clinician never has to know the cause of a patient's problem in order to establish a diagnosis. Consider, for example, the diagnosis of encephalopathy. The diagnosis, and to some extent even the prognosis, is established independent of knowing the cause of the problem, which could include a variety of diverse considerations. Similarly, the diagnosis of encephalitis can be established with near certainty without knowing that the patient was previously bitten and infected by a mosquito vector with a neurotrophic virus. The basis of this book involves the foundations of Clinical Medicine, Neurology, and Neuropsychology. The most important concept we hope to convey is that the primary responsibility of a clinician acting in the role of a clinical neurobehavioral toxicologist is to be a clinician first and a neurotoxicologist second. Importantly, the attributes related to neurobehavioral toxicology relate specifically to investigating items included in the complete differential diagnosis that could be explained by an exposure to a neurotoxicant. Given this clarification, consider the following presentations, two of which involve individual patients and a third which involves a group of patients. In reading these presentations, consider the issues common to each that are important and relevant to clinical neurotoxicology. The methodologies used to address these questions form the basis for much of what follows in this volume.

Case presentations

Patient with progressive dementia

Case presentation

A 66-year-old retired man was referred by his physician because of increasing forgetfulness and difficulty with activities of daily living of about 18 months' duration.[2] He complained of difficulty following and understanding conversations, but deferred to his wife when asked about specific details. The past medical and family histories were unremarkable, other than treated hypertension. He reported doing well in school, successfully completing high school with average grades, confirmed by subsequent review of his educational transcripts. He had worked as a welder for almost 40 years, retiring several years previously. The general medical examination results were normal, as was the neurological examination, except for abnormal mental status examination results. Specifically, he showed an impaired short-term memory, and he performed poorly on the Mini-Mental State Examination (MMSE), scoring 22 of 30 (Folstein, Folstein, & McHugh, 1975). Emotionally, he appeared mildly depressed. His wife indicated his loss of interest in most of his past work and leisure-time activities, although he denied feeling depressed.

On formal neuropsychological testing, he did poorly in all relevant domains. In terms of intellect, he earned scores that placed him near the border of deficient performance (Wechstler Adult Intelligence Scale – Revised [WAIS-R] Verbal Intelligence Quotient [VIQ]: 69, Performance Intelligence Quotient [PIQ]: 74) (The Psychological Corporation, 1981). Despite some difficulties with language (e.g., Vocabulary [SS = 5]), there was no indication of generalized aphasia. His performance was impaired on most cognitive measures. There was no indication of major affective disorder or thought disorder. Table 1.1 shows the results from neuropsychological examination of this patient, as well as data from two past examinations of the same patient. The significant decline in performance experienced by the patient over 2 years is readily apparent from these serial test results.

Clinical approach

At this point, the clinician is faced with several important tasks, none of which is concerned initially with identifying the cause of this patient's problem. The first task is to address the question of whether or not a neurobehavioral or neurological problem even exists. As trivial as this question may seem, it is the most difficult problem faced by the clinician (e.g., distinguishing normal from abnormal; see Chapter 4 for a fuller discussion of this issue), and the problem most frequently addressed during training. In the context of the present example, this initial task is to verify objectively the presence of dementia, regardless of its etiology. The primary difficulty for the clinician is

Table 1.1 Results of serial testing in a patient with symptoms of dementia.

Test administered	Domain measured	Test results		
		Year 0–2	Year 0–1	Year 0
WAIS-R, VIQ (The Psychological Corporation, 1981)	Verbal intellect	82	77	69
WAIS-R, PIQ	Performance intellect	98	77	74
WAIS-R, Vocabulary	Vocabulary level	8	6	5
WAIS-R, Similarities	Abstract conceptualization	7	6	4
WAIS-R, Block design	Visual–motor problem-solving	9	6	6
WAIS-R, Digit symbol	Psychomotor problem-solving	8	4	5
MMSE	General mental status	28/30	N/A	22/30
WMS, MQ (Wechsler, 1945)	General memory and orientation	82	87	60
WMS, Passages	Verbal recall, per cent retained	60	66	10
WMS, Visual reproductions	Visual recall, per cent retained	72	69	30
WRAT-3, Reading (Wilkinson, 1993)	Reading recognition	N/A	90	61
Depression ratings	Clinical ratings of depression	Moderate depression	Mild depression	Mild depression

Selected tests were chosen that were repeated across all three examinations and that reflected a range of neuropsychological domains sufficient to discern a meaningful clinical pattern.

MMSE, Mini-Mental State Examination; PIQ, Performance Intelligence Quotient; VIQ, Verbal Intelligence Quotient; WAIS-R, Wechsler Adult Intelligence Scale–Revised; WMS, MQ = Wechsler Memory Scale, Mental Quotient; WRAT-3, Wide Range Achievement Test–3.

establishing evidence of a decline in function beyond baseline (loss of function) which is greater than can be explained by 'normal' aging alone. Assuming that the answer to this question is 'yes', the next question involves localization of the patient's problem within the nervous system. For problems involving cognition, the localization is straightforward, and although dementia is a behavioral condition, a cortical neuroanatomical localization is implied by its presence. Only after the presence of a problem is established and localized within the nervous system is the differential diagnosis developed. As indicated elsewhere in this chapter, the differential diagnosis is simply a list of possible explanations for the patient's neurological or neurobehavioral problem. The methodology used to establish the differential diagnosis involves many factors, including the onset and temporal profile of the disorder (see Chapter 6 and elsewhere in this volume for more detailed discussion about the diagnostic process). In terms of 'dementia', the clinical diagnosis can be verified in terms of standard methodologies, and it is possible that other considerations, such a depressed mood, would also need to be investigated.

Some may find the process of separating the clinical diagnosis from the cause of the problem unnecessary, as many diagnoses seem to incorporate both. Consider, for example, the diagnosis of multi-infarct dementia – both the clinical diagnosis (dementia) and the cause (cerebrovascular disease) are included. However, the diagnosis of dementia is established independent of causal consideration because a host of disorders can underlie this condition. In general, the potential 'causes' of dementia include cerebrovascular, infectious, neoplastic, structural, hereditary, toxic, metabolic, psychological, psychiatric, and even iatrogenic considerations.

Once the presence of dementia has been documented and differentiated from other conditions that have similar clinical characteristics (e.g., delirium, schizophrenia, major depression, factitious disorder), the etiology must be determined. This is an important part of the diagnostic process in cases of dementia, because some causes are reversible or treatable, and early initiation of treatment is often critical (American Academy of Neurology, 2001). Once possible causes for the patient's condition have been identified, the clinician must independently verify or exclude each possibility. This is accomplished by comparison with formal criteria and reasoned argument. The approaches used to accomplish this task will be discussed at various points in the remainder of this volume (see especially Chapters 4–8). One set of formal criteria or questions used to establish causation are referred to as Hill criteria (Hill, 1965).[3]

Once developed, individual items listed as potential causes capable of producing the conditions in the differential diagnosis are evaluated, and the results of the evaluation are used to eliminate certain items, and, occasionally, to add others. For example, laboratory testing used to evaluate the problem of progressive dementia might show normal thyroid function results, thereby excluding hypothyroidism from consideration as a cause of the patient's dementia. Similarly, a normal cerebrospinal fluid examination would make an infection explanation unlikely. However, the results may have identified the presence of a substantial anemia, suggesting other systemic explanations, including vitamin B12 deficiency or even malignancy as causal considerations. Once the purported cause or etiology of the condition has been proposed, it must undergo review or verification, again using standard methodologies.

Additional questions relevant to the case presentation

Regarding verification of the diagnosis of dementia, the results of the clinical data would be compared with formal diagnostic criteria. For example, there are four primary elements in the DSM-IV (American Psychiatric Association, 1994) criteria for dementia, namely: (1) memory impairment; (2) multiple cognitive impairments, but at least one in addition to memory; (3) impaired social or occupational functioning; and (4) the impairments reflect a decline from prior levels of functioning. These criteria could be applied before establishing a final diagnosis. Concluding that there has been a decline in functioning from previously higher levels, the final element listed above can be one of the most challenging problems facing the clinician. To reach this conclusion, the clinician must find some objective basis for determining a baseline with which to compare the patient's present performance. Records of past schooling may contain the results of aptitude or achievement tests or even IQ tests. Similar information can sometimes be found in records of past employment or military service. When past records are unavailable, the clinician must rely on approximations of past levels of performance using information from current behavioral measures, e.g., reading and vocabulary levels, and other indices of past performance. Once a baseline has been established and the clinician has concluded a decline in function, it is necessary to consider the rate of that decline over time in comparison with expected normal aging (Berent & Giordani, 1998). On occasion, the advantage of having the results of serial testing on the patient permits us to go beyond the minimum criteria for establishing a diagnostic and statistical Manual (DSM)-based diagnosis of dementia (e.g., American Psychiatric Association, 1994) and speak to the progressive nature of the patient's condition (Table 1.1). In doing so, we may have evidence highly suggestive of a specific diagnosis, such as Alzheimer disease,[4] a disorder that can be diagnosed with substantial specificity, despite this being a disease of unknown cause.

Given these considerations, what aspects of the evaluation are changed when we consider the patient's occupational history? Certainly the history of any occupational exposure to a neurotoxicant does not influence the clinical diagnosis of dementia, a condition that was established without consideration of etiology. What does change is the possibility that an occupational exposure to some identified or suspected neurotoxicant now should appear in the list of potential causes for this patient's dementia. The list is then addressed using the same methodologies outlined above (and discussed in detail elsewhere in this volume) to establish causation. These considerations will reflect among other things current knowledge from the animal and human literature as well as the objective and evidence-based approaches presented in Chapter 4 and issues of causal attribution discussed in Chapter 8.

The final diagnosis in this case was *probable Alzheimer disease*. The reader might wish to consider why the potential exposure to toxicants in the patient's history was excluded in the final diagnosis. From the evaluating clinician's viewpoint, the best reasons for this exclusion were based on the fact that the patient's symptoms occurred after he was removed from exposure and, perhaps most important, his decline in ability was rapidly progressive. Still, one might ask, what other information would be important to further verify the final diagnosis?

Patient with depression and suspected dementia

The preceding case presentation contains a number of factors that must be considered in order to determine objectively the adverse effects of toxicants on the nervous system, or to exclude them as playing a causative role. In that patient, the clinician was challenged to go beyond a conclusion based solely on association (i.e., the patient's symptoms in the context of a history of work-related exposure to toxicants) in establishing a diagnosis of idiopathic Alzheimer disease. The example reflected issues related to a systematic approach to problem-solving that included the objective verification of presenting complaints, their nature, and consideration of the (scientifically derived knowledge regarding) biological and clinical plausibilities of the findings in reaching final conclusions. Now, consider how the medical information associated with the following case presentation influenced this patient's evaluation.

Case presentation

A 39-year-old female executive was referred for evaluation of depression and possible cognitive decline of about 2 years' duration. Her past medical history was remarkable for a similar 2-year history of significant weight gain with truncal obesity and abdominal striae, increased facial hair, facial flushing, rounded (moon) facies, and irregular menstruation. At the time of an earlier evaluation, she was found to have a persistently elevated blood glucose level, an elevated urinary free cortisol level, and a low adrenocorticotropic hormone (ACTH) level diagnostic of Cushing syndrome. Computerized tomography of the abdomen identified an adrenal mass. Treatment consisted of adrenalectomy with identification of a benign adrenal adenoma.[5] She subsequently developed amenorrhea, which was treated with hormone replacement. Her hypertension was controlled by dietary restriction, and her diabetes resolved. Her clinical diagnoses included Cushing syndrome,[6] depression, and mild hypertension.

Neurobehavioral disorders at the time of her initial evaluation included mood disorder, adjustment and treatment compliance issues, and the presence of possible cognitive dysfunction. Her neuropsychological examination showed a normal general mental status and normal intellectual ability. While her general intellect was in the normal range, the presence of mild difficulty with short-term memory and problem-solving raised the possibility that her intellect was potentially higher than manifested, i.e., that there had been some decline from her baseline functioning. Also, she was moderately depressed (Table 1.2). Both cognitive and affectual diagnoses fulfilled conventional diagnostic criteria, respectively. The more difficult issue involved identifying

Table 1.2 Selected scores from neuropsychological examinations for a patient with history of Cushing syndrome and adrenalectomy.

Test administered	Examination I: scores	Examination II: scores
WAIS-R, FSIQ (Wechsler, 1945)	99	117
WAIS-R, VIQ	100	119
WAIS-R, PIQ	98	115
Vocabulary	11	11
Comprehension	9	10
Similarities	11	14
Digit span	9	14
Picture arrangement	9	13
WMS MQ	105	120
WMS, IV, per cent recall	56	89
WMS, VI, per cent recall	100	96
Category test	47 errors	19 errors
Self-rating	Moderately depressed	Not depressed
SCL-90-R (Derogatis, 1977, 1983)	Elevated on somatic concerns, isolation, and hostility	No significant elevations
MMSE	30 of 30	30 of 30

FSIQ, Full Scale Intelligence Quotient; SCL-90-R, Symptom Checklist-90-Revised. For other abbreviations, see Table 1.1.

the cause of her neurobehavioral impairments. Thorough evaluation for potential causes of mild cognitive impairment showed normal results, including cerebral imaging, electroencephalogram studies, and additional routine tests of blood and urine, separate from the abnormalities associated with her diagnosis of Cushing syndrome. Unlike the first case presentation of dementia discussed above, there were no concerns about some exogenous exposure producing her problem. On the contrary, the primary concern was that of an endogenous 'exposure' associated with her systemic Cushing syndrome.

The important point is that the presence or absence of a suspected exposure should not influence the process by which causation is established. Important to the current case presentation were additional concerns related to the patient's life situation, which included psychosocial issues related to family concerns, issues surrounding her work as an executive, and emotional concerns related to her medical diagnoses, prognosis, and treatments. As will be discussed in Volume III, the primary diagnosis of Cushing syndrome is capable of explaining most, if not all, of the patient's symptoms and signs in this case. The 'neurotoxicant' involves exposure to excess cortisol produced by an adrenal tumor, and this medical condition appeared to explain all of the patient's symptoms. These included changes in her symptoms over time and, most importantly from a neurobehavioral viewpoint, the 2-year time course for these changes in her mood and cognition. However, the final explanation is not necessarily specific, and, as often is the case, findings related to the presence or absence of deterioration over time were important in establishing causation. The diagnosis of Cushing-related mood disorder anticipated almost perfectly the eventual improvement in her depression, with similar improvement in her clinical symptoms. A large body of consistent research evidence, including epidemiological and animal modeling that links excess cortisol to the kinds of symptoms experienced by the patient, supports this explanation. In addition, removal from the endogenous exposure through surgery and subsequent lowering of cortisol levels was accompanied by improved function in all areas that had been initially affected. Depression itself could arguably be presented as an alternative explanation for both her behavioral impairments on presentation and her improved functioning following treatment. This explanation was excluded, however, because the pattern of cognitive impairment revealed within and between the two examinations did not correspond to the expected clinical pattern for depression (Zakzanis, Leach, & Kaplan 1999). The pattern of strengths and weaknesses did fit those that have been associated with Cushing's syndrome (Starkman, Gebarski, Berent, & Schteingart 1992) and, as will be discussed below with expected changes that follow lowering of cortisol in the brain (Starkman *et al.*, 1999).

Issues related to the case presentation

While the patient in the present case study did not meet formal clinical criteria for dementia (American Psychiatric Association, 1994), her cognitive functioning was discernibly lowered as a result of her underlying medical condition. Both mood and cognition were adversely affected, and both these domains improved following resolution of the underlying pathology. It is conceivable that the patient's cognitive dysfunction was secondary to depression. However, and in addition to the mention above of the expected neuropsychological patterns in depression, there is ample evidence that cognition is directly affected in the type of medical condition suffered by the patient in this example, independent of depression (Starkman *et al.*, 1992; Zakzanis *et al.*, 1999). Nevertheless, it remains possible that depression, and its improvement, contributed to the patient's symptoms and the change in those symptoms that followed treatment. This possibility could most likely be further clinically verified or excluded over time through serial examinations. The biological effects of her medical condition at the time, however, appeared to represent the simplest explanation for the entirety of her clinical picture and were chosen as the most likely etiology (see Chapter 8 for a discussion of causal determination).

We do not yet have a complete understanding of the nature of neuronal dysfunction involved in cases such as the one presented above. However, it is known that limbic structures in the brain, and especially the hippocampus, are particularly sensitive to the impairing affects of excess cortisol (Starkman *et al.*, 1992). Until fairly recently, we believed that central nervous system neurons were incapable of regeneration. We now know this is not the case, and that there may be several ways in which such regeneration can occur (McEwen, 1999a, 1996b; Duman, Malberg, Nakagawa, & D'Sa 2000; Duman, 2001). Degeneration and regeneration of underlying neuronal function have been studied in relation to corticosteroids (Lupien & McEwen, 1997; Lupien, Nair, Briere, Maheu, Tu, Lemay, McEwen, & Meaney 1999), and these mechanisms may explain the changes that resulted in this patient's clinical presentation following successful medical treatment. In addition to its reflection of underlying neurological dysfunction as a result of a medical condition, this case represents an important type of disorder that is capable of producing reversible dementia, one of a number of conditions that are likely to occur relatively frequently in clinical practice. Yet, under the right circumstances, this type of case could be confusing in terms of etiology. For instance, what if the patient had presented to the clinician complaining of having been exposed to environmental toxicants?

Exogenous conditions producing endogenous change

An important consideration related to the preceding case presentation involves the possibility that changes in the environment produce changes in the chemistry and structure of the brain. This is accomplished through the brain's hormonal system, which, under the control of the pituitary gland and related structures, allows environmental stimuli to influence hormonal secretion of the adrenals, thyroid, and gonads (McEwen, 2000). In some instances, these chemicals have an enhancing effect, while at other times they may be functionally adverse (McEwen, 1999a). Nevertheless, the system can be seen as adaptive for the survival of the organism in that it contributes to homeostasis. Consider, for example, an instance where a person is confronted with a fearful, fight–flight, situation. If the person survives the encounter, he or she may learn to avoid that situation in the future. While this seems a reasonable outcome at first glance, there may be good reasons from the viewpoint of survival to return to the now feared location. All of us have had this type of experience, having to go back to a situation that had been adverse in some way. Sometimes, it requires considerable courage to accomplish this, and the renewed approach often is accompanied by a learned anxiety response that is in itself painful. If painful enough, the anxiety might even prevent us from completing the second encounter, or the person might decide on some strategy to deal with the anxiety, i.e., a specific psychological defense mechanism. If survival depends on going back to the now feared location, however, the most adaptive thing would be to forget (i.e., to extinguish) the previously learned response or, at least, to render it less intense. It has been shown that adrenal steroids enhance the extinction of a previously conditioned avoidance response (McEwen, 1999a; McEwen, De Kloet, & Rostene 1986). Such extinction, in turn, increases the likelihood that the organism will go back to a situation that it has learned to avoid. If food or some other necessary commodity is to be found there, then the process has restored a proper balance between self-protection and risk that lends to the organism's survival. In addition to enhancing learning extinction, the adrenal steroids have been implicated in selective attention, consolidation of learned information, and aspects of coping with repeated stresses (McEwen, Gould, Orchinik, Weiland, & Woolley 1995; McEwen & Sapolsky, 1995; Lupien & McEwen, 1997; McEwen, 1999a).

So, what is the price of these evolutionary adaptations? It has been convincingly shown that excesses of these chemicals in the brain are associated with a variety of neurobehavioral dysfunctions. Starkman *et al.* (1992), for instance, used magnetic resonance imaging and neuropsychological tests to show that hypercortisolemia was associated with reduced hippocampal volume in the human brain. In addition, they demonstrated significant positive correlations between hippocampal volume and scores on neuropsychological tests of verbal learning and memory. In a later work, the same group reported on the reversibility of these phenomena. That is, hippocampal volume increased, at least in part, once cortisol levels were decreased as a result of successful treatment of the patient's Cushing syndrome (Starkman *et al.*, 1999). These changes were also associated with improved neuropsychological functioning (Giles, Giordani, Ryan, Berent, Schteingart, Schultz, Kauszler, Gebarski, & Starkman 2001).

Importance of context with regard to toxic exposure

Exposure to toxicants always occurs within some context, and the nature of the experience can carry its own implications for the exposed person's reactions and, in the clinical setting, their symptoms. A person, for instance, might be knowingly exposed to toxic substances because these materials are being used as a component in a treatment regimen for a medical condition, e.g., cancer. In contrast, the exposure could occur as a result of the person's employment or in the course of having a home treated for insect infestation. The individual might view the exposure as a product of their own error, or they might perceive the exposure as the result of someone else's negligence, or even as an act of nature. Exposure could occur in the course of war or as the result of a terrorist act. Each of these possible circumstances, and others not here specified, can have unique psychological consequences for the individual as well as for the symptoms that subsequently follow exposure. Such factors, together with a host of additional individual differences in personal history and manner of coping style, present challenges to the researcher interested in discovering the effects of the exposure and to the clinician who must determine an accurate diagnosis. Often, these 'para-neurotoxic' variables represent significant confounders, if not complete explanations, for research findings. In clinical practice, these factors might also serve as partial or complete explanations for a patient's symptoms and signs. In the context of a specific research or clinical problem, these potential influences should be identified and addressed. They should always be considered in a differential diagnosis in clinical practice. Because of their importance, we will focus on this aspect of neurobehavioral toxicology at times. In the remainder of this chapter, such factors will be considered and discussed around specific cases when relevant. The scenario that follows demands such consideration in order to achieve a reasonable understanding of the situation. While some aspects of this understanding are directly related to the toxicant, it may be more important in this particular case to consider the context of exposure and to individual reactions to the situation.

Exposure to a neurotoxicant in the context of a terrorist act

On 20 March 1995, a terrorist attack occurred on the Tokyo subway system. Sarin, an agent that has been used in military actions as a 'toxic nerve gas', served as the weapon in this attack. Interestingly, this same gas was employed less than a year before (27 June 1994) in an incident in a residential area of Matsumoto, Japan, that also was believed to be the work of terrorists (Morita, Yanagisawa, Nakajima, Shimizu, Hirabayashi, Okudera, Nohara, Midorikawa, & Mimura 1995). Five thousand five hundred people were injured in the Tokyo incident, with eleven fatalities, while 600 were injured in Matsumoto, with seven fatalities (Morita *et al.*, 1995; Matsui, Ohbu, & Yamashina, 1996). Sarin is an organophosphorus AChE inhibitor (Matsui *et al.*, 1996), although its actions are complex and adversely effect multiple aspects of the cholinergic system. Dysregulation can occur as a result of sarin exposure by way of its impact on choline acetyltransferase, anticholinesterase, receptor sites, and various other aspects of the nervous system. In both incidents in Japan, the symptoms were initially surprisingly mild and transient in most individual survivors and reportedly included visual changes and ocular pain, vomiting, dyspnea, headaches, and some mild cognitive problems. One report of the 1994 incident described five patients with critical cardiopulmonary or respiratory arrest. Two of these patients died and three recovered completely (Matsui *et al.*, 1996). One hundred and six patients were described as having mild to moderately severe symptoms, with the remaining patients suffering only mild symptoms as a direct result of exposure to the toxicant. Most were released within 6 hours of hospital admission, and, except for traumatic stress reactions, all signs and symptoms disappeared within a few weeks (Matsui *et al.*, 1996). With regard to stress, emotional reactions were reportedly not uncommon, and these were attributed to post-traumatic stress disorder in at least two reports (Matsui *et al.*, 1996; Yokoyama, Araki, Murata, Nishikitani, Okumura, Ishimatsu, & Takasu,

1998). Almost all symptoms of the sarin exposure itself as reported in these studies were said to have resolved within 30 days of exposure, with no sequelae in most people (Morita *et al.*, 1995).

Discussion

CONSIDERATION OF THE TOXICANT

AChE is a particularly well-studied, although less than completely understood, substance whose role in neurotransmission has been known since the 1920s (Cooper *et al.*, 1996) or even earlier (Siegel *et al.*, 1999). ACh serves as the active neurotransmitter, with varying actions depending on multiple receptor types. The enzyme choline acetyltransferase is the catalyst in ACh synthesis, while the enzyme AChE serves as a catalyst to the hydrolysis of the choline ester and inactivates ACh (Cooper *et al.*, 1996). Although the distribution of ACh goes beyond the nervous system (Siegel *et al.*, 1999), it is the primary neurotransmitter in the peripheral nervous system (PNS). In the central nervous system (CNS), ACh is found in several nuclear clusters with extensive projections to various cortical and subcortical areas of the brain, including frontal and parietal cortex and the hippocampus (Gilman & Newman, 1996).

The cholinergic system, of course, is much more complex than described here. For instance, ACh may serve multiple roles in the nervous system, as a hormone or modulator of neurotransmission in addition to the more strict role of neurotransmission (Cooper *et al.*, 1996). There are also multiple types of cholinergic receptor, the two primary classes being muscarinic and nicotinic, each further divided into subclasses. Likewise, there are multiple cholinesterases, with differing susceptibility to chemical inhibitors. The various receptor sites of the cholinergic system are often found in discrete anatomical locations, with direct implications for physiological functions mediated by these areas. For instance, the ACh stimulation in sweat glands can lead to diaphoresis, while blockade may produce anhidrosis. Muscarinic and nicotinic receptors are found in both the PNS and CNS, and both are widespread in the CNS (Siegel *et al.*, 1999).

There are natural and synthetic agents, endogenous as well as exogenous, that have the capacity to disrupt cholinergic-mediated neurotransmission. The mechanisms by which such disruption can occur is better understood for some aspects of neurotransmission than it is for others. A number of substances are known to cross the blood–brain barrier and, through specifically differing mechanisms of action, cause disruption of ACh-mediated neurotransmission. Atropine and scopolamine, for instance, are both known to decrease brain ACh levels (Siegel *et al.*, 1999). Acute overdoses of organophosphorus compounds, as occurred in the sarin incidents described above, inhibit cholinesterase (ChE) and AChE, leading to an over-accumulation of ACh (Maroni & Catenacci, 1994) and producing a variety of changes in the behaviors mediated by these systems. These changes include weakness, fasciculation, hypersalivation, dizziness, visual disturbances, sweating, bradycardia, tremor, convulsions, psychotic symptoms, coma, and death (Bleeker, 1994). Some of the adverse effects of cholinesterase inhibition can be antagonized with atropine, presumably because of its inhibition of ACh. There is also evidence from animal studies that even one pretreatment with AChE can significantly reduce the behavioral and lethal effects of acute organophosphate exposure (Doctor, Blick, Caranto, Castro, Gentry, Larrison, Maxwell, Murphy, Schutz, & Waibel, 1993). In actuality, these processes are more complex than this scenario might suggest. For instance, AChE inhibition can occur through a number of differing mechanisms. Also, the consequences of inhibition may differ from one synapse to another and from one receptor type to another (Siegel *et al.*, 1999). The antagonistic effects of atropine, for example, are muscarinic. Other factors of course (e.g., dose, duration) contribute to the effect of a substance in any given instance. With regard to the sarin incidents in Japan, we know very little about the amount of exposure in the individual cases. However, serum ChE values were measured in many instances, and it was reported that the more severely injured of the victims had the lowest values (Matsui *et al.*, 1996). Regardless of dose, however, it appeared from the reports that those who survived the period of acute intoxication went on to full recovery (Matsui *et al.*, 1996), underscoring the reversibility of many toxic exposures.

CONSIDERATION OF THE CONTEXT IN WHICH THE EXPOSURE OCCURRED

Disasters are often described as being 'natural' (e.g., the result of a storm or earthquake) or 'human made' (e.g., industrial accidents or, as in the present instance, acts of terrorism) (Baum, 1991). According to Baum, the effects of human-made disasters are likely to be more persistent than are those that result from natural disasters, becoming chronic distress in some cases.

   The exposures in Japan occurred within a context of a human-made disaster: terrorism. There is a substantial body of literature on the effects of terror and other acts of aggression on human functioning (VandenBos & Bryant, 1991). One aspect to such events is the stress it represents to those involved, and we discussed above some aspects of the relationship between stress and biological function. Aside from these biological considerations, there are predictable behavioral sequelae that can be expected to occur within the context of such acts (Frederick, 1991). While we may know more about human reactions to disasters other than those caused by terrorist acts (e.g., physical trauma, assault, sexual abuse), there are some common elements to be found in all of these disasters (VandenBos & Bryant, 1991). According to Frederick (1991), and with regard to survivors of terrorism specifically, one can expect to see emotional disturbance in the majority of cases to some degree. This reaction is independent of the type of stressors involved, i.e., toxicant or other weapon. Reactions can be pervasive and affect other aspects of the individual's life – family, work, or personal comfort. Depending on individual circumstance, these reactions can persist for long periods, in some cases with only superficial adjustment. A few psychological reactions that can be expected might include anxiety, phobias, recurrent thoughts, depression, fearfulness, feelings of guilt, flattened affect, loss of concentration, difficulties with memory, and self-blame. Psychophysiological reactions can also occur and might include sleep disturbance, gastrointestinal problems, sexual dysfunction, respiratory disorders, vertigo, hypertension, diaphoresis, weight change, hyper-alertness/startle, tachycardia, and others (Frederick, 1991).

CONSIDERATION OF INDIVIDUAL REACTIONS

As described in the Japan sarin incidents, anxiety disorder (more specifically, Post-traumatic Stress Disorder or PTSD) was a relatively common diagnostic finding and may have accounted for continuing symptoms beyond initial treatment in many cases. Also, as just reviewed, reactions to stress can in themselves produce many symptoms in common with reactions to toxic exposure. Symptoms of anxiety often coexist with depression and are commonly seen in clinical practice, whether or not a toxicant is involved (Nisenson, Pepper, Schwenk, & Coyne, 1998). There are those who view the occurrence of emotional symptoms (anxiety and depression) following exposure to a toxicant to be the direct result of toxicity (Bolla & Roca, 1994). While this could be true in a given case, it is unlikely that such a reaction would occur in isolation or persist in the absence of amelioration of other toxicant-induced symptoms, as was the case in the sarin incident. Regardless of one's theoretical predilection, each individual case will have to be evaluated on its own merits and within the context of considering all of the potentially relevant factors in order to arrive at accurate conclusions regarding both effect(s) and cause(s). The individual history will be critical in such evaluation. Since emotional disturbance is fairly common in the general population, one might expect to find a number of people with such problems in evaluating a group as large as that seen following the Japan incidents. It would be wrong to assume that these findings were the result of exposure to the toxicant, or even to the disaster experience, without first exploring all factors that might predict such a condition. It is equally important to recognize that factors other than the direct effects of exposure to a toxicant can explain and account for many of the debilitating symptoms that accompany an exposure incident.

Comments

The preceding discussions reveal that we are dealing with very complex systems in attempting to discern the effects of toxicants on the nervous system and behaviour. In so doing, we rely on a scientifically derived database that is revealing in many ways, but also incomplete and continuously changing. Care should be taken in attempting to attribute clinical signs and symptoms to a specific chemical using partial or circumstantial evidence. Even in those instances where our knowledge of some aspect of neurotransmission is more complete, e.g., nicotinic receptors of the cholinergic system, one should always keep in mind that there is a difference between what *can* occur and what *does* occur. Because of this, we have focused here on many factors that may at first appear to be only remotely related to the topic of toxicology. Our approach is founded on the bias that toxicants do not cause adverse effects in isolation. That is, the human organism is a complex array of interactions (e.g., the actions of a substance on the organism, the organism's reactions to those actions, and the multitude of interactions that accompany both), and that one has to consider a variety of component parts in order to understand the effects of one.

In the chapters that follow, we will detail the clinical and clinical research approaches to understanding the effects of toxicants on humans, as a group as well as in a given individual.

Notes

1   For all clinical case material, details of the history have been modified to preserve the anonymity of patients and their families.
2   Details of the history have been modified to preserve the anonymity of the patient and his family.
3   See Chapter 4 and elsewhere in this volume for a fuller description of these criteria for establishing a toxic etiology.
4   Since the results of pathological examination are required to make a final and conclusive designation of Alzheimer disease, convention leads to the addition of a modifier, 'probable,' which can be removed once the results of the pathology report are known.
5   Details of the history have been modified to preserve the anonymity of the patient and her family.
6   The term 'Cushing syndrome' has been applied traditionally to a clinical picture that results from excess of cortisol, regardless of cause. The term 'Cushing disease' has been used to refer specifically to hyperfunction of the adrenal cortex as a result of excess pituitary ACTH (Berkow, 1982; Hudson, Hudson, Griffing, Melby, & Pope, 1987).

References

American Academy of Neurology (2001). *AAN guideline summary for point of care: detection, diagnosis and management of dementia*. American Academy of Neurology (available at: http://www.aan.com/professional/practice/index.cfm).

American Psychiatric Association (1994). *Diagnostic and statistical manual of mental disorders* (4th ed.). Washington, DC: APA.

Baum, A. (1991). Toxins, technology, and natural disasters. In G. R. VandenBos and B. K. Bryant (Eds.), *Cataclysms, crises, and catastrophes* (pp. 9–53). Washington, DC: American Psychological Association.

Berent, S., & Giordani, B. (1998). Functional neuroimaging correlates of memory dysfunction in neurodegenerative disease. In A. I. Troster (Ed.), *Memory in neuro-degenerative disease: Biological, cognitive, and clinical perspective* (pp. 128–139). Cambridge: Cambridge University Press.

Berent, S., Giordani, B., Foster, N., Minoshima, S., Lajiness-O'Neill, R., Koeppe, R., & Kuhl, D. E. (1999). Neuropsychological function and cerebral glucose utilization in isolated memory impairment and Alzheimer's disease. *Journal of Psychiatric Research, 33*, 7–16.

Berkow, R. (1982). *The Merck manual* (14th ed.). Rahway: Merck & Co., Inc.

Bleeker, M. L. (1994). Clinical presentation of selected neurotoxic compounds. In M. L. Bleeker and J. A. Hansen (Eds.), *Occupational neurology and clinical neurotoxicology* (pp. 207–233). Baltimore: Williams & Wilkins.

Bolla, K. I., & Roca, R. (1994). Neuropsychiatric sequelae of occupational exposure to neurotoxins. In M. L. Bleeker and J. A. Hansen (Eds.), *Occupational neurology and clinical neurotoxicology* (pp. 133–159). Baltimore: Williams & Wilkins.

Cameron, O. G., Starkman, M. N., & Schteingart, D. E. (1995). The effect of elevated systemic cortisol levels on plasma catecholamines in Cushing's syndrome patients with and without depressed mood. *Journal of Psychiatric Research, 29*, 347–360.

Cooper, J. R., Bloom, F. E., & Roth, R. H. (1996). *The biological basis of neuropharmacology* (7th ed.). New York: Oxford University Press.

Davis, K. L., Hollister, L. E., Overall, J., Johnson, A., & Train, K. (1976). Physostigmine: effects on cognition and affect in normal subjects. *Psychopharmacologia, 51*, 23–27.

Derogatis, L. R. (1977). *SCL-90 Administration, Scoring, & Procedures Manual–I, for the R (revised) Version*. Baltimore: Johns Hopkins University School of Medicine.

Derogatis, L. R. (1983). *SCL-90-R Manual II*. Towson: Clinical Psychometric Research.

Doctor, B. P., Blick, D. W., Caranto, G., Castro, C. A., Gentry, M. K., Larrison, R., Maxwell, D. M., Murphy, M. R., Schutz, M., & Waibel, K. (1993). Cholinesterases as scavengers for organophosphorus compounds: protection of primate performance against soman toxicity. *Chemico-Biological Interactions, 87*, 285–293.

Duman, R. S. (2001). A neurotrophic hypothesis of depression. In *The twelfth annual Albert J. Silverman research conference: Vol. 12*. Ann Arbor: University of Michigan Press.

Duman, R. S., Malberg, J., Nakagawa, S., & D'Sa, C. (2000). Neuronal plasticity and survival in mood disorders. *Biological Psychiatry, 48*, 732–739.

Folstein, M., Folstein, S. E., & McHugh, P. R. (1975). 'Mini-mental state.' A practical method for grading the cognitive state of patients for the clinician. *Journal of Psychiatric Research, 12*, 189–198.

Forno, L. S. (1992). Neuropathologic features of Parkinson's, Huntington's, and Alzheimer's diseases. In J. W. Langston and A. Young (Eds.), *Neurotoxins and neurodegenerative disease* (pp. 6–16). New York: New York Academy of Sciences.

Frederick, C. J. (1991). Psychic trauma in victims of crime and terrorism. In G. R. VandenBos and B. K. Bryant (Eds.), *Cataclysms, crises, and catastrophes* (pp. 59–108). Washington, DC: American Psychological Association.

Giles, J., Giordani, B., Ryan, K., Berent, S., Schteingart, E., Schultz, M., Kauszler, S., Gebarski, S., & Starkman, M. (2001). Hippocampal, glucocorticoid, and cognitive disorder changes in treated Cushing's disease. In *The twelfth annual Albert J. Silverman research conference: Vol. 12*. Ann Arbor: University of Michigan Press.

Gilman, S., & Newman, S. W. (1996). *Manter and Gatz's essentials of clinical neuroanatomy and neurophysiology* (9th ed.). Philadelphia: F. A. Davis.

Goetz, C. G. (1985). *Neurotoxins in clinical practice*. New York: Spectrum.

Greenwald, B. S., & Davis, K. L. (1983). Experimental pharmacology of Alzheimer disease. *Advances in Neurology, 38*, 87–102.

Grunhaus, L., Dilsaver, S., Greden, J. F., & Carroll, B. J. (1983). Depressive pseudo-dementia: a suggested diagnostic profile. *Biological Psychiatry, 18*, 215–225.

Harte, J., Holdren, C., Schneider, R., & Shirley, C. (1991). *Toxics A to Z*. Berkeley: University of California Press.

Hill, A. B. (1965). The environment and disease: association or causation. *Proceedings of the Royal Society of Medicine, 58*, 295–300.

Hudson, J. I., Hudson, M. S., Griffing, G. T., Melby, J. C., & Pope, H. G., Jr (1987). Phenomenology and family history of affective disorder in Cushing's disease. *American Journal of Psychiatry, 144*, 951–953.

Krall, W. J., Sramek, J. J., & Cutler, N. R. (1999). Cholinesterase inhibitors: a therapeutic strategy for Alzheimer disease. *Annals of Pharmacotherapy, 33*, 441–450.

Lupien, S. J., & McEwen, B. S. (1997). The acute effects of corticosteroids on cognition: integration of animal and human model studies. *Brain Research – Brain Research Reviews, 24*, 1–27.

Lupien, S. J., Nair, N. P., Briere, S., Maheu, F., Tu, M. T., Lemay, M., McEwen, B. S., & Meaney, M. J. (1999). Increased cortisol levels and impaired cognition in human aging: implication for depression and dementia in later life. *Reviews in the Neurosciences, 10*, 117–139.

Maroni, M., & Catenacci, G. (1994). Biological monitoring of neurotoxic compounds. In M. L. Bleeker and J. A. Hansen (Eds.), *Occupational neurology and clinical neurotoxicology* (pp. 43–90). Baltimore: Williams & Wilkins.

Matsui, Y., Ohbu, S., & Yamashina, A. (1996). Hospital deployment in mass sarin poisoning incident of the Tokyo subway system – an experience at St. Luke's International Hospital, Tokyo. *Japan-Hospitals, 15*, 67–71.

McDonald, E. S., & Windebank, A. J. (2000). Mechanisms of neurotoxic injury and cell death. In J. W. Albers and S. Berent (Eds.), *Clinical neurobehavioral toxicology* (pp. 525–540). Philadelphia: W. B. Saunders.

McEwen, B. S. (1999a). Endocrine effects on the brain and their relationship to behavior. In G. J. Siegel, B. W. Agranoff, S. K. Fisher, R. W. Albers, and M. D. Uhler (Eds.), *Basic neurochemistry: Molecular, cellular and medical aspects* (pp. 1007–1026). Philadelphia: Lippincott-Raven.

McEwen, B. S. (1999b). Stress and the aging hippocampus. *Frontiers in Neuroendocrinology, 20*, 49–70.

McEwen, B. S. (2000). Effects of adverse experiences for brain structure and function. *Biological Psychiatry, 48*, 721–731.

McEwen, B. S., De Kloet, E. R., & Rostene, W. (1986). Adrenal steroid receptors and actions in the nervous system. *Physiological Reviews, 66*, 1121–1188.

McEwen, B. S., Gould, E., Orchinik, M., Weiland, N. G., & Woolley, C. S. (1995). Oestrogens and the structural and functional plasticity of neurons: implications for memory, ageing and neurodegenerative processes. *Ciba Foundation Symposium, 191*, 52–66.

McEwen, B. S., & Sapolsky, R. M. (1995). Stress and cognitive function. *Current Opinion in Neurobiology, 5*, 205–216.

Merriam-Webster, A. (1993). *Merriam-Webster's collegiate dictionary* (10th ed.). Springfield: G. & C. Merriam.

Morita, H., Yanagisawa, N., Nakajima, T., Shimizu, M., Hirabayashi, H., Okudera, H., Nohara, M., Midorikawa, Y., & Mimura, S. (1995). Sarin poisoning in Matsumoto, Japan. *Lancet, 346,* 290–293.

Nisenson, L. G., Pepper, C. M., Schwenk, T. L., & Coyne, J. C. (1998). The nature and prevalence of anxiety disorders in primary care. *General Hospital Psychiatry, 20,* 21–28.

The Psychological Corporation (1981). *Wechsler Adult Intelligence Scale – Revised Manual.* San Antonio: Psychological Corporation.

Reed, D., Crawley, J., Faro, S. N., Pieper, S. J., & Kurland, L. T. (1963). Thallotoxicosis: acute manifestations and sequelae. *Journal of the American Medical Association, 183,* 96–102.

Risch, S. C., Cohen, R. M., Janowsky, D. S., Kalin, N. H., & Murphy, D. L. (1980). Mood and behavioral effects of physostigmine on humans are accompanied by elevations in plasma beta-endorphin and cortisol. *Science, 209,* 1545–1546.

Shipley, J. T. (1995). *Dictionary of word origins.* New York: Dorset.

Siegel, G. J., Agranoff, B. W., Albers, R. W., Fisher, S. K., & Uhler, M. D. (1999). *Basic neurochemistry: Molecular, cellular and medical aspects* (6th ed.). Philadelphia: Lippincott-Raven.

Starkman, M. N., Gebarski, S. S., Berent, S., & Schteingart, D. E. (1992). Hippocampal formation volume, memory dysfunction, and cortisol levels in patients with Cushing's syndrome. *Biological Psychiatry, 32,* 756–765.

Starkman, M. N., Giordani, B., Gebarski, S. S., Berent, S., Schork, M. A., & Schteingart, D. E. (1999). Decrease in cortisol reverses human hippocampal atrophy following treatment of Cushing's disease. *Biological Psychiatry, 46,* 1595–1602.

VandenBos, G. R., & Bryant, B. K. (1991). *Cataclysms, crises, and catastrophes.* Washington, DC: American Psychological Association.

Wechsler, D. (1945). A standardized memory scale for clinical use. *Journal of Psychology, 19,* 87–95.

Wilkinson, G. S. (1993). *Wide Range Achievement Text – 3.* Delaware: Wide Range.

Yokoyama, K., Araki, S., Murata, K., Nishikitani, M., Okumura, T., Ishimatsu, S., & Takasu, N. (1998). Chronic neurobehavioral and central and autonomic nervous system effects of Tokyo subway sarin poisoning. *Journal of Physiology (Paris), 92,* 317–323.

Zakzanis, K. K., Leach, L., & Kaplan, E. (1999). *Neuropsychological differential diagnosis.* Lisse: Swets & Zeitlinger.

2 Classification and management of toxicant-related information

Introduction

In *Silent spring* (1962, 1994), Rachel Carson presented a dire scenario about the use of pesticides and other toxicants and their effects on the environment. She dedicated her work to Albert Schweitzer's prediction that man has lost the capacity to 'foresee' and 'forestall' and will eventually destroy the Earth. Despite this theme, an underlying and more positive note that goes beyond a simple prediction of doom can be seen in her book. That is, she detailed, rightly or wrongly, what she saw as the correct changes needed in society's environmental practices in order to avoid the catastrophes that she believed would otherwise occur.

Individuals vary in their views of the correct way to deal with toxicants in the environment. Some advance political and regulatory solutions, others propose scientific, philosophical or even theological answers. In his introductory comments to a later edition of *Silent spring* (Gore, 1994), then US Vice-President Al Gore called for political reform as a necessary component in attempting to deal with toxicants in our environment, stating 'Cleaning up politics is essential to cleaning up pollution.' He also called for increased regulatory solutions, emphasizing what he termed the 'Clinton–Gore ... imperatives: tougher standards, reduced use, and broader use of alternative biological agents.' Although less directly emphasized than the regulatory and political aspects in his writings, Gore's introduction can also be interpreted as implying the need for an objective approach to knowledge generation. This interpretation is based on his use of terms such as 'thorough' and 'honest testing', 'testing the effects of ... chemicals on children, not just adults ...' and testing 'a range of varying combinations'.

The authors of the present work also have a philosophical bias. Simply stated, we believe regulatory and other standards should be based on objective, scientifically derived knowledge to the fullest extent possible. We would hope, for example, that the details of the aforementioned Clinton–Gore imperatives, or those that take their place in the future, include direct involvement of scientifically derived knowledge. Scientific method provides the most effective means at this time for generating such knowledge. Science is an institution as well as a methodology. As such, it reflects a history that includes the evolution of a variety of components needed maximally to ensure the generation of relevant and accurate knowledge within the framework of ethical and safe inquiry. Clinical approaches should be based upon and be compatible with these scientifically derived data. Philosophical speculations and other methods of acquiring knowledge may be valuable to the extent that they are viewed as hypothesis generating, lending themselves to the mechanics of scientific refinement, refutation, or validation. To paraphrase from a presentation delivered to the Environmental Protection Agency (EPA) scientific advisory groups (Berent & Albers, 1999), the alternative to a scientific approach, to rely solely on regulation without the benefit of peer-reviewed and objective experimentation, represents a slippery slope, one that invites a few to decide what might be best for all. Such an approach disrupts the balance, the relationship between objective knowledge and regulatory decisions. At the least, it invites political expediency or other vested interest considerations to drive these decisions and may do nothing in the long-term to solve the problems to which such regulations are directed.

Assessment and management of risk

Objective assessment of toxic risk is a necessary component to the advancement of scientific knowledge about toxicants and the development of effective regulations. Systematic risk assessment is considered to be a process that involves four parts (Gaylor & Slikker, 1992). These parts consist of the following:

- Hazard identification. What are the potential effects of exposure? The data used to answer this question ideally would be based on animal and human scientific research.
- Description of dose–response relationships. What is the relationship between an effect, usually adverse, and the amount of exposure under various conditions? This question is ideally addressed objectively using data from epidemiological and laboratory research.
- Exposure assessment. What are the circumstances of exposure to a particular toxic substance, its nature, and extent? Individual and environmental measurements are used to address this question, data are related to the presence of the substance in the environment and the resulting dose through inhalation, ingestion, or through the skin.
- Quantitative risk estimation. What generalizations can be drawn from the information generated in the first three steps above? This question may be addressed through modelling that often includes a number of assumptions. This is the most subjective part of the risk-assessment process.

From a scientific perspective, the results of the risk assessment process, especially the fourth step above, could be viewed as hypothesis generating. That is, the process represents a systematic approach to the development of hypotheses for further and formal study to validate or refute the findings. However, the process may at times be offered as a basis for regulatory development without further inquiry. Some argue that regulatory decisions should be based on these estimates since we cannot afford to postpone regulations until more precise knowledge is obtained (Gaylor & Slikker, 1992). How often have you heard the phrase 'better safe than sorry'? When human safety is concerned, a conservative response, especially to the unknown, is not unusual. You could think of this type of response as 'high-tea reasoning'. That is, an English colleague once taught us that milk should always be simmered but never brought to boil before adding it to tea. We noticed, however, that he never asked for his milk to be warmed when eating out. When asked why, he replied that since in a restaurant there is no way to ensure that the milk had not been boiled, it was better to not ask for it to be warmed. While the practical expediency of 'high-tea reasoning' might have a claim to justification in the regulatory arena, the scientist and the clinician should continue to rely on precise information to the extent possible in pursuing their tasks. This is especially true when addressing questions of causality in suspected toxic disorders.

In actuality, the consensus view among those who appear to be the strongest proponents of 'risk assessment' strategies is one that calls for objective and prospective research. At the same time, there appears to be further consensus in this group that enough information has already become available to conclude that environmental toxins are responsible for a host of human illnesses, including neurodegenerative and delayed neurodegenerative illnesses (National Research Council, 1992). These conclusions do not appear to be accepted within the larger scientific community (e.g. Langston & Young, 1992). While it is clear that environmental toxicants (those that are extrinsic to the organism) can, and do at times, cause damage to the nervous system,[1] there is no firm evidence that links these compounds to chronic neurodegenerative disease. Spencer, Ludolph, & Kisby (1992), for instance, stated, 'it seems unlikely that progressive neurodegenerative diseases, such as amyotrophic lateral sclerosis, Parkinson disease, and dementia of the Alzheimer type, are triggered by environmental agents with excitotoxic potential.' In support of this conclusion, they pointed out the 'self-limiting' nature of damage to the nervous system from such agents. That is, the patterns of neuronal deficit reflect selective chemical exposure, e.g., damage consistent with the distribution of glutamate receptors and consequent functional symptoms that are served by the affected pathways, e.g., memory. To quote comments by Calne, Hochberg, Snow & Nygaard (1992) on the possible role of environmental toxicants in neurodegeneration, 'We have no idea whether acute, subacute, or chronic exposure might be relevant. We do not know whether damage would be immediate or delayed. Nor is there any compelling evidence on whether organic or inorganic toxins are more likely to have an etiologic role.' Calne *et al.* go on to list several competitors for a causative role in neurodegeneration, including infection, failure in DNA repair, auto-immunity, failure of some vital function (e.g., defective nutrition), and late expression of a lethal gene (programmed cell death). These investigators concluded, 'we are faced with the dilemma of too many theories and not enough facts.'

Fortunately, the regulatory process appears to have made consistent efforts to achieve a balance between various interests while maintaining a scientific basis for its work. According to Dow (1994), the first federal law in the USA to regulate pesticides was enacted in 1910, and replaced in 1947 with the expanded Federal Insecticide, Fungicide and Rodenticide Act (FIFRA). The Environmental Control Act 1972 changed the emphasis of FIFRA from consumer protection to human and environmental health, with further emphasis on risk–benefit analyses. Further, according to Dow, these changes, together with an expanding toxicology knowledge base, necessitated the improvement and standardization of exposure assessments. The Federal EPA was established in 1970. Historically, the direction taken by regulatory efforts appears to have been towards strengthening the balance between objective science, industry, societal needs, and public safety. The Code of Federal Regulations 1989 (40 CFR 160) demanded that all studies done after that date and submitted in support of pesticide regulation would have to be performed following 'good laboratory practices' (Dow, 1994). This put a demand on industry for good science, but it also reflected a welcome philosophical orientation on the part of the agency.

Classification

Aside from the consideration that anything can be toxic in sufficient dose, there are thousands of substances that possess the capacity to do harm and in low enough doses to be considered 'toxic'. There are over 10 000 chemical substances described in *The Merck Index* (Merck Research Laboratories, 2001). Almost 3000 substances have been described as toxic to the visual system alone, and this number may represent less than 20% of all compounds (Mattsson, Boyes & Ross, 1992). The problem of numbers becomes even greater when the multifactorial nature of many chemicals is considered, e.g., the fact that various metabolites and other by-products can have their own toxic effects, and the possible effects of interactions. These interactions might occur between chemical-specific variables, but they might also involve environmental factors as well as variables within the exposed organism. Without attempting to calculate the possible permutations and combinations, it is easy to see that we are dealing with very large numbers in terms of chemically related variables that might explain an observed effect.

Despite these hurdles to understanding, and the challenge they pose for scientific inquiry, an objective approach to problem-solving calls for an effective system of classification. Classification is a basic and necessary component of the systematic approach to studying any topic. Various schemes have been used in attempts to increase objectivity and quantification in the study of toxicants. There is, however, no universally agreed upon standard for the classification of neurotoxic substances (Schaumburg & Spencer, 2000). As will become clear from the following discussions, the nature of toxicants, to some extent because of the incomplete nature of our knowledge base, makes classification difficult. In publication, authors often will organize their discussions around an agent's chemical properties (e.g., whether it is viewed as a metal, gas, or solvent), on the basis of its intended use (e.g., pesticide or medication), on its selective neuroanatomical target (central nervous system or peripheral nervous system), or on the basis of the type of damage caused (e.g., effects on cell body or myelin).

The Environmental Protection Agency (EPA) has worked with science and industry in attempts to develop systems to classify substances in terms of their relative toxicity. A No Observed Adverse Effect Level (NOAEL), for instance, is required of all commercially produced agents designed for use as pesticides or related applications (EPA, 1991). The NOAEL is defined as the highest dose that does not lead to an adverse effect. For non-carcinogenic substances (carcinogens have different regulatory requirements), the NOAEL is to be established through regulated methods of experimentation. To determine the allowable 'safe dose', the EPA adjusts the established NOAEL by dividing by a safety factor (SF) or uncertainty factor (UF). The SF is usually a factor of ten to account for possible differences in sensitivity between animals and humans and another ten for possible individual variations in sensitivity, a total SF = 100, or an assumed 'no or negligible' risk level of NOAEL/100 (Gaylor & Slikker, 1992).

The rationale for NOAELs rests on the assumption of a threshold effect, a dose level below which no toxic effect will occur. Since scientific knowledge is probabilistic and never absolute, however, it is difficult to determine the exact level for all exposed individuals, or if the level is actually zero (Gaylor & Slikker, 1992). While there are some attempts at objectivity in this system, there is considerable subjectivity as well as ample opportunity for various political and vested interest groups to influence the process. These factors influence the final safety level as well as the methods used to arrive at the NOAEL in the first place. For instance, EPA guidelines called for NOAELs to be established on the basis of animal or human experimentation. With recent concerns about the ethical use of human subjects in research, there has been growing pressure to limit such studies to animals. While this would protect human volunteers, it would also seriously limit the ability to generalize, a critical step in scientific methodology (see Chapter 3), from the results of such experimentation.

The EPA also employs a system for determining the level of acute toxicity that is based upon determination of the LD_{50} for the specific agent. The LD_{50} is defined as the dose at which 50% of the test animals die (the lethal dose).

The lower the LD_{50} in terms of dose, the more toxic the substance is considered. This is then translated to a four-point scale that ranges from 'caution' to 'danger, poison' (Harte, Holdren, Schneider, & Shirley, 1991).

Many substances have multiple potential applications. Since our regulatory agencies have been developed largely in response to special-interest groups, a number of paradoxes emerge as a result of the clash between these interests and the actual properties of the substances to be regulated. For instance, while the EPA is charged with regulating pesticides and similar products, it is the Food and Drug Administration (FDA) that has responsibility for medicinal safety. At times, this may mean that very similar substances are regulated differently, depending on whether its manufacturer intends to market the final product as a medicine or as a herbicide or insecticide. Anticholinesterase compounds, for example, have been used as pesticides, as weapons of war, but also as drugs for the evaluation and treatment of myasthenia gravis, Alzheimer disease, and other diseases. As a result of these peculiarities, different regulations can exist for the intended use of a specific substance.

Schaumburg & Spencer (2000) proposed a model of classification based on potential susceptibility of cellular neurotoxic targets, mechanisms of injury for these targets, the consequent disorder, and the types of substances that can lead to structural or functional damage to the target. They divided the cellular material into two classes: (1) neurons and their processes and (2) neuroglia and myelin. They then listed primary mechanisms of injury and gave examples of substances that can cause such injury. For example, organophosphates and carbamates through their inhibition of acetylcholinesterase can induce chemical disruption of enzymatic function in neurons. Botulinum toxin inhibits release of acetylcholine, while black widow spider venom leads to over-release of acetylcholine (Goetz, 1985). In each case, normal neurotransmission may be seriously compromised, though via different routes. Many will like the system proposed by Schaumburg & Spencer (2000) for a number of reasons, a primary one being its compatibility with the current state of scientific knowledge regarding cell structure and function.

As acknowledged by Schaumburg & Spencer, however, their classification scheme may not be as attractive as are some alternative systems to regulators and industry because the scheme does not easily relate substances to one another under some one functional application, e.g., pesticides. Schaumburg & Spencer point out that their system is also limited by the potential for some agents to affect sequentially or simultaneously more than one site in the nervous system, to differ in effects depending on exposure variables (e.g., varying effects from the same agent at different dose levels). Another limitation comes from the fact that an inconsistent knowledge base exists across all substances of interest.

Major problems face any attempt at classification of neurotoxicants. To list a few, many substances are not unitary in effects, multiple substances have similar effects, and there is an inevitable lack of inclusiveness in listing substances. Also, the varying levels of completeness in our knowledge lead to differences of opinion and controversies with regard to the effects of a given substance and the mechanisms of damage (Albers & Berent, 2000b). As an example, fenfluramine has been used to study eating behavior in animals and is used as a diet drug and for other medical applications in humans. This substance elicits the release of and inhibits the reuptake of serotonin (5-hydroxytryptamine). While fenfluramine has been reported to deplete brain serotonin at high-dose levels in animal models, a comparable effect at therapeutic levels has not been documented in humans (Christensen, Yurgelun-Todd, Babb, Gruber, Cohen & Renshaw, 1999). Despite this lack of evidence, some have argued that fenfluramine produces an effect in humans comparable with that seen in animals (Schenck & Mahowald, 1996; Koury, Stone, Stapczynski & Blake, 1999).

Other challenges to classification include difficulties associated with differentiating primary from secondary effects of a given agent, identification of metabolites and their effects, lack of standard definitions in some instances, and different facets of function, e.g., biochemical versus physiological. In addition, cross-classification is difficult to achieve, e.g., looking up by chemical class, functional class, or other potential variables related to class.

To give an example of the complex actions of a given compound, Zonisamide (ZNS) or Zonegran, two brand names for a somewhat novel drug with anticonvulsant properties, is a chemical compound with complex and differing effects depending on dose. It is a sulfonamide derivative with the chemical name 1,2-benzisoxazole 3-methanesulfonamide. In the nervous system, ZNS and its metabolites have multiple effects. It has been shown, for instance (Suzuki, Kawakami, Nishimura, Watanabe, Yagi, Seino & Miyamoto, 1992; Kito, Maehara & Watanabe, 1996), that ZNS blocks or reduces T-type calcium current, allowing fewer channels to open during depolarization of the cell membrane. It is through this process that the drug is believed to exert its anticonvulsant qualities (Oommen & Mathews, 1999). ZNS has also been shown to affect the dopaminergic system (Okada, Kaneko, Hirano, Mizuno, Kondo, Otani & Fukushima, 1995). More interestingly, the ZNS effect on dopamine is biphasic in a dose-dependent manner. Lower doses (in the 20–50 mg/kg range) enhance dopamine function, whereas higher doses (around 100 mg/kg) inhibit dopamine function (Oommen & Mathews, 1999). In a small preliminary study of the effects of ZNS on cognition (Berent, Sackellares, Giordani, Wagner, Donofrio & Abou-Khalil, 1987), findings were reported that, in retrospect, are consistent with the now known biphasic effects of ZNS on neurotransmission. In an earlier work, higher doses of ZNS were accompanied by a decline in specific cognitive functions, primarily the acquisition and consolidation of new information, without more general cognitive dysfunction. A significant linear relationship also was found between the extent of cognitive impairment and ZNS plasma concentrations. Interestingly, the findings suggested the development of tolerance to these adverse cognitive effects over time. ZNS is now used effectively and safely through a slow titration schedule and by maintaining a therapeutically appropriate dose (Faught, Ayala, Montouris, Leppik & the Trial Group 2001).

To emphasize further the complexities inherent in the topic of neurotoxicity, consider the case of snake venoms. These venoms are mixtures of proteins and polypeptides that can be classified into two major categories depending on the mode of action (Mebs, 1988). According to Mebs, one type includes curariform toxins (alpha toxins) that block neuromuscular transmission by action on the postsynaptic membrane, targeting nicotinic acetylcholine receptors. The second type acts presynaptically, and these can be further subdivided, one subtype acting to inhibit transmitter release, the other to facilitate transmitter release. There are also other types of snake venom, and more than 100 different snake venoms have been identified to date (Mebs, 1988). These venoms vary in mode of action depending on the chemical composition in a given type.

Despite these challenges to classification, as illustrated by the brief presentations on ZNS and snake venoms, there are many reasons to continue with our attempts at classification. For instance, an effective classification lends to the systematic and standardized approach in science, allows for an orderly treatment of knowledge and the limitations on such knowledge, and provides an interface between basic and applied science and, hopefully, between science, industry, and government.

In Table 2.1 we have organized a number of substances, modifying the suggestions for classification made by Schaumburg & Spencer (2000). Listed are primary neuron, glia, and myelin target sites, substances that can damage them, and the ways in which such damage can occur. In addition, included are some of the possible physiological (e.g., anhidrosis) and functional (e.g., emotional lability)[2] consequences of toxicity. While such an approach to classification has some appeal, there are also problems with it. The enormous number of substances makes it difficult to list a sufficient number even to approach inclusiveness. The nature of such a list will suit the informational needs of some disciplines but be of limited value for others. Related to discipline issues is the fact that what information is included in such a list will involve a good deal of subjective judgment on the part of the author of the table. In addition, one's our factual understanding is constantly changing. Any list, like that shown in Table 2.1, will quickly become dated.

Table 2.1 Classification of selected toxicants by site and nature of action, when known, and the possible physiological and functional consequences of neurotoxicity.[3]

Target site	Vulnerability	Substance	Consequence
Axon	Inhibition of protein synthesis	Ricin (a phytotoxin)	Axonal degeneration
Axon (degeneration, axon terminal, axonal transport)	Disruption of normal axonal flow, antero- and retrograde	Acrylamide, *n*-hexane	Peripheral neuropathy
Cell membrane	Disruption of sodium (Na$^+$) channels	Tetrodotoxin, ciguatoxin (fish toxins)	Sensory nerve dysfunction, dizziness, visual changes, ptosis, progressive paralysis
Neuron (dopaminergic neurons in the basal ganglia)	Nigrostriatal degeneration	MMP+ (metabolite of MPTP)	Acute Parkinsonism
CNS neurons, motor neurons	Glycine receptor antagonism	Tetanus toxin	Hyperreflexia, seizure
Neuron	Mitochondrial DNA chain growth	Some antiviral drugs used in the treatment of AIDS (zalcitabine)	Peripheral neuropathy
Neuron	Degeneration of cells in striatum and basal ganglia, mechanism not fully understood	Manganese	Atypical Parkinsonian syndrome, dystonia, irritability, emotional liability, illusions, hallucinations
Neuron, neurotransmission	GABA enhancement	Benzodiazepines	CNS depression: somnolence, dysarthria
Neuron, neurotransmission	GABA inhibition	Picrotoxin, penicillin	CNS stimulation: hyperactivity, tremor, seizure
Corticospinal neurons	Glutamate receptor excitotoxicity and resultant neuro-degeneration	Some varieties of chickpea (*Lathyrus*)	Lumbar pain, lower extremity weakness, stiffness, paresthesias, clonic tremor, spastic paraplegia (lathyrism)

Target site	Vulnerability	Substance	Consequence
Neuron	Anticholinergic effects	Mushroom toxins (e.g., *Amanita*)	Agitation, muscle spasms, ataxia, myoclonus, convulsions, death
CNS neurons	GABA receptor excitotoxicity or inhibitory	Cassava, some algies (mussels), ketamine, kainate	Varies with affected site in CNS and whether specific toxic agent is agonist (e.g., NMDA) or antagonist (e.g., ketamine); can include anesthesia, memory loss, behavioral alterations
Neuron	Enzymatic inhibition producing hypoxia, demyelination. Blocks cytochrome oxidase/adenosine triphosphate production	Cyanide	Headache, delirium, agitation, Parkinsonism, dystonia, seizure, coma, death
Neuron cell body, especially sensory	Disruption of DNA and RNA synthesis	Doxorubicin (an antineoplastic drug)	Chromatin fragmentation, cell degeneration, sensory neuropathy, progressive ataxia
Neuron, especially in cerebellum and pons	GABA and glutamate enhancement, other actions dependent on various metabolites of toxicant and their interactions	Benzene	Nausea and vomiting, drowsiness, ataxic gait, paralysis, coma, death
Neuron, neurotransmission, adrenergic alpha receptor	Norepinephrine and its precursor (dopamine) inhibition	Cocaine, amphetamine, tricyclic antidepressants, phenothiazines, S-cathinone (Khat)	Hyperactivity, extrapyramidal dysfunction, ischemia, severe behavioral changes

Target site	Vulnerability	Substance	Consequence
Neuron, neurotransmission	Serotonergic reuptake inhibition	Some antidepressants (e.g., fluoxetine), MDMA, Ecstasy)	Disturbances in mood, cognition, perception
Neuron, neurotransmission	Serotonergic enhancement	LSD	Disturbances in mood, cognition, perception
Neurons, especially in smooth muscle, heart and endocrine systems	Disruption of L-type calcium (Ca^{2+}) channels	Snake venoms (e.g., Mamba) and some drugs (e.g., verapamil)	Progressive weakness and paralysis
Neurotransmission	Inhibition of acetylcholinesterase	Organophosphates (e.g., some pesticides)	Multiple, including anxiety, depression, other behavioral and cognitive disorders, paresthesias, peripheral neuropathy
Neurotransmission	CNS neurons, motor neurons	Strychnine	Disinhibition of motor neurons
Neurotransmission	Dopamine enhancement	Gamma hydroxy butyrate ('date rape drug')	Seizures, coma, respiratory depression, amnesia

CNS, central nervous system; GABA, gamma-aminobutyric acid; LSD, lysergic acid diethylamide; MDMA, 3,4 methylenedioxymetamphetamine; MMP+, 1-methyl-4-phenylpyridirum ion; MPTP, 1-methyl-4-phenyl-1,2,3,6-tetrahydrophyridine NMDA, *N*-methyl-D-aspartate.

More traditionally, tabular information on toxicants has been presented in the form depicted in Table 2.2. It presents a number of toxic substances, organized by class and with an indication of the practical applications for each substance. A third column includes some of the adverse effects that have been purported to result from over-exposure to the specific substance. Many toxicology-related textbooks have been organized around similar themes. Problems with this approach include the limited number of substances that can be included, the lack of verification for the listed information that usually exists in such tables, difficulties with keeping information current and consistent with new knowledge, and the limited information and over-simplified implications in terms of adverse effects included in the table. Also, there is a non-specific nature to the listed adverse effects, usually with no verification of a cause-and-effect relationship between the effect and its presumed toxic etiology. The last point especially represents a major drawback with systems

Table 2.2 Selected substances ordered by general class, with partial information about practical applications and purported neurotoxic effects.[4]

Specific substance	Applications	Some purported adverse effects[5]
Metals and metalloids:		
Aluminium	Building structures, electrical, smelting, medicinal	Dementia
Arsenic	Smelting, pesticides, herbicides, wood preservatives	Peripheral neuropathy, other organ damage
Barium	Paints, glass, pesticides, automotive parts	Hypokalemic paralysis
Bismuth	Semiconductors, solders, ore refining, medicinal	Encephalopathy
Cobalt	Pigments, drying solutions, histology stains	Possible visual changes
Gold	Jewelry, industry, medicine	Possible peripheral neuropathy and CNS effects
Lead	Batteries, petroleum, solder, plumbing, ammunition, paints	Encephalopathy (children), peripheral neuropathy (adults)
Lithium	Alloys, lubricants, ceramics, medications	Tremor, peripheral neuropathy, CNS toxicity
Manganese	Steel, batteries, ceramics, glass, fertilizers, antiseptics	Emotional disturbances, Parkinsonism-like disorder (manganism)
Mercury, inorganic	Pharmaceuticals, fungicides, pesticides, goldsmithing, mirrors	Tremor, peripheral neuropathy, ataxic gait, dysarthria, irritability, mania, concentration problems, emotional problems
Organotins	Polymers, disinfectants, fungicides, insecticides	Headache, visual problems, mental confusion, seizure, loss of consciousness
Platinum	Electronics, jewelry, chemical catalysts, medicinal	Peripheral neuropathy, auditory damage
Thallium	Jewelry, alloys, fireworks, glass, pesticides	Emotional disturbances, ataxia, lethargy, peripheral neuropathy, seizure
Zinc	Sheet metal, alloys, batteries, household utensils, astringents, antiseptics	Apathy, tremor, ataxia (Brazers' disease)

Specific substance	Applications	Some purported adverse effects[5]
Solvents:		
Benzene	Petrochemicals, fuels	Mental changes, CNS depression, seizure, somnolence
Carbon disulfide	Textiles, cellophane, chemical synthesis	Peripheral neuropathy, irritability, anorexia, behavioral changes
Ethyl alcohol (ethanol)	Beverage, pharmaceutical, chemical synthesis	Inebriation, narcosis, vertigo, tremor, ataxia, mental alterations, peripheral neuropathy, seizure, cerebral atrophy
Formaldehyde	Plastics, textiles, chemical industry	Excitation, insomnia, anorexia, paresthesias, weakness
Methylene chloride	Paint-remover, degreasing	Inebriation, stupor, lethargy
Methyl alcohol (methanol)	Fuel, chemical synthesis	Blindness, delirium, tremor, hallucinations, paresthesias, coma
Methyl chloride	Plastics, rubber, chemical synthesis	Personality changes, ataxia, tremor, confusion, speech impairment
Perchloroethylene	Dry cleaning, textiles, degreasing, electrical transformers	Somnolence, dizziness, incoordination, headache
Trichloroethylene	Degreasing agent	Anesthesia, confusion, incoordination, CNS depression, cranial neuropathy (most often trigeminal)
1,1,1-Trichchloroethane	Metal and plastic moulds cleaning	Headache, lassitude, CNS depression
Styrene	Plastics, polymers, resins	Stupor, weakness, tremor, depression
Toluene	Dyes, explosives	Inebriation, narcosis, CNS depression, ataxia, balance impairment, cerebral atrophy
Xylene	Petrochemicals	Confusion, tremor, vertigo, memory impairment

Specific substance	Applications	Some purported adverse effects[5]
Gases:		
Carbon monoxide	Product of incomplete combustion	Excitement, anxiety, delirium, stupor, parkinsonism, hypoxic encephalopathy
Hydrogen sulfide	Reagent	Narcosis, CNS suppression, nervousness, sleep disturbance
Carbon dioxide	Beverage industry, dry ice, fire extinction, aerosol propellant, entertainment industry, antiseptic	Headache, dizziness, restlessness, paresthesias, asphyxia, coma, seizure
Nitrous oxide	Anesthetic, propellant	Altered consciousness, narcosis, myelopathy
Insecticides:		
Carbamates (in general)	Insecticide	Irritability, mood lability, memory loss, confusion
Chlorinated hydrocarbons (in general)	Insecticide	Nervousness, depression, anxiety, mood lability, memory loss, hallucinations
Dichlorodiphenyl-trichloroethane (DDT)	Pesticide	Weakness, tremor, seizure, emotional lability
Dieldrin	Insecticide	Fatigue, tremor, vertigo, convulsions
Organophosphates (in general)	Pesticide	Neuromuscular blockade, skeletal muscle weakness, respiratory depression, pupillary constriction, and other cholinergic-related symptoms
Herbicides:		
Agent Orange	Herbicide, a mixture containing dioxin and other substances	*See* dioxin
Dioxin	Herbicide	Headache, dizziness, nausea, muscle pain, emotional disturbance, dyspnea
Miscellaneous:		
Caffeine	Beverages, medicine	Excitement, restlessness, tinnitus, seizure
N,N-diethyl-meta-tolu-amide (DEET)	Insect repellent	Slurred speech, confusion, insomnia, seizure, psychosis, coma

Specific substance	Applications	Some purported adverse effects[5]
Miscellaneous:		
Methyl bromide	Fumigant	Tremor, convulsants, delirium, paresthesias
Nicotine	Recreational drug, insecticide	Dose-dependent blockade of acetylcholine synapses resulting in neuromuscular disorder
Silicone(s)	Three major types: fluids, resins, elastomers; multiple applications, e.g., dental moulds, medical implants, 'silly putty'	Controversial adverse CNS and peripheral nervous system effects have been proposed but not substantiated
Uranium	Nuclear power	Mental disorder, restlessness,
Vinyl chloride	Plastics	Anesthesia, CNS depression, sensory disturbance
Sarin	Weapon of war and terrorism	Skeletal muscle weakness or paralysis with respiratory arrest, anxiety (acute and Post-traumatic Stress Disorder, possibly situational and related to circumstances of exposure)

CNS, central nervous system.

that list various substances and their purported effects since it implies a specific causal relationship between the listed symptoms and the named substance. The models make it tempting to 'deduce' a causal connection when none might be present in a given case. A simple cookbook-type of approach to the study of neurobehavioral toxicology is antithetical to the philosophy of the present work. Here, we have emphasized the need to employ traditional and scientifically based methods for solving research and clinically related problems. This approach applies to conclusions about cause. We discuss the problems associated with making causal attributions in detail in Chapter 8.

Complicating matters is the fact that symptoms that have been attributed to a toxic etiology in a list such as depicted in Table 2.2 are often non-specific. Patients, too, may present with non-specific complaints. When these complaints are similar to those reflected in Table 2.2, they could as likely have resulted from a host of causes other than toxicity. Many, in fact, are as likely to result from the effects of aging or other life events as from neurotoxicants.

In their chapter on the effects of chemicals on behavior, for instance, Anger & Johnson (1987) provided a list of behavioral effects that were reported in the literature they reviewed. This list contained 200 or more behavioral effects, divided into major behavioral domains, and none specific to a toxic etiology. In the domain they termed 'Affective/Personality', for example, Anger & Johnson listed approximately 50 symptom areas. Without repeating them all, the list included almost every possible behavioral manifestation. Included were symptoms reflecting emotional expression (e.g., anxiety, depression, crying, exhilaration, emotional lability), thought disturbances (e.g., confusion, dementia, perceptual distortion), motivational and character disturbance (e.g., impulsiveness, withdrawal, psychopathic behavior, substance abuse), vegetative signs (sleep disturbance, loss of libido), and others. Since adverse behavioral symptoms often share commonality with normal behavioral expressions, the lack of an estimate of severity in such lists leaves interpretation of their significance difficult. Anxiety, for instance, can be an appropriate response to certain life events that may carry some threat to our well being, or it may be an expression of pathology.

The multidisciplinary nature of neurobehavioral toxicology in itself presents a challenge to classification. For instance, the information that might be needed by the neurochemist will contain details that go well beyond those that might be useful to a practicing clinician. Also, a given field's unique knowledge may at some point leave the non-initiated (i.e., a professional from another discipline) unable to comprehend concepts or terms as might be needed in the primary communication. Of course, this is a problem more generally and one that provides a rationale for involving multiple disciplines in the work of neurobehavioral toxicology. Using a team of individuals from varying disciplines to solve classification problems, however, is different than developing a single classification scheme that is utilitarian, accurate, and comprehensible to each team member.

A Physician's Desk Reference type of listing could be useful, especially as it lends itself to computerization. The effort would have to be multidisciplinary and, again, there is the problem of the amount of information needed to satisfy the needs of all relevant disciplines. Comprehensiveness is a problem. If we tried to cover all compounds that have the capacity to affect adversely the nervous system, we would likely end up with a reference like *The Merck Index* (Merck Research Laboratories, 2001), a listing of thousands of chemicals. There would be no guarantee that the final product would contain the basic information needed by the clinician to render an accurate diagnosis or to determine a causal relationship. In most instances, knowledge about the effects of specific substances is too limited to allow for a DSM-type approach (American Psychiatric Association, 1994), and systems such as the 'WHO Criteria' (World Health Organization Workgroup, 1985) for establishing toxic etiology are non-specific and overly inclusive in terms of pathology.

Textbook treatments tend be aimed at specific disciplines or specialties, e.g., neuropsychology or neurology, and the contents often emphasize some aspect that is unique to a given field, e.g., neuropsychological test patterns associated with exposure to specified chemicals (e.g., Hartman, 1995). These treatments may lack sufficient consideration of information from other fields. In the field of neuropsychology, for instance, neuropsychological test results are in isolation non-specific and represent only one part of the neuro-psychological clinical enterprise (see Chapter 5). Patterns of test scores may take on more specificity than any one score, and test patterns can at times be used as a basis for operationally defining a specified condition. For instance, one could define a learning disability on the basis of a ratio between intellectual level and achievement in a specified subject area, e.g., reading. Almost always, however, there is a need to go beyond the test results themselves to reach clinical conclusions, especially in the determination of etiology (see Chapter 8). With regard to using a test pattern to define a learning disability, for example, a positive finding of learning disability tells us little about its etiology or how to intervene to correct the situation.

Various authors have approached the problem of how best to present the effects of toxicants in a variety of ways. Many approach the topic by reviewing specific chemicals and presenting conclusions about its effects on the exposed individual. A problem with this approach is that the effects are often non-specific and wide ranging, to the end that the information is of little practical value. Other reference works are informational, even entertaining (e.g., Goetz, 1985). Still other works focus on specific topics, e.g., the role of toxicants in mood disorders, reviewing specific chemical substances and their purported effects (e.g., Albers & Berent, 2000a). This type of approach can be informative and provide information relevant to a number of specialties, but it does not necessarily provide a useful reference source in everyday practice.

Feldman (1998) represents a model that approaches each covered substance in some depth, e.g., providing informative background from the published literature and relating that review to clinically relevant information. The scholarly orientation used by Feldman reflects an excellent model. A major weakness in the approach, however, is that only a limited number of substances can be described in this way, specifically about 20 by Feldman. Although such reference works usually attempt to include substances that represent certain chemical classes, e.g., metals or solvents, it is not clear how well the agents chosen for focus generalize to others in the same class. Also, there is the problem common to all texts of keeping the information current in relation to an ever-changing knowledge base. Nevertheless, the substances covered in such works usually represent the major compounds seen in practice, and, as a result, such works can be extremely useful from a practical viewpoint.

A very useful approach from our viewpoint might be a case presentation model (see Table 2.3 for an outline and example of this approach to organizing toxicant-related information). These cases can be drawn from actual patients seen by the clinician, or they might come from material that has been

Table 2.3 Outline for case presentation format.[6]

Introduction and background: Here the topic is introduced with identification of the specific substance or clinical symptoms and signs that will be presented. A literature review should be included that is sufficient to introduce the reader to the topic.

Case presentation: The specific case is presented, e.g., including the patient's chief complaints, relevant history, and past examination and test results. A description of the present examination and its results are presented here.

Differential diagnosis: The working diagnosis is presented based upon the evaluation and consideration of all past examination results. Considerations should include all possible alternative diagnoses that compete with or that might be in addition to the initial, or working, diagnosis.

Additional information: Information from any further tests or examinations is presented here. This will include information from psychometric examination as well as any laboratory tests, imaging, or other medical tests done as part of the present examination, or elsewhere.

Comments: Relevant comments can be made at any time and might include conclusions or information from others who have seen the patient.

Alternative diagnoses: Provide a list of diagnoses that still compete to explain the patient's symptoms, or that remain in addition to the primary diagnoses, after consideration of the further tests and other additional information.

Discussion: The case is discussed around the topics of interest. Here, what is known about the various conditions being considered is presented in a critical review that includes a review of the relevant literature to support the writer's expressed opinions.

Verification of the clinical diagnosis: Verification of the final primary diagnosis is made within the context of supporting criteria, e.g., referring to published diagnostic criteria such as those by Richardson, Wilson, Williams, Moyer & Naylor (2000) or others, as relevant.

Verification of alternative or additional clinical diagnoses: The process of verification is repeated for any alternative diagnoses and should include the rationale for excluding items in the differential diagnosis.

Cause/etiology: A cause for the patient's condition is specified when known.

Verification of cause/etiology: Discussion is presented around specific criteria to argue why the conclusion of cause is probably accurate or to document why it is not known for all diagnoses listed.

Conclusion: Discuss the findings generally, including arguments as to why certain suspected explanations for the patient's condition were excluded.

---

described in the published literature or from an investigator's research. Each case can then be presented in the context of how the clinical problem was approached, how the results of additional information influenced the diagnostic results, and how well the final outcome was predicted. Drawbacks again include the very large number of examples needed to be comprehensive. The fact that every case has a degree of uniqueness in terms of chemical, environmental, and organism-related variables potentially limits the generalization of the reported findings to other settings. Nevertheless, this approach has been effective and useful in teaching as well as in published communications that describe group as well as individual findings (Albers, Hodach, Kimmel & Treacy, 1980; Albers & Bromberg, 1995). Through this mode of presentation, the author has the opportunity to emphasis specific substances while explaining the various contingencies that needed to be dealt with in order to reach his or her conclusions. Differential and co-morbid considerations can be explained, and the final conclusions can be verified. Another benefit of such a model is that it encourages the professional to attend to all of the relevant information in reaching and verifying conclusions.

Conclusion

In the final analysis, the professional working in the area of neurobehavioral toxicology needs to approach every case, or research question, on its own individual merits. The methods to use when solving these clinical problems and answering research questions will be presented in the following chapters. These methods will hopefully provide the reader with a guide and the tools needed effectively to address these important and complicated problems.

Notes

1   The story of how 1-methyl-4-phenyl 1,2,3,6-tetrahydropyridine (MPTP) was found to be a dopaminergic neuron neurotoxicant is well known within the scientific community (Albin, 2000). It has been estimated that several hundred intravenous drug users were exposed to MPTP, the result of an error by a chemist making a 'designer' drug. The intent by the chemist had been to produce an analog to meperidine (MPPP) and to disseminate the drug as a heroin substitute, but mistakes produced batches of both MPPP and MPTP. A number of individuals who used this drug developed acute parkinsonism whereas others showed no apparent symptoms or signs but were subsequently found on quantitative position emission tomography evaluations also to have dopaminergic abnormalities. There was no clinical evidence of neurotoxic injury occurring outside the basal ganglia (Albin, 2000).

2   In describing the functional consequences of a substance, we have chosen to use terms that are compatible with the World Health Organization (WHO) International Classification of Functioning, Disability and Health (ICF) (formerly ICIDH) system of functional classification. First published in 1980, ICIDH underwent several revisions, e.g., the 2001 implementation manual (World Health Organization, 2001). ICF provides a systematic and comprehensive description of functions in a manner that lends to research as well as to clinical applications. It can be applied in a quantitative or descriptive context and is not limited to disease or other abnormal conditions. The example given, 'emotional lability', would be listed under 'emotional functions' in the ICIDH system and would be designated as 'b152' (World Health Organization, 2000).

3   Table 2.1 was modified after a model suggested by Schaumburg & Spencer (2000), with table contents drawn from Schaumburg & Spencer (2000), Albers & Berent (2000a), Klaassen & Watkins (2003), and Siegel, Agranoff, Fisher, Albers & Uhler

(1999). It is presented primarily to illustrate an approach to classification. The information, however, is simplified, and the reader should consult primary sources for more comprehensive information.

4   Information in Table 2.2 was adopted from a variety of reference sources, including: Merck Research Laboratories (2001), Brown (2002), Anger & Johnson (1987), Marsh (1987), Katz (1987), and Klaassen & Watkins (2003).

5   As discussed in the present chapter, Table 2.2 is presented as an example of one way in which toxicants are sometimes classified. The information about adverse effects of specific substances in such listings is often, as in the present example, without comprehensive scientific verification. Even when by citation to the relevant scientific literature, the information presented is most likely to be oversimplified, e.g., lacking details such as dose and duration required to produce the stated adverse effect. Nevertheless, such lists can represent a starting place for the professional to learn more about a particular substance.

6   The outline in Table 2.3 is intended only as a guide to encourage the reader to include all relevant topics in a systematic approach in communicating clinical findings.

References

Albers, J. W., & Berent, S. (2000a). *Clinical neurobehavioral toxicology*. Philadelphia: W. B. Saunders.

Albers, J. W., & Berent, S. (2000b). Controversies in neurotoxicology: current status. *Neurologic Clinics, 18*, 741–764.

Albers, J. W., & Bromberg, M. B. (1995). Chemically induced toxic neuropathy. In N. L. Rosenberg (Ed.), *Occupational and environmental neurology* (pp. 175–233). Boston: Butterworth-Heinemann.

Albers, J. W., Hodach, R. J., Kimmel, D. W., & Treacy, W. L. (1980). Penicillamine-associated myasthenia gravis. *Neurology, 30*, 1246–1250.

Albin, R. L. (2000). Basal ganglia neurotoxins. In J. W. Albers and S. Berent (Eds.), *Clinical neurobehavioral toxicology* (pp. 665–680). Philadelphia: W. B. Saunders.

American Psychiatric Association (1994). *Diagnostic and statistical manual of mental disorders* (4th ed.). Washington, DC: APA.

Anger, W. K., & Johnson, B. L. (1987). Chemicals affecting behavior. In J. L. O'Donoghue (Ed.), *Neurotoxicity of industrial and commercial chemicals* (pp. 51–148). Boca Raton: CRC Press.

Berent, S., & Albers, J. W. (1999). Presentation to the joint Science Advisory Board (SAB) and Scientific Advisory Panel (SAP). Arlington: Environmental Protection Agency.

Berent, S., Sackellares, J. C., Giordani, B., Wagner, J. G., Donofrio, P. D., & Abou-Khalil, B. (1987). Zonisamide (CI-912) and cognition: results from preliminary study. *Epilepsia, 28*, 61–67.

Brown, J. S. (2002). *Environmental and chemical toxins and psychiatric illness*. Washington, DC: American Psychiatric Publishing.

Calne, D. B., Hochberg, F. H., Snow, B. J., and Nygaard, T. (1992). Theories of neurodegeneration. In J. W. Langston and A. Young (Eds.), *Neurotoxins and neurodegenerative disease* (pp. 1–5). New York: New York Academy of Sciences.

Carson, R. (1962). *Silent spring*. New York: Houghton Mifflin.

Carson, R. (1994). *Silent spring*. New York: Houghton Mifflin.

Christensen, J. D., Yurgelun-Todd, D. A., Babb, S. M., Gruber, S. A., Cohen, B. M., &

Renshaw, P. F. (1999). Measurement of human brain dexfenfluramine concentration by ^{19}F magnetic resonance spectroscopy. *Brain Research, 834,* 1–5.

Dow, M. I. (1994). Worker exposure studies. *Quality Assurance, 3,* 275–278.

Environmental Protection Agency (1991). *Pesticide Assessment Guidelines.* Washington, DC: EPA Office of Programs.

Faught, E., Ayala, R., Montouris, G. G., Leppik, I. E., & the Trial Group (2001). Randomized controlled trial of zonisamide for the treatment of refractory partial-onset seizures. *Neurology, 57,* 1774–1779.

Feldman, R. G. (1998). *Occupational and environmental neurotoxicology.* Philadelphia: Lippencott–Raven.

Gaylor, D., & Slikker, W., Jr (1992). Risk assessment for neurotoxicants. In H. A. Tilson and C. L. Mitchell (Eds.), *Neurotoxicology* (pp. 331–343). New York: Raven.

Goetz, C. G. (1985). *Neurotoxins in clinical practice.* New York: Spectrum.

Gore, A. (1994). Introduction to R. Carson's *Silent Spring.* In R. Carson (Ed.), *Silent spring* (pp. xv–xxvi) New York: Houghton Mifflin.

Harte, J., Holdren, C., Schneider, R., & Shirley, C. (1991). *Toxics A to Z.* Berkeley: University of California Press.

Hartman, D. E. (1995). *Neuropsychological toxicology: identification and assessment of human neurotoxic syndromes* (2nd ed.). New York: Plenum.

Katz, G. V. (1987). Metals and metalloids other than mercury and lead. In J. L. O'Donoghue (Ed.), *Neurotoxicity of industrial and commercial chemicals* (pp. 171–191). Boca Raton: CRC Press.

Kito, M., Maehara, M., & Watanabe, K. (1996). Mechanisms of T-type calcium channel blockade by zonisamide. *Seizure, 5,* 115–119.

Klaassen, C. D., & Watkins, J. B. (2003). *Casarett and Doull's essentials of toxicology.* New York: McGraw-Hill.

Koury, R., Stone, C. K., Stapczynski, J. S., & Blake, J. (1999). Sympathetic overactivity from fenfluramine-phentermine overdose. *European Journal of Emergency Medicine, 6,* 149–152.

Langston, J. W., & Young, A. (1992). *Neurotoxins and neurodegenerative disease.* New York: New York Academy of Sciences.

Marsh, D. O. (1987). The neurotoxicity of mercury and lead. In J. L. O'Donoghue (Ed.), *Neurotoxicity of industrial and commercial chemicals* (pp. 159–169). Boca Raton: CRC Press.

Mattsson, J. L., Boyes, W. K., & Ross, J. F. (1992). Incorporating evoked potentials into neurotoxicity test schemes. In H. A. Tilson & C. L. Mitchell (Eds.), *Neurotoxicology* (pp. 125–145). New York: Raven.

Mebs, D. (1988). Snake venom toxins: structural aspects. In J. O. Dolly (Ed.), *Neurotoxins in neurochemistry* (pp. 3–12). New York: Wiley.

Merck Research Laboratories (2001). *The Merck index: An encyclopedia of chemicals, drugs, and biologicals* (13th ed.). Whitehouse Station: Merck & Co.

National Research Council (1992). *Environmental neurotoxicology.* Washington, DC: National Academy Press.

Okada, M., Kaneko, S., Hirano, T., Mizuno, K., Kondo, T., Otani, K., & Fukushima, Y. (1995). Effects of zonisamide on dopaminergic system. *Epilepsy Research, 22,* 193–205.

Oommen, K. J., & Mathews, S. (1999). Zonisamide: a new antiepileptic drug. *Clinical Neuropharmacology, 22,* 192–200.

Richardson, W. S., Wilson, M. C., Williams, J. W., Jr, Moyer, V. A., & Naylor, C. D. (2000). Users' guides to the medical literature: XXIV. How to use an article on the clinical manifestations of disease. Evidence-Based Medicine Working Group. *Journal of the American Medical Association, 284*, 869–875.

Schaumburg, H. H., & Spencer, P. S. (2000). Classification of neurotoxic responses based on vulnerability of cellular sites. *Neurologic Clinics, 18*, 517–524.

Schenck, C. H., & Mahowald, M. W. (1996). Potential hazard of serotonin syndrome associated with dexfenfluramine hydrochloride (Redux). *Journal of the American Medical Association, 276*, 1220–1221.

Siegel, G. J., Agranoff, B. W., Fisher, S. K., Albers, R. W., & Uhler M. D. (Eds.) (1999). *Basic neurochemistry: molecular, cellular and medical aspects* (pp. 1007–1026). Philadelphia: Lippincott-Raven.

Spencer, P. S., Ludolph, A. C., & Kisby, G. E. (1992). Are human neurodegenerative disorders linked to environmental chemicals with excitotoxic properties? In J. W. Langston and A. Young (Eds.), *Neurotoxins and neurodegenerative disease* (pp. 154–160). New York: New York Academy of Sciences.

Suzuki, S., Kawakami, K., Nishimura, S., Watanabe, Y., Yagi, K., Seino, M., & Miyamoto, K. (1992). Zonisamide blocks T-type calcium channel in cultured neurons of rat cerebral cortex. *Epilepsy Research, 12*, 21–27.

World Health Organization (2000). *International classification of functioning, disability and health: Prefinal draft*. Geneva: WHO.

World Health Organization (2001). *International classification of functioning, disability and health (ICF)*. Geneva: WHO.

World Health Organization Workgroup (1985) *Chronic effects of organic solvents on the central nervous system*. Geneva: WHO and Nordic Council of Ministers.

3   Clinical and clinical research considerations

Introduction

The energies of many disciplines are directed toward problems associated with toxicants and their effects on behavior and the nervous system, what we have termed 'human neurobehavioral toxicology.' Emphases differ between these disciplines and their various specialties and subspecialties. Some are more laboratory based while others are clinically oriented. It is clear, however, that the knowledge generated by any one of these disciplines will be needed by all if a full and accurate understanding of this topic is to be attained. Costa (1992) stated it well when he said 'only the full integration of these multidisciplinary approaches can provide satisfactory answers to neurotoxicological questions.'

While the present book emphasizes only two disciplines, Neurology and Neuropsychology, the material draws heavily from knowledge generated by a wider professional community. A common denominator between these various disciplines is found in their bases in science. While artful skills often are required in all of these endeavors (e.g., laboratory techniques by the basic scientist, interviewing or testing techniques by a clinician), science provides the methods for knowledge generation.

Two general types of research have been described to study the effects of toxicants on the nervous system. Anger (1992) termed these: (1) experimental laboratory research, and (2) quasi-experimental. For Anger, the distinction between the two types of studies relates to the active manipulation of the independent variable in the former and the absence of such manipulation in the latter. Others have used similar wording to classify research (Kazdin, 1998). While this distinction may be accurate in many instances, there are problems with characterizing research in this manner. First, many studies that most of us would consider to be basic and, therefore, experimental do often contain considerable subjectivity. For instance, laboratory research might involve characterization of exposure, or some other independent variable, by analog estimation or observation of serendipitous differences in stimulus presence or magnitude. Second, the term, 'quasi-experimental' has a somewhat pejorative connotation because of its derivation through comparison with something else that is implied to be the ideal model.

In actuality, there are many types of research. Perhaps the most meaningful distinctions are descriptive and based on factors such as methodological distinctions, e.g., cohort in comparison with cross-sectional studies, or based on interest, e.g., clinical in comparison with basic research. Each type of study carries with it certain limitations and benefits. The continued development of methods and procedures will allow for increasingly sophisticated scientific inquiries of human neurobehavioral toxicology. The value of a distinction such as 'experimental' versus 'quasi-experimental' is questionable, and the distinction is probably inaccurate.

One could view all scientific research as being experimental. In the early days of science, the practitioner of science was often referred to as an 'experimentalist' (Woodworth & Schlosberg, 1938). In a later edition of their now historical book on experimental psychology, Woodworth and Schlosberg (1964) described the experimenter's requirements primarily as actions of controlling the conditions under which an event occurs. They went on to detail the then known ways to achieve the necessary controls, to control the events under study, to vary the conditions, to verify results, and to draw meaningful conclusions. They suggested, prophetically as it turns out, there might be any number of ways to accomplish such control, some known at the time and some yet to be discovered. For Woodworth, in particular, who started writing on the applications of science to psychology as early as 1910, any subject of inquiry was fair game for the scientist so long as a means could be found to bring the problem into the experimental process (Woodworth & Schlosberg, 1964). Of course, a large number of methodological, procedural, and mathematical advances have been introduced over the years that now allow the scientist to address questions in ways not possible in Woodworth's time.

Both Psychology and Neurology are fields based in science. These scientific foundations are manifested in several ways. Both fields, for instance, employ objective and quantitative methods to the extent possible. The work of both is aimed at contributing to an expanding knowledge base, knowledge which is archived through publication and related professional communications. Both fields attempt to deal with observable and operational variables in the conductance of their research as well as in clinical work, and both employ the scientific method to address research problems. Therefore, in terms of method as well as subject interest, the two fields are overlapping. Where the overlap ends, each brings unique knowledge and skill to the problems of common interest. In short, the two are compatible and invite collaboration with one another.

Scientific method

In its most simple expression, the scientific method consists of five basic steps:

- Problem.
- Hypothesis.
- Experiment.
- Analysis.
- Conclusions.

Each of these essential steps will be discussed below in more detail.

Definition of the problem to be addressed

A scientific problem is usually expressed as a question(s) that relates to some unknown aspect of the topic of interest. Such questions are formulated on the basis of thorough and systematic review of previous work by the investigator or others in order to identify what is known and what questions still need to be addressed to comprehend the topic more fully. Unknowns and inconsistencies in the literature should be identified at this step in the process and used to formulate new research questions.

Not all questions lend themselves to this approach. The problem must be testable (i.e., the question must be answerable) by the methods of science. The data that will be needed to address the question(s) must be observable and obtainable through a systematic approach. In some cases, e.g., psychometric data, this will be easier to effect than in other instances, e.g., historical information from interview. Methodological designs, procedures, and techniques need to be available to meet this qualification. For instance, at the time that the anatomical distribution and physiological mediation of several cholinergic muscarinic receptor subtypes had been fairly well studied *in vivo*, the use of pharmacological approaches to address additional questions could not be undertaken. This delay resulted from the fact that no adequate, selective receptor subtype antagonist had yet been identified (Kuhar, Couceyro, & Lambert, 1999). Once the antagonist had been discovered, it became possible to learn more about these receptors.

Hypothesis

The hypothesis is a proposed answer to the question raised in the problem step of the method. It is stated as, or reducible to, an 'if, then' proposition (e.g., If a subject (s) is exposed to 100 units of substance X, then s will evidence a change in speed of performance on test A). A given problem may necessitate several hypotheses (or several experiments) for a complete answer. The hypothesis should be written clearly and succinctly and should derive logically from the literature review and problem development. Also, it should reflect meaningful information that will advance our understanding of some important aspect of a topic area. For instance, studies are published too frequently that repeat hypotheses that were supported numerous times previously.

Experiment

A research design is created that allows for observations of variables relevant to testing the hypothesis while controlling for extraneous factors that could confound the results obtained. Usually, this involves a controlled experiment to test the proposed hypothesis, but other systematic approaches to controlled observation are sometimes employed. The research design is crucial to a systematic study of any topic. The ideal design is one that allows for substantial control over experimental variables. Such control is accomplished through a variety of methods, including the ability to randomize in subject selection and experimental group assignment. A combination of randomization and 'masking'[1] (i.e., 'single' if only one class, subject or experimenter is masked, and 'double' when keeping both subject and experimenter unaware of the exact treatment group to which the subject has been assigned), is seen as an effective way to control for potential experimenter and subject biases (Byar, Simon, Friedewald, Schlesselman, DeMets, Ellenberg, Gail, & Ware, 1976). Another challenge to human neurobehavioral research is found in the high variability associated with many behavioral variables. While ideal control is not always possible in human neurobehavioral research, it should be approximated to the fullest extent possible. The difference between the ideal and this approximation will limit what can be said about the results of a given study and should be discussed at the conclusion step in the scientific method (see below).

A good research design is one that plans for all aspects of the study. Not only does it reflect a plan for relevant data collection, but it is also directly connected to a planned statistical analysis. There are a variety of ways to accomplish these aims, depending on the specific research design chosen, e.g., mean comparisons, analysis of variance, regression models. A 'one-way classification' design, for instance, allows for comparison of results between two or more groups, while in a 'two-way' or 'cross-over' design, every subject can receive all treatments. Combining such basic designs produces a factorial design. A factorial design is often employed in neurobehavioral research, at least when meaningful control can be exerted over the intended variables of study. The employment of two (independent) variables – 'A' and 'B' – for example, allows for the statistical comparison of direct effects and interactions between and within multiple levels of two independent factors, A and B, as well as analysis of the possible interactions between A and B. A longitudinal or repeated measures aspect can also be incorporated into such a design by adding a third variable, e.g., 'C = time'. The data representing the outcome (dependent) variables, e.g., scores on a test of memory, can be analysed through the design in terms of the main effects of variables A or B, and in terms of the interactions between these independent variables. The ability to analyse these interactions represents an important value in the factorial research design because many behavioral events are contingent on other aspects of the organism or on the environment in which the study occurs. If, for instance, variable 'A' in a hypothetical study represented exposure to a given substance and 'B' represented subject age, a significant interaction between A and B would indicate that a meaningful effect for exposure was dependent on subject age, whether the subjects were older or younger. It is helpful for the investigator to depict the design graphically, and there are several ways to create such as image. Techniques for doing this, as well as more detailed information about experimental and statistical design, can be found in any number of textbooks on the topic (e.g., Edwards, 1985; Fisher, 1991; Pearson, 1993).

An experimental design must also account for what are variously termed 'intervening', 'nuisance', or, as in the field of epidemiology, 'confounding variables' or, simply, 'confounders'. Such variables are those whose effects the investigator is not interested in but that might influence the study outcome. Especially in the area of neurobehavioral toxicology, the effects of potential confounders must be identified or controlled in order to determine the effects of an identified substance on some outcome measure. It is likely that failure to account properly for potential confounders represents the one most important criticism that might be aimed at published reports in this research area (e.g., Albers & Berent, 2000). Garabrant (2000b) describes three primary ways to account for confounding variables: 'restriction' (limiting the range of a factor, e.g., age, to remove its contribution effectively to the observed outcome), 'matching' (e.g., matching control subjects identically to experimental subjects on one or more confounding variables like sex, race, IQ, or some other factor), and 'randomization' in subject selection. At times, an investigator will deal with a potential confounder by making it an independent variable and, thus, a primary focus of study. Garabrant (2000a) proceeds to describe three types of epidemiological study to which these controls apply. These studies actually apply to any field, and they certainly represent important designs for neurobehavioral research. The first is the 'cohort study'. A cohort study is longitudinal. It relies on the comparison over time of two or more disease-free groups for which objective exposure histories are known. The outcome variable is usually some disease factor hypothetically or actually known to result from the specific substance of interest. A 'case-control study' is the second type of research. 'Cases' are identified from a 'source' population. Controls are selected from the same population, and the exposure histories for both groups are compared. Since these histories are often obtained on the basis of self-report or inferred from historical descriptions of job assignments, there is a strong subjective component to the research data that potentially limits the reliability of the case control method. Finally, there is the 'cross-sectional study', where the prevalence of a dependent variable, usually a disease characteristic or analog, is measured and compared at one point in time between a sample and its control group. The factorial design discussed above can be employed with any of these epidemiological models.

While not an actual research design, the literature on the effects of various substances on neurobehavioral function contains many case reports. Case reports usually are systematic clinical descriptions of cases that the author believes are the result of some exposure. The primary value of the case report model is in its hypotheses-generating capacity. Nevertheless, there are situations when the case report method may be the only available tool for learning more about a particular topic. One such situation, for instance, relates to the concept of a study's *power* (i.e., the ability of the study to detect a statistically significant difference between groups when it exists). A combination of the size of the effect and the size of the sample is used to determine the power of a given study. The bigger the effect, the smaller the sample required to detect a group difference. Since the expected effect in many human toxicological studies is subtle, one method used by investigators to increase the power of a study is to increase the size of the sample. However, it is not always possible to identify a sufficient number of subjects to achieve sufficient power, especially when confirmed cases of exposure are rare. In these instances, a detailed case report study (a systematic study that employs several cases of the same nature) may be the only way to provide information about the hypothesized relationship. Again, the value in terms of hypothesis confirmation or causal determination will be very limited using this study method. Case report studies, in fact, may be of most value when they lead to a finding of a 'counter-instance' of a previously supported relationship (Kazdin, 1998).

Before leaving the topic of a study's power, it should be mentioned that while increasing the number of subjects enhances the power of the study to detect significant differences, it can also increase sensitivity to the point that small and clinically insignificant differences become statistically significant. An example of this might be a cross-sectional study in which a clinically meaningless difference in IQ (e.g., less than five points) is reported to have important practical implications based solely on a statistically significant difference between groups. A knowledge of the effect size and the clinical implications of the effect should, therefore, always be considered in determining the practical significance of a reported finding (Kraemer, 1992).

Regardless of the experimental design employed, the data required to address the hypothesis(es) must be objectively obtainable and relevant. Clinical research will often employ tests and procedures used in routine practice as a means for obtaining data by systematizing their collection to fit the parameters of the research design. The disciplines of Neuropsychology and Neurology both lend themselves to research that employs data collected in the clinical setting because both have developed standards of practice that are fairly consistently systematic. As a result, clinical research problems can often be approached via designs that are made retrospectively; that is, designs that employ previously collected information. Whether the design is retrospective or prospective, i.e., planned after or before the collection of data, the investigator needs to adhere to the human use considerations discussed below. Whether prospective or retrospective in design, the tools and procedures used to collect the data should be valid and reliable and used in an acceptably standardized manner. Since retrospective studies are planned after data have been collected for some other purpose, e.g., as part of a clinical examination, the experimental design is somewhat different than in the case of a prospective study. The primary difference reflects the absence of actual experiment. In its place, the design contains a plan for identifying the data that will be used and how those data will be handled. Other aspects of the scientific method remain relevant, and before analysing any data, there should be a stated problem, hypothesis, identification of data relevant to test the hypothesis and control of extraneous variables, planned analysis, conclusions and limitations on what can be said as a result of the study.

The experiment in science is in many ways analogous to the collection of data in the clinical setting (Table 3.1). In both instances, the data needed are determined by the questions asked. If psychological tests are employed, for example, the behavioral domains to be measured should be limited to those relevant to the stated question. The relevance can be determined by considering what is needed to answer the question directly, e.g., a test of verbal memory if the question specifies that area of functioning. There may be a need to consider additional data to control for confounders or otherwise

Table 3.1 Comparable steps in research and clinical practice

Research		Clinical practice	
Step	*Activity*	*Step*	*Activity*
Problem	Literature review and identification of relevant and unanswered questions	Problem	Interview and review of past medical and psychological history, identification of symptoms
Hypothesis	Define questions	Working diagnosis	Define relevant questions and information needed to address them
Experiment	Experimental design and data collection	Clinical examination	Perform relevant tests and procedures
Analysis	Descriptive and analytic statistical treatment of data	Analysis, including the integration of clinical findings with information from published research	Differential diagnosis and clinical decisions
Conclusions	Report of findings, generalizations and generation or new questions	Conclusions	Recommendations for treatment and further tests as needed

to understand the meaningfulness of the primary data (e.g., a measure of reading level when a paper-and-pencil-type test is employed, or a measure of limb temperature when performing nerve conduction studies). Whereas, in research, one must control for potential confounders and exercise caution when inferring causality from the results of study, the process of differential diagnosis serves a similar function in the clinical enterprise (see Chapter 4). While Clinical Neuropsychology and Neurology strive to approximate the scientific approach, the approximation is never perfect, and careful attention must be given to the limitations of the knowledge obtained from either the research or the clinical arena.

The common term used to refer to the collection of a wide range of data with disregard for their relevance to the proposed question is 'shot gunning'. Investigators and clinicians give various reasons for engaging in this practice. The investigator might argue, for example, that it is more economical to collect as much information at one time as possible since the subject or patient might not be available later. Another might argue that he or she wants to collect as much information as possible because the state of knowledge about a given topic is too scant to know what will be important beforehand. Regardless of the justifications, the practice is ill advised and usually reflects the lack of adequately stated questions, hypotheses, or other aspects of planning the investigation.

There are many reasons not to engage in the shot gun approach to data acquisition. To continue with the marksmanship analogy, for instance, there is a folk description of the person who repeatedly fires a hand gun at the side of a barn and then finds where the bullets have struck. The gunman then draws a circle around some of the bullet holes that seem to be close together and brags about his or her ability to shoot a 'tight cluster.' Since such a cluster is the usual index of accurate shooting, others who are unaware of the actual randomness of the aiming are likely to believe the gunman to be a better 'shot' than is actually the case. The practice is sometimes light-heartedly referred to as 'Texas sharp shooting' to distinguish it from real marksmanship.

Shot gunning in science and clinical practice can lead to the same inaccurate outcome. Toss several coins in the air multiple times, and all will occasionally come up heads. Include magnetic resonance imaging data in a study when they have no direct connection to the study hypothesis and the test might reveal positive findings that are in actuality unrelated to the study question, or may even lack clinical meaningfulness. The authors once had occasion to reanalyse data that consisted of well over 300 physiological and behavioral variables and on which the original investigator had reported significant correlation (with no error corrections) among about 5% of these variables. By chance alone, one might expect this percentage of significant comparisons. When these data were reanalysed with proper control for multiple comparisons, the meaningfulness of the findings concluded by the original investigator disappeared. Also, it is important always to keep in mind that correlation does not imply causality. This was another aspect of research analysis ignored by the investigator in the work just described. That investigator attributed his correlation findings to exposure to toxic substances on the basis of his 'significant' (actually non-significant when properly controlled) correlation findings, but he ignored the relationships between variables that did not fit his hypothesis. Setting aside for the moment the ethical violation of his selective reporting, one of those variables was the subjects' educational levels. Interestingly, the educational variable continued to be significantly correlated with most of the investigator's primary study variables even after control for multiple comparisons. Following the investigator's correlation analyses, he performed a between-groups analysis and reported a significant difference in terms of exposure to the study toxicant. When education (a pre-exposure measure in this instance) was included in our reanalysis of these same data using a covariance model, however, there was no statistically significant difference between experimental and control groups in terms of 'exposure'.

It may be helpful to comment on the distinction between quantitative and qualitative research. While the ideal in science is to conduct research that is as quantitative as possible, there are occasions when quantification is not completely possible. A case report that describes the occurrence of a rare disorder or a scholarly theoretical review of an important topic represent two examples of work that are sometimes referred to as 'qualitative research'. Instances of improper analyses should not be confused with qualitative research. When done properly, a less than completely quantitative study may enlighten our understanding of the importance of problems, help us formulate pertinent questions, and generate relevant hypotheses (Woodworth & Schlosberg, 1964). Qualitative research is almost always hypothesis generating rather than hypothesis testing. Qualitative research can be seen as improper only when the author of such a study, or others, attempt to draw conclusions from the work that are not justified by the limitations of the method.

Analysis

The results of the experiment are analyzed mathematically, leading to a probability statement about the likelihood that the hypothesis is true. As already implied, analysis and design are intimately bound to one another. The experimental design anticipates the statistical treatment of the data, leading to the collection of data suitable for analyses and relevant to the research hypothesis(es). In the research setting, this step in the process involves descriptive and inferential statistics, usually to determine if two or more comparison groups are representative of a common population of scores. The analogous step in clinical practice involves the comparison of an individual's scores, or other clinical data, with historical controls or normative data.

Even when significant results are obtained, a single study may not be sufficient to establish cause-and-effect relationships. Also, there is a difference between statistical significance and clinical significance. A cross-sectional study reviewed by one of the present authors, for instance, found a statistically significant difference in IQ scores between a group of subjects purportedly exposed to a toxicant and their controls. The investigator of that study discussed the meaningfulness of the findings in terms of the adverse effects of the exposure on the exposed subjects. While the results were statistically significant, the mean difference between the groups in the reported study was about three points, less than the standard measurement error for the test employed. Clinically, it would be very difficult to draw much in the way of a significant conclusion from this finding. Such results can have theoretical value, nevertheless. For instance, the finding can be added to those of other studies and the patterns of research outcomes examined and evaluated. Formal quantitative review techniques, such as meta-analysis, exist that permit comparison of research outcomes and effect sizes across a series of studies, and which are preferable to a less formal description of positive and negative findings (Hartman, 1995). In carrying out such analyses, however, it is important to keep in mind that the validity of the findings of a meta-analysis will be limited by the quality of the original research upon which the analyses are based.

Conclusions based on the scientific method

Following the analysis step in the scientific method, conclusions are drawn concerning the correctness of the initially stated hypotheses. Statements are also made about the extent to which the findings generalize to others in the population under study as well as to populations not directly represented in the study. The ability to generalize is critical, but over-generalization is to be avoided. Woodworth and Schlosberg (1964) wrote: 'The experimenter would like, of course, to reach a conclusion of some generality, but often he feels in duty bound to confess that he is not sure of it except under the specific conditions of his experiment.' The authors continued, 'He would like to "extrapolate" from the laboratory setup to the conditions of daily life, but he is not sure. . . . He does right to qualify his conclusion.' Science must simplify to understand nature better. This simplification occurs through sampling, control of variables, and the various other constraints of design discussed above. These technical necessities also limit what we can conclude from the results of our studies. While ultimately we may be interested in establishing cause-and-effect relationships between variables, most results from research do not reach that level. Just as the clinician's differential diagnosis is limited by the information obtained, the researcher must be careful not to over-generalize from study results.

The researcher's findings should be communicated with the wider professional community. This is accomplished usually through publication or other formal communication. Sufficient detail should be included in the communication to allow others to replicate the work, as replication in itself helps to establish the factualness and generalizability of a finding. It is generally wise to resist the temptation to announce prematurely study results through news media or other public vehicles. This is especially true when results are provocative. Just as a clinician would never share a partially substantiated diagnosis with a patient without considerable qualification, especially when that diagnosis might be anxiety provoking, the scientist needs to be cautious in communicating the results of inquiry. The scientific method is not a speedy process, but it does allow for such public announcements at appropriate times, e.g., following verification of the results by replication and further study. There are exceptions, of course, as when findings may indicate an immediate threat of harm.

Special research considerations

Animal models

Animal models are used extensively in toxicological research for a number of reasons. The information from these animal studies help to identify techniques and procedures that might eventually have application in humans and also helps in the determination of cause-and-effect relationships (Hill, 1965; Stanton & Spear, 1990). Animals can be randomly assigned to exposure conditions of varying dose, frequency, duration, and timing, as well as to dosage levels that are higher than would be safe in humans. There are limitations to the usefulness of animal models, however. As subjects in research where the ultimate aim is to advance knowledge about human responses to a stimulus, the animal model is an imperfect substitute. The meaningfulness of the results (i.e., the generalizability of the findings) to human populations will be determined by the similarity between the species. There are considerable differences in function and susceptibility between most species, to the extent that it is insufficient to rely solely on animal models to study toxic effects in humans.

Non-human primates, for example, have been reported to be more vulnerable than are humans to the toxic effects of polychlorinated biphenyls (PCBs) (Kimbrough, 1995). Generalizing the results of such studies to people might, therefore, fit a 'better safe than sorry' consideration as discussed in Chapter 2, but the results may not increase our understanding of the actual causal relationships in people. In addition, there are behaviors that may be unique to humans, may differ qualitatively between species, or for which no adequate means has been discovered for studying the behavior in animals, e.g., thinking. Even when creativeness leads to a technique for measurement of such behaviors in animals, there is no guarantee that the construct is similar between the species. While experimental control is usually viewed as a desirable aspect of experimental design, the ability to exert more control in animal studies may, in itself, serve also to limit the generalizability of findings (Kazdin, 1998). For example, some procedures that increase the regulation of dose or other aspects of exposure to a substance, e.g., intravenous administration of a substance, might not be allowed in comparable studies in humans. This could lead to different procedures being employed between species (e.g., injection in animals and dermal absorption in people), with possibly different outcomes as a consequence of exposure (Baelum, 1999). Animal studies can provide models that increase our understanding of such factors as relative toxicity, probable mechanisms of action, and functional neuroanatomical involvement for a given substance. Nevertheless, the determination of a causal relationship between exposure to a substance and specific neurobehavioral outcomes in humans ultimately requires evidence from human research (Berent & Trask, 2000).

Additional issues related to sample selection

When selecting subjects to participate in a study, the goal is to select a sample that represents a larger population of interest. The comparison groups should, except for the treatment variable, be comparable in as many ways as possible. The strength of the study will be directly related to the success of controlling for potential group differences. Random assignment of subjects to experimental and control groups is viewed by many scientists as the ideal way to achieve equivalent groups (Kazdin, 1998). Sample size influences this process, however, and equivalence between groups through randomization may be difficult to achieve when working with small samples (Hsu, 1989). Also, random assignment of human subjects to experimental or control conditions has at times brought ethical challenges on the basis that, especially in medical settings, being randomized to a control group could put a patient at a treatment disadvantage (Schafer, 1985; Weinstein, 1974b). Some have argued to allow randomization only when the evidence clearly supports true 'equipoise' between treatment conditions (Freedman, 1987).

   Many studies in the area of human neurotoxicology have been characterized as having failed to control adequately for relevant confounding factors (Baker, 1985). When potential confounding variables are identified, the investigator can attempt to control their moderating effects by statistical designs such as matching the groups on the potential confounders or through the use of statistical controls, such as analysis of covariance. Bias can enter a study at any point, and some of these biases begin with the selection of study participants. Potential biases in the selection of subjects for human study can occur in many ways. Neurobehavioral toxicological studies often rely on serendipitous samples, individuals who, because of occupation or other circumstances, may have been more likely than others to become exposed to some specified substance. Often, this is the only way to identify an 'exposed' sample since the toxicity of many substances precludes purposeful exposure. In industrial settings, the investigator must contend with a number of phenomena that can bias the sampling and lead to selection bias. For instance, limiting the study participants to active workers might exclude a number of people who are not active due to exposure to the study agent. Also, there is the overall tendency for working populations to have lower morbidity and mortality than the general population, a phenomenon referred to as 'the Healthy Worker Effect' (Garabrant, 2000b). In psychiatric settings, the investigator must contend with what has been termed 'Berkson's bias', the observation that patients with more complex, comorbid disorders are more likely to seek treatment than are those without such conditions (Galbaud du, Newman, & Bland, 1993).

Selection bias can also occur with regard to age, sex, socio-economic status, education or reading level, or, depending on the study hypothesis and proposed dependent variables, a multitude of neurobehavioral or physical considerations. In a study in which learning and memory are important outcome variables, for example, uncontrolled differences in reading level between treatment groups or between the study sample and overall population can lead to false conclusions and improper generalizations. Failure to consider differences in age, height, weight, or body mass index in a study employing nerve conduction study results can lead to similar errors (Albers, Wald, Werner, Franzblau, & Berent, 1999).

Volunteerism itself can produce inadvertent bias in sampling. People who volunteer for research tend to be better educated, have a higher occupational status, be more self-disclosing, have a higher need for social approval, and be more sociable than the general public (Rosenthal & Rosnow, 1975, 1991). In order to minimize these potential volunteer effects, the investigator should actively recruit subject participation and increase the range of potential subjects rather than relying solely on those that simply volunteer through newspaper or other advertisements. When possible, randomized selection of subjects from the study population can be employed as a way of reducing bias.

Protection of subjects in research

'Research procedures likely to cause serious or lasting harm to a participant are not used unless the failure to use these procedures might expose the participant to risk of greater harm or unless the research has great potential benefit (to the participant) and fully informed and voluntary consent is obtained from each participant.'

(American Psychological Association, 1987, p.6).

Determination of toxicity in animals and humans is an important aspect in the development of new drug treatments for disease. Toxicants are also studied for their potential usefulness as pesticides, cleaners, combustibles, and other practical applications. Since toxicity is often a by-product of some other primary, benign intent (e.g., in the manufacture of products such as glass or plastics), we also need to understand the impact of these secondary outcomes. Our need to study these various issues, together with the fact that we are often trying to understand aspects of toxicity through its applications, brings legal and ethical considerations into focus. The situation produces tension and, at times, conflicts between our need to know and our need to protect the animal and human subjects who would take part in these studies. Everyone involved in these activities should have a clear understanding of these considerations and the historical and rational explanations for them. For the most part, we will limit our discussion in this section to regulations and guidelines in the USA. With this in mind, it should be mentioned that some uncertainty remains regarding to whom the formal regulations apply. That is, do they apply only to federally funded projects or to all research more generally? These comments aside, most nations have regulations governing the conductance of research, especially with humans, as do the professional organizations to which the research investigators belong and the institutions in which they work. In fact, familiarization with the various regulations governing research has become increasingly required of research investigators. The following paragraphs are intended to provide a review and discussion of some of these considerations.

Title 45, Code of Federal Regulations, Part 46 (Department of Health and Human Services, 1991), commonly referred to as '45 CFR 46', is the primary document containing federal regulations about the protection of human subjects in research. The complete collection of federal policies regarding research, referred to as 'The Common Rule,' is contained in a number of documents published by various branches of government, e.g., Department of Agriculture (7 CFR Part 1c), Department of Energy (10 CFR Part 745), and Environmental Protection Agency (40 CFR Part 26).[2] For most practical purposes, however, 45 CFR 46 is the source document for individuals concerned with human research subjects and reflects the basic policy governing all federally supported research (National Institutes of Health, 1995).

Research is defined in 45 CFR 46 as the following: 'a systematic investigation, including research development, testing and evaluation, designed to develop or contribute to generalizable knowledge' (Department of Health and Human Services, 1991: Section 46.102 d).

A human subject is defined as a living individual about whom information is obtained. The information may be data obtained through intervention or interaction with the person, or it may be identifiable private information obtained by any means (Department of Health and Human Services, 1991: Section 46.102 f). These regulations apply regardless of the status of the investigator(s), e.g., student or professional.

Before beginning any research with human subjects, the investigator is required to submit the intended protocol to an institutional review board (IRB) for the board's review and approval of the study. In the process of their review, the IRB is empowered to suggest modifications to the proposed study protocol, to approve or disapprove the protocol. While these regulations technically apply to projects conducted, sponsored, or regulated by the US Federal Government, their application in practice is almost universal.

An institution is likely to have formally assured the government that it will comply with the policies on human research (through completion of a formal statement termed the 'assurance of compliance'). This means, of course, that the institution is speaking for its employees and the employees' students and collaborators as well (local or anywhere else in the world). This is an important observation because it provides a basis for understanding why institutions are so sensitive to regulatory details. It should also sensitize us to how interdependent we are on every individual complying with these regulations in their research. These various research regulations are said to provide only a framework for documenting that serious efforts have been made to protect human subjects in research and are not intended as a rigid set of rules. Nevertheless, it is also stated that failure to comply with policies can lead to loss of research privileges for an individual, a laboratory, or for an entire institution (National Institutes of Health, 1995). Each of these possible actions has occurred.

The ethical conduct of research is viewed by almost all, investigators and regulators alike, as a necessary prerequisite to involving humans in research projects. This is reflected in the ethical standards of many professional organizations (e.g., American Psychological Association, 1992) and other societal institutions. Nevertheless, whether through ignorance or malintent, investigators have not always behaved ethically in conducting their research. These instances of unethical behavior, and the historical reasons for society's emphasis on the need for formal regulatory oversight of human research, are complex and beyond the scope of the present book. Some of the more important events deserve mention nevertheless.

Until early in the 20th century, ethical concerns about inquiries involving humans centered on a medical therapeutic model. As clinical research became more widely practiced, concerns about safety and the ethical treatment of the subjects in such research also grew. These concerns were enhanced by a number of adverse experiences that, in turn, resulted in formal guidelines and rules for the conduct of research involving humans. One of the most dramatic of these experiences involved research conducted by Nazi physicians in the period leading up to and during the Second World War. In 1946, 23 of these physicians were tried at Nuremberg for crimes associated with their treatment of prisoners (National Institutes of Health, 1995). An outcome of those trials was the codification of a set of ethical standards for the conduct of research involving humans, now known as The Nuremberg Code. Among other things, The Nuremberg Code emphasized the idea that voluntary consent by subjects in research was absolutely essential (United States Government, 1949). As a result of these events, the National Institutes of Health established the first federal policy for the protection of human subjects in 1953, paving the way for the establishment of IRBs and prospective review of research (National Institutes of Health, 1995). In 1964, the World Medical Association (later the World Health Organization) adopted the *Helsinki Declaration*, which emphasized the safety of subjects in research, including respect for animals used in research, and set the stage for formal protocol and risk-to-benefit analyses in biomedical research.

Several events in the 1970s led to further regulations of human research. The best publicized of these events, perhaps, was the Tuskegee Syphilis Study, a longitudinal project funded by the government which began in the 1930s (National Institutes of Health, 1995). Approximately 400 African–American men were involved in the study without their knowledge. These men were systematically denied penicillin for treatment, of their syphilis, even after the drug became the standard of treatment, in order to study the natural history of the disease (National Institutes of Health, 1995). This and other negative research-related events led to Senate hearings and the National Research Act 1974 (Public Law 93–348), eventuating in 45 CFR 46 described above. The National Commission for the Protection of Human Subjects of Biomedical and Behavioral Research was also formed. In 1979, this commission issued *The Belmont Report*, which attempts to summarize the basic ethical principles that should guide human research. It emphasizes the three fundamental principles relevant for all research with human subjects:

- Respect for persons.
- Beneficence.
- Justice.

Respect for persons acknowledges dignity and autonomy. Because this principle necessitates informed consent, it also calls for special treatment of persons with diminished autonomy who might be asked to participate in research they might not completely understand, e.g., children and those with mental disabilities or severe illnesses. Since the subject matter of neurobehavioral toxicological research often calls for the study of people with diminished autonomy, this principle may be especially relevant. It should also be mentioned that a waiver of informed consent, or even a complete exemption from research review for a specific project, can be appropriate under some conditions of study, and the researcher should work closely with their IRB to ensure that in all cases proper procedures are followed.

Beneficence calls for careful analysis of risks and benefits before entering a human subject in research. It invites identification of alternative ways of generating knowledge when these might be available. In evaluating this principle in its review, an IRB will closely examine the proposed research design to ensure that it reflects sound, safe, and ethical practices. A good research design is a requirement for the proposed study to be considered ethical (Levine, 1988).

To meet the principle of justice, subjects must be treated fairly. Decisions to include or exclude classes of subjects must be carefully justified to prevent inequitable treatment of one group or another. Also, an IRB might ask if the subjects of study are likely to benefit from the results, and, if not, why they are being proposed as participants.

The implications of the distinctions and overlap between clinical work and research may be obvious, but they are far reaching, nevertheless. For instance, common procedures might be used in both instances, clinical or research. The neurologist or neuropsychologist might decide to employ data derived from clinical interview in subsequent research. In so doing, the clinician has engaged in practice that meets the definition of research as described in 45 CFR 46. At what point should the clinician prepare and submit a protocol for this activity to an IRB? In the simple example just given, the answer to the question is not difficult. The interview might have occurred in the context of clinical work, that work meeting the usual standards of practice, i.e., nothing was done differently for the sake of research independent of clinical considerations. In this case, it is likely that the subsequent use of these data to address a research hypothesis is retrospective. If, on the other hand, the clinical interview was part of a planned research methodology, then it might be prospective. In either instance, the IRB approval should be sought before the time the research is initiated. If retrospective, that may well be after the clinical work has been completed. If prospective, it may be required before the interview. Of course, every case will be unique, and it is difficult to make a general rule that will apply in all instances of clinical research. There are also instances when a project might be exempt from IRB review, or even the requirement that informed consent be obtained to use the information. The exemption might be because of subject anonymity and lack of *linkability* of subject to data, for example. Each case needs to be evaluated on its own merits, but the clinical investigator should be sensitive to the ethical issues associated with research, know and adhere to the regulations.

Bias

Attending to ethical concerns can influence the design of a research study in ways that introduce additional bias. For example, the principle of *Respect for Persons* necessitates that subjects in most studies be informed about the nature of the proposed study and give their consent before participating. The process of informing and obtaining consent is in itself an intervention with the subject, and it has been suggested that the subjects' behavior could be altered (i.e., biased) as a result of these interventions (Kihlstrom, 1995). Put another way, the intervention might produce an iatrogenic effect (Myers Cairns & Singer, 1987). When such a change occurs, the referent study could be said to be *reactive* (Williams, Lees & Brown, 1993; Lees-Haley & Brown, 1992). A participant might be told during the process of consent, for instance, that a particular study would seek to identify possible side-effects of a substance to which he or she may have been exposed. This could imply that certain symptoms are to be expected following such exposure and increase the likelihood that the participant will report those symptoms. Importantly, such information might enhance the subject's sensitivity to a host of non-specific symptoms, some or all of which might represent variations of normality, that he or she might then associate with the exposure. If the study is one that is concerned with a sample of potentially exposed persons, as in a work setting, the effect is likely to be different between groups because the information will remove any masking that might otherwise have been in place with regard to exposed or non-exposed conditions.

Many of the symptoms that are reported across human neurotoxicological studies are non-specific and similar from one study to another, including complaints experienced by non-exposed as well as exposed individuals, e.g., headache, dizziness, fatigue, forgetfulness. Williams, Lees, & Brown (1993) have written that the non-specific nature of these symptoms suggests that some general 'psychological' confounder is responsible for these observations rather than their being a reflection of the effects of a specific toxicant. In terms of the Hill (1965) criteria, discussed in more detail below, the pattern of these study reports would probably be neither consistent (criterion 7) nor specific (criterion 8) in addition to possibly failing to meet other Hill criteria.

Since the phenomenon of *reactivity* is a likely occurrence in studies with human subjects, it is probably wise to attempt to determine its presence and, when possible, control for its influences. This experimental control might be accomplished through the use of instruments designed to measure a subject's susceptibility to influence or test the participant's sophistication regarding the effects of a given toxicant. The researcher might also include items in self-report inventories that reflect expected as well as non-expected effects of a given substance, or use other devices that are designed to measure the specificity as well as the sensitivity of the participant's reports. The results of such techniques can be employed to define potential confounder variables that can then be incorporated into the analyses of results. *Expectation bias* can be present that is not the product of the investigator's intervention, of course, and should be specifically evaluated before interpreting research results. Also, attention should be given to these areas of possible confounds in reading and evaluating published studies as well as when planning to conduct a study (Berent & Trask, 2000).

Masking and placebo controls

As already mentioned, it is often difficult or impossible to directly administer a stimulus to humans in toxicological research. There are exceptions, and one of these is found in studies designed to establish the effectiveness and safety of substances to be used as medications. In these and other instances when the investigator controls the stimulus variable, an available method for experimental control is to conduct a double-masked, placebo-control study. 'Placebo' refers to an inert agent that would not ordinarily be expected to alter the outcome variable. In such a model, the experimental group would receive the active substance, while the control group would receive the

placebo. 'Double-masking' refers to the situation when neither the participant nor the researcher knows who is receiving the active drug or who is given
the placebo. In a single-masked study, it is usually the subject who is unaware
of which agent, active drug or placebo, he or she is receiving. Although
studies are done without masking, e.g., 'open labeled designs', these carry the
risk that either or both experimenter or subject expectancies may exert an
effect on the outcome. In a review of studies concerned with the effects of
carbon monoxide, for example, Benignus (1993) stated that 75% of the single-
masked (participant-masked) studies reported significant results in comparison with only 26% of double-masked studies reporting significance.
However, masking alone is no absolute guarantee that all potential influence
will be eliminated since the investigator, subject, or both may still be able to
'guess' the identity of who is receiving the active substance and who is
not (Margraf, Ehlers, Roth, Clark, Sheikh, Agras & Taylor, 1991; Carroll,
Rounsaville & Nich, 1994).

The use of technicians to administer tests and procedures, who are kept
uninformed about the exact nature of the study hypothesis, may aid in over-
coming potential bias from inadequate masking. Another suggested technique is to measure routinely the efficacy of masking by having investigators
and participants guess the status of selected participants (Beatty, 1972). Case-
control studies present an added challenge because participants may be self-
identified as 'exposed' or not, and masking may be impossible. Ney, Collins, &
Spensor (1986) have suggested that investigators should measure the participants' and the observer's assessment for a possible attribution factor, that is,
whether they believe that an observed change resulted from the study agent or
from some other factor. Although the use of masking techniques is well
known, it is rare for investigators systematically to evaluate the effectiveness
of these techniques in a study (Ney *et al.*, 1986; Oxtoby, Jones, & Robinson,
1989).

Evaluation of research claims regarding causality

Professionals interested in human neurobehavioral toxicology may manifest
that interest through research or clinical applications. Whether directly
engaged in the planning and implementation of research, or a consumer of
published reports of research, the principles discussed in this chapter should
be considered in the evaluation of research findings. These principles are put
in question format and summarized in Table 3.2. In addition, Hill (1965)
listed 10 criteria that should be considered when establishing a toxic etiology for a given substance. Causality is an important but complex topic
and differs from the clinical concept of etiology (see Chapter 8 for a full
discussion of the topic of causality). We rely on published studies to document conclusions regarding cause in a given case or in a group of cases.
Criteria, such as those listed by Hill, can aid in evaluating the implications of conclusions from a research investigation and can also help in

Table 3.2 Factors to consider in the planning or evaluation of human neurobehavioral research

Factors	Questions
General	Does the research plan iterate clearly the five steps in the scientific process?
Problem	Is the literature review relevant, representative and inclusive?
	Is the research question testable?
Hypothesis	Is the hypothesis stated clearly and in a form that is reducible to an 'if, then' proposition?
	Does the hypothesis follow logically from the literature review and problem statement?
Experiment	Does the experiment reflect a systematic method for collecting data that are relevant to the hypothesis?
	Are primary or independent variables specified, and is there an appropriate plan for their statistical treatment?
	Is the study prospective or retrospective?
	Do subjects represent a population that is relevant to the research question and hypothesis?
	Are control subjects appropriate?
	How are subjects selected and assigned to research conditions? Is the selection equitable in addition to representative?
	Is the study institutional review board reviewed and approved, i.e., is it ethical?
	Is the study peer reviewed?
	How are the data collected, e.g., observation, self-report, report by others, psychometric, neurometric, other?
	What is the method for obtaining exposure information? Is it described clearly and adequate in terms of objectivity and accuracy? Is it inclusive in terms of time, duration, and dosage? Is it based on laboratory findings or self-report? Is it specific in terms of substance? Is it actual or analog?
	Is an appropriate experimental design described clearly and in sufficient detail that the study could be replicated by others?
	Are the proposed procedures valid, reliable, and safe? Are standardized procedures used in their administration?
	What type of design is planned, e.g., cohort, cross-sectional, other?
	What are the potential subject and experimenter biases and is there a plan for their control?
	What is the informed consent process? Is it reasonable? How does it potentially affect the subject's responses to the research?
	Are all potential confounders identified?

Is there an adequate plan for the control of potential confounders?

What type of controls are used, e.g. restriction, masking, randomization, other?

Is there a plan for evaluating the effectiveness of control methods?

Is an expected level of significance defined, e.g., an alpha level?

Analysis
Does the analysis include an appropriate number of comparisons, and were these specified in the design?

What is the planned level of analysis, e.g., descriptive, statistical inference?

Are the data quantitative (if so, at what level, e.g., nominal, ratio) or qualitative?

Are the data based on valid and reliable instruments and collection procedures?

Are comparisons based on control groups or historical controls, i.e., normative data?
Are the norms used appropriate?

Does the analysis follow logically from the experiment, and was it anticipated in the design?

Are there controls for a Type I error from multiple comparisons, e.g., Bonferroni?

What is the level of statistical significance?
How is this expressed, e.g., odds ratio, p value?

Conclusion
Are conclusions consistent with and do they follow logically from the stated problem, hypothesis, and data?

Do the results confirm or fail to confirm the study hypothesis?

Are weaknesses identified and discussed?

Are speculative statements or conclusions clearly identified as such?

Does the investigator set reasonable limits on generalizations?

Are the results consistent or contrary to prior findings, fact, or theories?

Do the findings suggest causal relationships?
How do they relate to Hill's criteria?

If simply descriptive, do the results add meaningfully to present understanding?

Does the study generate new hypotheses?

establishing etiology in a given clinical case. The criteria listed by Hill cover the following:

- Is the timing of exposure and onset of signs appropriate?
- Is there evidence of a high relative risk based on sound epidemiology studies or case reports?
- Is the proposed cause–effect relationship biologically plausible?
- Is there evidence of an anticipated dose–response relationship?
- Does removal from exposure modify the adverse effect?
- Has the existence of an animal model been established?
- Is there consistency among studies conducted at different times and in different settings?
- Is the cause–effect relationship relatively specific?
- Is there evidence of analogous problems caused by similar agents?
- Have other potential causes (explanations) been investigated and eliminated?

Also, Richardson, Wilson, Williams, Moyer, & Naylor (2000) listed related criteria specific to the evaluation of research literature that purports to establish clinical diagnoses or studies that report on some aspect of specified diagnoses. The criteria listed by Richardson *et al.* relate strongly to a process of differential diagnosis. These criteria include such considerations as the adequacy of the diagnosis in explaining major symptoms, how closely and simply the diagnosis fits the reported clinical observations, whether or not it is the best explanation for all of the patient's symptoms, if the diagnosis is capable of disproof, and how well it coincides with the patient's clinical course. While these criteria are aimed at the verification of a patient's clinical diagnosis, they also provide a useful guide in planning and evaluating research studies. Also, Richardson *et al.* listed guides for use in evaluating articles that specifically report on the clinical manifestations of disease. Richardson *et al.* provided points that specifically address studies reporting on the clinical manifestation of disease. Because of the specific relation to disease, these criteria may provide a useful addition to those provided in Table 3.2. Topics that should be considered in such review, drawing from Richardson *et al.*, pertain to a study's validity, detail, results, and practical clinical utility. Some questions reflecting these general considerations include the following:

- Was the presence of disease credibly verified independent of disease manifestations?
- Did the patient sample comprehensively represent those with the disorder?
- Were the clinical evaluations that served as a basis for describing clinical manifestations sufficient in detail and description?
- Were the reported results adequately precise and comprehensive?
- How relevant were the results to the reader's own clinical practice?

Most research designs, and certainly most published research in Neuro-behavioral Toxicology, provide evidence suggestive of a causal relationship or fail to provide such evidence, but very few can be said to provide confirmation of causal relationships using Hill's or similar criteria. In most instances, the greatest value of the results of even well-designed studies is to be found in providing, or failing to provide, support for prior hypotheses or in the generation of new hypotheses. Consistent findings over a series of studies and from a variety of perspectives are the most likely way in which causal criteria are met (see Chapter 8).

Conclusion

The present chapter emphasized research in human neurobehavioral toxicology, recognizing the intimate relationship between research and clinical practice in this field. In 1914, Whipple explicitly differentiated behavioral research from clinical approaches, distinguishing the two based on their objectives. The aim of the clinician was seen by Whipple as diagnostic or therapeutic, while the objective in research was theoretical, to discover new facts, principles, or laws for science. In other words, the goal of research is to increase our scientific knowledge base. Others, such as Stern (1911) and Dunlap (1922), further developed the distinctions made by Whipple.

Within research, the scientific method is applied to assess the merit of specific hypotheses. The selection of the research design and statistical tools for analysis create particular strengths and limitations for each study. Although ethical and practical concerns often preclude the use of basic experimental models, a body of research from clinical experimental and analogue studies can be used to evaluate the strength of presumed causal relationships between environmental agents and neuropsychological symptoms in humans. Attempts to measure and control for potentially biasing factors, such as experimenter expectancies, demand characteristics, and other moderating variables, can strengthen the quality of research results.

As we will discuss more fully in the following chapters, the clinical approach focuses on the individual. The results of the clinical examination, together with information from interview and other sources, are used to make individual diagnostic and related conclusions and to advance recommendations for treatment or further tests if indicated. In the research setting, the conclusions should increase our understanding of the original problem, but they should also lead to new questions and proposed hypotheses. A primary difference between research and clinical practice is that while the clinical enterprise allows us to make conclusions about an individual, the group serves as the focus in research. Conclusions about an individual can seldom be made solely on the basis of the results of a scientific study; however, the knowledge from such studies is essential to formulate and verify our clinical conclusions.

Notes

1 Traditionally, the word 'blind' was used instead of the term 'mask.' Sensitivity to social correctness in the use of language has led increasingly to substitution of the word 'mask,' as employed here.
2 All are available from the US federal government (Washington, DC: Government Printing Office).

References

Albers, J. W., & Berent, S. (2000). Controversies in neurotoxicology: current status. *Neurologic Clinics*, *18*, 741–764.

Albers, J. W., Wald, J. J., Werner, R. A., Franzblau, A., & Berent, S. (1999). Absence of polyneuropathy among workers previously diagnosed with solvent-induced toxic encephalopathy. *Journal of Occupational and Environmental Medicine*, *41*, 500–509.

American Psychological Association (1987). *Ethical principles in the conduct of research with human participants*. Washington, DC: APA.

American Psychological Association (1992). *Ethical principles of psychologists and code of conduct*. Washington, DC: APA.

Anger, W. (1992). Assessment of neurotoxicity in humans. In H. Tilson and C. Mitchell (Eds.), *Neurotoxicology* (pp. 363–386). New York: Raven.

Baelum, J. (1999). Acute symptoms during non-inhalation exposure to combinations of toluene, trichloroethylene, and *n*-hexane. *International Archives of Occupational and Environmental Health*, *72*, 408–410.

Baker, E. L., Jr (1985). Epidemiologic issues in neurotoxicity research. *Neurobehavioral Toxicology and Teratology*, *7*, 293–297.

Beatty, W. W. (1972). How blind is blind? A simple procedure for estimating observer naivete. *Psychological Bulletin*, *78*, 70–71.

Benignus, V. A. (1993). Importance of experimenter-blind procedure in neurotoxicology. *Neurotoxicology and Teratology*, *15*, 45–49.

Berent, S., & Trask, C. L. (2000). Human neuropsychological testing and evaluation. In E. Massaro (Ed.), *Neurotoxicology handbook*, Vol. 2. Totowa: Humana.

Byar, D. P., Simon, R. M., Friedewald, W. T., Schlesselman, J. J., DeMets, D. L., Ellenberg, J. H., Gail, M. H., & Ware, J. H. (1976). Randomized clinical trials. Perspectives on some recent ideas. *New England Journal of Medicine*, *295*, 74–80.

Carroll, K. M., Rounsaville, B. J., & Nich, C. (1994). Blind man's bluff: effectiveness and significance of psychotherapy and pharmacotherapy blinding procedures in a clinical trial. *Journal of Consulting and Clinical Psychology*, *62*, 276–280.

Costa, L. G. (1992). Effect of neurotoxicants on brain neurochemistry. In H. Tilson and C. Mitchell (Eds.), *Neurotoxicology* (pp. 101–123). New York: Raven.

Department of Health and Human Services (DHHS) (1991). Title 45 Code of Federal Regulations Part 46 Protection of Human Subjects. Washington, DC: Government Printing Office.

Dunlap, K. (1922). *The elements of scientific psychology*. St Louis: C.V. Mosby.

Edwards, F. A. (1985). *Experimental design in psychological research*. New York: Harper & Row.

Fisher, R. A. (1991). *Statistical methods, experimental design, and scientific inference*. New York: Oxford University Press.

Freedman, B. (1987). Equipoise and the ethics of clinical research. *New England Journal of Medicine, 317*, 141–145.

Galbaud du, F. G., Newman, S. C., & Bland, R. C. (1993). Psychiatric comorbidity and treatment seeking. Sources of selection bias in the study of clinical populations. *Journal of Nervous and Mental Disease, 181*, 467–474.

Garabrant, D. H. (2000a). Epidemiologic principles in the evaluation of suspected neurotoxic disorders. In J. W. Albers and S. Berent (Eds.), *Clinical neurobehavioral toxicology* (pp. 631–648). Philadelphia: W. B. Saunders.

Garabrant, D. H. (2000b). Epidemiologic principles in the evaluation of suspected neurotoxic disorders. In J. W. Albers and S. Berent (Eds.), *Clinical neurobehavioral toxicology* (pp. 631–648). Philadelphia: W. B. Saunders.

Hartman, D. E. (1995). *Neuropsychological toxicology: identification and assessment of human neurotoxic syndromes* (2nd ed.). New York: Plenum.

Hill, A. B. (1965). The environment and disease: association or causation. *Proceedings of the Royal Society of Medicine, 58*, 295–300.

Hsu, L. M. (1989). Random sampling, randomization, and equivalence of contrasted groups in psychotherapy outcome research. *Journal of Consulting and Clinical Psychology, 57*, 131–137.

Kazdin, A. E. (1998). *Research design in clinical psychology* (3rd ed.). Boston: Allyn & Bacon.

Kihlstrom, J. (1995). *From the subject's point of view: The experiment as conversation and collaboration between investigator and subject.* New York: American Psychological Society.

Kimbrough, R. D. (1995). Polychlorinated biphenyls (PCBs) and human health: an update. *Critical Reviews in Toxicology, 25*, 133–163.

Kraemer, H. C. (1992). Reporting the size of effects in research studies to facilitate assessment of practical or clinical significance. *Psychoneuroendocrinology, 17*, 527–536.

Kuhar, M. J., Couceyro, P. R., & Lambert, P. D. (1999). Catecholamines. In G. J. Siegel, B. W. Agranoff, R. W. Albers, S. K. Fisher, & M. D. Uhler (Eds.), *Basic neurochemistry: molecular, cellular, and medical aspects* (pp. 243–262). Philadelphia: Lippincott-Raven.

Lees-Haley, P. R., & Brown, R. S. (1992). Biases in perception and reporting following a perceived toxic exposure. *Perceptual and Motor Skills, 75*, 531–544.

Levine, R. J. (1988). *Ethics and regulation of clinical research* (2nd ed.). New Haven: Yale University Press.

Margraf, J., Ehlers, A., Roth, W. T., Clark, D. B., Sheikh, J., Agras, W. S., & Taylor, C. B. (1991). How 'blind' are double-blind studies? *Journal of Consulting and Clinical Psychology, 59*, 184–187.

Myers, M. G., Cairns, J. A., & Singer, J. (1987). The consent form as a possible cause of side effects. *Clinical Pharmacology and Therapeutics, 42*, 250–253.

National Institutes of Health (1995). *Guidelines for the conduct of research involving human subjects at the national institutes of health.* Washington, DC: Government Printing Office.

Ney, P. G., Collins, C., & Spensor, C. (1986). Double blind: double talk or are there ways to do better research. *Medical Hypotheses, 21*, 119–126.

Oxtoby, A., Jones, A., & Robinson, M. (1989). Is your 'double-blind' design truly double-blind? *British Journal of Psychiatry, 155*, 700–701.

Pearson, J. C. G. (1993). *Statistical methods in environmental health*. New York: Chapman & Hall.

Richardson, W. S., Wilson, M. C., Williams, J. W., Jr, Moyer, V. A., & Naylor, C. D. (2000). Users' guides to the medical literature: XXIV. How to use an article on the clinical manifestations of disease. Evidence-Based Medicine Working Group. *Journal of the American Medical Association, 284*, 869–875.

Rosenthal, R., & Rosnow, R. L. (1975). *The volunteer subject*. New York: Wiley.

Rosenthal, R., & Rosnow, R. L. (1991). *Essentials of behavioral research: Methods and data analysis* (2nd ed.). New York: McGraw-Hill.

Schafer, A. (1985). The randomized trial: for whose benefit. *IRB: Review of Human Subject Research, 7*, 4–6.

Stanton, M. E., & Spear, L. P. (1990). Workshop on the qualitative and quantitative comparability of human and animal developmental neurotoxicity, Work Group I report: comparability of measures of developmental neurotoxicity in humans and laboratory animals. *Neurotoxicology and Teratology, 12*, 261–267.

Stern, W. (1911). *Die differentielle psychologie in ihren methodischen grundlagen*. Leipzig: J. A. Barth.

The National Commission for the Protection of Human Subjects of Biomedical and Behavioral Research (1979). *The Belmont Report: Ethical principles and guidelines for the protection of subjects in research*. Washington, DC: Government Printing Office.

United States Government (1949). *Trial of war crimes before the Nuremberg Military Tribunals under control of Council Law No. 10. 2, 181–182*. Washington, DC: Government Printing Office.

Weinstein, M. C. (1974). Allocation of subjects in medical experiments. *New England Journal of Medicine, 291*, 1278–1285.

Whipple, G. M. (1914). *Manual of mental and physical tests*. Baltimore: Warwick & York.

Williams, C. W., Lees, H., PR, & Brown, R. S. (1993). Human response to traumatic events: an integration of counterfactual thinking, hindsight bias, and attribution theory. *Psychological Reports, 72*, 483–494.

Woodworth, R. S., & Schlosberg, H. (1938). *Experimental psychology*. New York: Rinehart & Winston.

Woodworth, R. S., & Schlosberg, H. (1964). *Experimental psychology*. New York: Rinehart & Winston.

World Medical Association (1964). *Helsinki Declaration*. Helsinki: WMA.

4 Clinical approaches

Introduction

The preceding chapter reviewed some basic aspects of clinical neurobehavioral research. While important contrasts were described between clinical research and direct clinical applications, we also emphasized the corollaries between these two types of professional activities (see Table 3.1). As mentioned in that chapter, little distinction was made between these two endeavors before the turn of the last century (Berent & Trask, 2000). At that time, clinical practice was almost entirely medical and was usually viewed as experimental and consisting of systematic and empirical interventions with the goal of discovering the best way to correct a patient's symptoms (Woodworth & Schlosberg, 1964). The need for a more formal distinction between the two arose as both research and clinical practice became more sophisticated.

A simple way to define the distinction between research and clinical practice is based on the difference in objectives between the two. This, of course, is no new idea, having been suggested by Whipple (1914). The immediate goal of the researcher is to generate new generalizable knowledge while the clinician seeks to identify individual problems and respond to them therapeutically. While this distinction is viable, the practice of modern psychology and medicine calls for interaction between the two. At least in terms of clinical research, if not more generally to include basic investigations, there should be, by necessity, a seamless interaction between research and clinical practice. Even if a given clinician chooses to focus solely on service delivery, there exists the need to remain current with regard to advances in relevant knowledge. To accomplish this, the clinician must obtain and maintain the requisite knowledge to understand meaningfully the principles and methods as well as the limits of science and the products that derive from those efforts.

Because clinical neurobehavioral toxicology is a multidisciplinary endeavor, the research literature relevant to the clinician's practice will derive from diverse sources. This represents a challenge to the practitioner in this area, who will be required to know something of each of the disciplines involved (e.g., Physiology, Biochemistry, Epidemiology, etc.). This is not to say that every clinician should, or even could, be an expert in all of these fields. On the contrary, a professional knows where his or her expertise begins and ends. A multidisciplinary effort represents the interaction between many individuals, each making their unique contribution to a problem solution. Nevertheless, and to avoid the failure encountered in the building of the Tower of Babel, knowledge sufficient to communicate effectively with individuals from disciplines other than your own is required. This challenge is made easier because the scientific approach is the basis for the respective disciplines. This is certainly true for Psychology and Neurology, the two fields that represent the focus of the present book. As a result, the information in Table 3.2 will be applicable to research reported by any of the various disciplines concerned with neurobehavioral toxicological issues. The criteria implied by the questions in Table 3.2 also can be used by the clinician or research investigator to evaluate the overall merit of specific investigations as well as in the planning of one's own research.

Clinical neurology and clinical neuropsychology

Chapters 5 and 6 will present the unique and specific aspects of the two clinical approaches with which this book is primarily concerned, i.e., Neurology and Clinical Neuropsychology, a specialty area of Psychology. In the present chapter, we will briefly discuss some commonalties and differences between the two disciplines, how these contrasts leave the two complementary to one another, and some aspects of interaction between the two fields.

Neurology and Neuropsychology share many commonalties not only in terms of interest area, but also in shared philosophies, concepts and, in many aspects, methodologies. As discussed in Chapter 3, both fields are grounded in science. This foundation has led both Neurology and Neuropsychology to evidence-based approaches to the clinical enterprise. These approaches will be discussed in more detail below as well as in Chapter 8 and elsewhere in these volumes. Each field also approaches the study of the nervous system from different perspectives. The totality of these commonalties and differences leave the two disciplines truly complimentary.

Both disciplines, Neurology and Neuropsychology, rely on a database in terms of research and other scholarly writings that is more shared than divergent. Many of the same events and individuals appear in the written histories of both – names like Charles Darwin, William James, John Hughlings Jackson, Sir Francis Galton, and others (Berent & Trask, 2000) – and both are firmly rooted in the scientific method. Like Psychology, Neurology is concerned with normal as well as abnormal behavior; and as in Neurology, the neuropsychologist is concerned with health as well as disease. The overlap between the two disciplines leaves it difficult to make sweeping statements about differences between the two. As a medical specialty, however, Neurology brings to the clinical enterprise the unique perspective of medicine, with its inclusion of the general medical physical examination and knowledge of systemic and other disease processes that may be important in developing a proper differential diagnosis in a given case. Neuropsychology, on the other hand, contributes from its strong background in knowledge of normal behaviour and psychopathology, motivation, social considerations, interpersonal and group processes, and the other topical areas of the field of Psychology, as well as its strong foundation in statistical and psychometric methods. While both fields rely increasingly on the results of other laboratory tests, e.g., results of electrodiagnostic evaluation and brain imaging studies (see Chapter 7), Neurology might incorporate directly into the evaluation a number of invasive techniques, e.g., blood draw and analyses, needle electromyography, tissue biopsy, and angiography.

Although not true of the field of Psychology in general, Clinical Neuropsychology has traditionally focused clinically on the central nervous system (CNS), giving less attention to the peripheral nervous system (PNS) (Bieliauskas, 1997). The PNS is especially important in the study of the effects of toxicants on the nervous system as many substances evidence a tendency adversely to affect one or the other (CNS or PNS), or both, in ways that are critical from a diagnostic viewpoint. To attribute dysfunction to one or the other of these systems might well require a differential exclusion of the other. While not completely arbitrary, the distinctions between the PNS and CNS are sometimes ambiguous, as discussed further in Chapter 6 and elsewhere in these volumes. For instance, all of the cranial nerves originate in the CNS but have components in the PNS. Sensory nerves originate in the PNS, with long PNS and CNS extensions, while motor nerves originate in the spinal cord but have major projections into the PNS. The autonomic nervous system, in general, has both CNS and PNS components. Neuropsychologists do routinely measure behaviors that may have a PNS component, and sophisticated sensory and motor batteries exist that allow for a comprehensive evaluation of this area of human functioning. Especially in the area of neurobehavioral toxicology, the neuropsychologist may need to incorporate these measures into what is usually an already full battery of behavioural measures.

The referral model

The neurologist and neuropsychologist often work as a team, other specialists being brought into the process as a given clinical problem dictates, e.g., referral to a cardiologist on the basis of the patient's historical report or in response to a suspicious finding in the examination. A patient might enter this clinical milieu initially in one of several ways. Contact might be on the basis of a referral to either the psychologist or the neurologist from another physician or psychologist, some other professional, an institution such as a school system or business, as a self-referral, or through some other route. At times, the referral might be from an attorney or directly from a third-party payer.

Although either of these disciplines, Neurology or Psychology, might consult to others, the clinical neuropsychologist, especially, is accustomed to working within a referral model. In Neuropsychology, when the request is for consultation to a primary treating professional, including the neurologist, it can be helpful in the early phase of the process to communicate directly with the referring person. This contact will serve to clarify the clinical questions that will need to be addressed and to ensure that he or she is the appropriate specialist to respond to these questions. When consulting to another person about a clinical matter, it is generally wise to reach an understanding with the referring person about the expectations and possible time constraints or other considerations that might affect the evaluation. For instance, there may be time constraints as to when a report might be needed in order to meet some treatment or, even, some regulatory demand. Also, as early in the process as possible, the patient's understanding and expectations must be addressed. It is advisable, and in many instances required, formally to obtain the patient's informed consent to undergo the evaluation as well as to clarify with the patient to whom the results can be communicated. To give an example, a patient was referred by his place of employment to a neuropsychologist. The patient's supervisor was concerned about the employee's competence because of an apparent decline in performing his job duties. The supervisor requested that a neuropsychologist formally evaluate the employee. It was made clear to the psychologist by the supervisor that the results of the evaluation would be used to make a work-related decision about the employee, e.g., if his condition could be treated in some way or if he would be terminated from his position with the company. When the issues were directly discussed with the patient, however, he indicated that he wanted to be examined but did not want his employer to know the results of the evaluation. The employee reported that he worked with chemicals in his job and believed these were responsible for his symptoms. By eliciting the patient's and the employer's expectations before beginning the formal examination, it was fairly easy to resolve the apparent conflict between the two. The situation was explained to the patient, and the choice was left up to him whether to be seen as a referral from his employer, with a report sent to the employer, or in a more private manner. Following consultation with his own attorney, the employee chose to have the report sent to his employer, with agreement that a copy also be sent to the attorney. Clarifying such issues early will avoid considerable difficulties later.

Managing the professional interaction

In referring to one another, the neurologist or psychologist might view the interaction in one or more of several ways. The referral, for instance, could be a request for a complete and complementary evaluation to supplement, or even substitute for, the referring person's own evaluation. Second, the referral might be more limited in its request, the referring person's examination having produced specific questions that might be effectively addressed by their colleague's techniques. The neurologist, for example, might wish for a formal measurement of the patient's short-term memory to use as verification of the clinical findings or to use as a baseline for later comparison in a case that is otherwise diagnostically straightforward. For example, the neurologist in the present instance might view the neuropsychological examination in much the same way as another ancillary test. The neuropsychologist, on the other hand, could experience a similar situation. Of course, each field brings its own unique expertise to bear on the clinical problem at hand, and either professional might request advice and consultation from the other on that basis alone. Regardless of the basis of the referral, once made, the referring person will need to allow the responding professional to use clinical judgment, as well as the standards of his or her respective discipline, in determining the most appropriate way to proceed in addressing the clinical issues.

Clinical interventions may be emergent, of course, and require immediate response, e.g., acute stroke, suicidal threat, status epilepticus. Fortunately, most cases seen in the office practices of neurologists or neuropsychologists are non-emergent, though no less important because of that. In these more routine situations, effective communication between the collaborating disciplines will contribute greatly to a clinically effective response. Such communication is a two-way street, and the referring and responding individuals should make every attempt to clarify issues as mentioned above, e.g., time constraints on responding and other expectations surrounding the referral. A question a number of psychologists have found to be helpful is: 'What can I tell you from my evaluation that will affect your management of this case?' This question can be seen as an overture for further discussion that is designed to clarify the referring person's questions and allow the responding person to decide if he or she is in fact the appropriate person to address these issues and, if so, to determine the procedures that will be needed to respond effectively.

As shown in Table 3.1, the examination in clinical practice can be seen as analogous to the experiment in research. Just as the experiment should be tied carefully to the hypothesis(es), the clinical evaluation should be related to questions relevant to the working diagnosis. This does not preclude, of course, the fact that there is a standard examination that is always administered (see Chapters 5 and 6). A specific neurological working diagnosis, for example, includes the history of relatively recent and acute (within seconds to minutes) or subacute (within hours to a few days) onset of symptoms. The question to the neuropsychologist in this example might be something like the following: 'Are the results of neuropsychological evaluation consistent with changes in behavior that would be expected following an acute or subacute onset of cognitive impairment?' A positive answer to this question might be revealed in the pattern of resultant test scores, e.g., higher measured functioning in well-learned and repeatedly rehearsed areas like a fund of general information and vocabulary with contrasting low performance in tests of new learning and memory. Other common diagnostically related questions include queries regarding localized versus generalized dysfunction, patterns of functional strengths and weaknesses, consequences of identified dysfunction for everyday role performance, the presence of and the role of emotional disturbance, evidence for PNS versus CNS involvement, and other general or more specific questions (see Table 5.2). Positive findings on the psychometric portion of the neuropsychology evaluation might prompt the neuropsychologist to query the neurologist about the presence or absence of corroborating findings on the neurology examination. These questions may be related to any aspect of the clinical evaluation, diagnosis, treatment, prognosis, or etiology. While the results of examination from either profession remain independent, the discovery of discrepant findings between the two should be carefully considered before reaching a final diagnostic conclusion.

As two or more professionals work together over time, they become increasingly knowledgeable about the other's concerns and needs with regard to clinical information, to the point that many questions can be anticipated. As an aside, an ideal point to begin such interdisciplinary interaction is at the training level. When such a working history is absent, however, there is a need to include an educational component in the consultative relationship. There are times when one of the parties may be naive with regard to what can be asked. In those instances, the responding professional will need to assist the referring party in developing questions that are maximally suited to fit the need for relevant information as well as the expertise and technology available. In all cases, however, the responding party should formulate specific questions before conducting the evaluation. These questions will serve as a basis for determining the kinds of information that will be needed from historical records, what to ask in the clinical interview, and what types of test or other ancillary data will be required. Just as clinical research might lead to additional questions, so might the clinical evaluation. These new questions are pursued through further referral or through the incorporation of additional information from other sources into the analysis, e.g., job performance evaluations, military medical records, results from scholastic aptitude tests administered by the school system, and the like.

The clinical process

Some commonalties across fields

While there are specific differences in such things as the questions asked and the tools used by each professional, the underlying clinical approach is similar, if not essentially the same, in both Neurology and Clinical Neuropsychology. In both instances, the process focuses on problem solving and proceeds systematically, beginning with the patient's complaints and ending with diagnostic impressions and treatment recommendations. In general, the patient's symptoms are discovered by interview. Available and relevant past records are reviewed when possible with the aim of determining the presence of other pertinent information (e.g., a history of substance abuse) that might not have disclosed in the interview. Signs are then identified on the basis of examination and a differential diagnosis is formulated. This differential diagnosis is developed within the context of considering all possible explanations for the patient's condition to the extent that it is understood at this point in the process. This working diagnosis is then used to formulate additional questions that will need to be addressed in order to arrive at a final impression. A plan, analogous to the *experimental design* in research, is advanced that will include the types of tests and procedural information that will be needed to reach definitive conclusions. For example, in a patient in whom a seizure disorder is suspected, the plan would include electroencephalographic evaluation. While there are times when clinical objectives may be more limited (e.g., when formally determining IQ or other psychometric criteria for purposes of an individual's program eligibility), the plan generally would consider all aspects of the clinical management of the patient and not be limited solely to a specific diagnosis. There are times, for instance, when response to treatment may be required for various aspects of the patient's problem before a final diagnosis is determined. Until the final diagnosis is achieved, the process of developing the differential diagnosis continues and may be modified as additional information is obtained. Included in the clinical process are estimates of the severity of the patient's condition, estimates of the expected course of symptoms, prognosis in general, and determination of the etiology or cause of the patient's condition, if possible. Because there are a number of areas that remain unknown, each step in the process reflects some autonomy and can produce results that are important to the patient's therapeutic management even when questions that are associated with some of the steps in the process might not be answerable. For example, we are presently able to diagnose Alzheimer disease (AD) in a given patient, at least at some point in what is likely a relatively prolonged prodromal period (Berent, Giordani, Foster, Minoshima, Lajiness-O'Neill, Koeppe, & Kuhl, 1999). Also, we have the capacity to identify the functional strengths and weaknesses and the implications of this functional picture for the AD patient's activities of daily life. We can also identify some direct therapeutic interventions that are aimed at slowing cognitive decline (e.g., cholinesterase inhibitors such as donepezil hydrochloride, i.e., Aricept). However, despite the fact that we have learned a considerable amount about the biochemistry and physiology of AD, including some knowledge about what it is likely not, we are unable to identify the specific etiology of this disease at present. Nor do we need to specify the etiology in order to respond to these other aspects of the clinical process.

The need for objectivity

It is important for the clinician to remain as objective as possible through all phases of the clinical process. Objectivity does not equate to a lack of sensitivity or caring. Nor does it imply that the clinician cannot advocate for his or her patient. In fact, the clinical process itself can be viewed as a relationship that includes advocacy. This advocacy, however, is not manifested in an uncritical acceptance of whatever the patient reports. It is directed towards helping the patient clinically, and the best way to help the patient is to arrive at an objective diagnosis and treatment plan. To achieve this sometimes requires a response to the patient that might appear to be contrary to the patient's own opinion. For instance, it is not unusual for a patient to present his or her complaints as a diagnostic statement rather than in terms of symptoms. When asked to describe his primary complaints, for example, a patient responded, 'I have a solvent-induced toxic encephalopathy'. The patient's response included a diagnosis and an etiology but conveyed nothing about the symptoms he was experiencing. The tendency to respond in this fashion may be even more prevalent in the area of behavioral neurotoxicology than in some other areas because of the general and reasonable concerns in a well-informed society regarding this topic. The patient may have read about a condition in the newspaper, or another professional may have previously diagnosed the patient with the reported condition. Also, it is possible that the patient is involved in litigation related to the condition presented. Regardless of such circumstances, the clinician should attempt to elicit a description of the symptoms the patient is experiencing rather than accept uncritically the conclusion offered by the patient.

The effects on the individual of being involved in litigation are discussed below as well as elsewhere in these volumes. For now, however, it is worth mentioning that evaluating a plaintiff who is involved in litigation represents a special challenge to the clinician and demands a disciplined approach to the evaluation. Whether the clinician is hired by a plaintiff or defense attorney, or directly asked by the court to conduct such an examination, the clinician needs to avoid, to the extent possible, becoming entangled in the adversarial climate that often characterizes this area of endeavor. In our experience, the best way to accomplish this is to conduct the evaluation in a manner that approximates to what is done in regular clinical practice. This also holds for the conclusions that are reached, and the clinician should avoid taking any side in the dispute other than the side of defending his or her own findings. These findings, as in any other evaluation, should be arrived at in an objective manner, as discussed elsewhere in these volumes, and presented without concern for what appear to be the other parties' wishes. That is, whether the clinician is working for defense, plaintiff, or court, the findings are presented as they are. While this approach is almost always met with hostility from someone, our experience, again, has been that reasonable people want to hear the truth, whether or not that truth might hinder or help their initial cause. Accurate findings help all parties to arrive at a reasonable compromise in their disputes.

Also, the clinician can at times expect to be the recipient of some hostility when probing beyond the patient's stated presentation. This may be especially true with regard to topics that are anxiety provoking, and that anxiety has been controlled in part through the use of a diagnostic label. A young female patient, for example, stated to the clinician at the beginning of the examination that she had been sexually abused as a child and, as a result, had been hospitalized for psychiatric treatment on several occasions. Her present symptoms, she went on to emphasize, were unrelated to those earlier experiences and were instead solely the result of exposure to mercury through her dental amalgams. This attempt to constrain the clinician's ability to consider all possible causes for the patient's complaints could be very problematic, especially if, as in the case described, the patient's primary complaints appeared to be possibly based in longstanding anxiety disorder and not the result of exposure to toxicants. The young woman's resistance to consider alternative explanations for her symptoms may reflect a set of complex personal dynamics, but it is not surprising. If, for no other reason, Festinger's theory of *cognitive dissonance* (Festinger, 1957, 1962) would predict that when a person is confronted with a view that is logically inconsistent with one already held, that person will be motivated to reduce the resulting dissonance. To most people, perhaps, the seemingly easiest way to achieve such dissonance reduction is to reject the opposing viewpoint. Establishing rapport and a good working relationship, a relationship that includes mutual respect and allows for patient education, will help the clinician to minimize potential hostile reactions and to deal effectively with such situations. Maintaining objectivity will help in this regard.

Before moving from this topic, it is worth mentioning that providing the patient with education about his or her condition can, in itself, have a very therapeutic effect. Such education includes clarification of misconceptions the patient might hold about the condition or that others might have communicated to the patient. Such education can be accomplished without challenging another professional's opinion, and it should always be based upon the objective evidence at hand. One patient confided, for instance, that a 'friend' had told him that he could expect to deteriorate to a vegetative state within 2 years because of his exposure to solvents in the workplace. This misinformation was believed by the patient and had led to depression and suicidal ideation. In fact, the examination revealed a reasonably healthy individual with little or no cognitive impairment. Correcting the misinformation given to the patient by his perhaps well-meaning friend had a substantial and positive effect on the patient's demeanor.

The need for an evidence-based approach to the clinical process

We have referred numerous times to the scientific foundation of the clinical work in Neurology and Neuropsychology as well as to the ideal of striving for a seamless interaction between research and clinical applications. In the field of Psychology, this scientific approach to clinical work has been reflected in the scientist–practitioner model (Baker & Benjamin 2000; Belar, 2000). In the medical field, this concept has found expression in recent years in what has been termed 'evidence-based medicine' or 'evidence-based healthcare'. Evidence-based medicine is the term used to describe an approach to clinical care that underlies a series of articles published in the *Journal of the American Medical Association* (Guyatt, Haynes, Jaeschke, Cook, Green, Naylor, Wilson, & Richardson, 2000). The approach consists of a sequence of guidelines that permit the clinician to integrate information derived from published research into the care of individual patients. The strategies reported in the series of papers were designed initially for physicians, but they apply to all healthcare conditions and practitioners. Although the term 'evidence-based medicine' is well established, the rubric 'evidence-based healthcare' is equally appropriate (Guyatt *et al.*, 2000).

Evidence-based medicine has as its foundation the scientific method, and several aspects of evidence-based medicine are directly important to the concepts established herein for neurobehavioral toxicology. Clinicians appropriately rely on knowledge obtained from clinical research, independent of the intended use of the information. For example, strategies that evaluate the validity of published research apply equally well to diagnostic or treatment decisions. Inherent in the acquisition of new knowledge derived from the literature is information about clinical manifestations of a given disease.

A fundamental premise of evidence-based medicine is that clinical intuition, unsystematic clinical experience, and authoritative statements based on unscientific rationale are inadequate methodologies for deriving clinical decisions about diagnoses or treatment (Guyatt *et al.*, 2000). This point may be especially relevant in the case of neurotoxic disease since symptoms are often vague or poorly defined, and reported exposures are at times temporally removed from the patient's presentation to the clinician. As observed by Schaumberg & Spencer (1987), there is 'an unfortunate temptation' to attribute illness to chemical exposure when no other cause is readily apparent that would explain the patient's complaints. An important aspect of evidence-based medicine involves a methodology to determine whether available evidence fulfils certain basic standards involving the validity of the results of research and applicability of those results in a given clinical situation. The methodology of evidence-based medicine emphasizes a set of defined hypothesis-generating and -testing rules that emulate the scientific method and are complementary to professional training and common sense. Particularly relevant to the purposes of neurobehavioral toxicology are the evidence-based criteria used to verify a patient's diagnosis (Richardson, Wilson, Williams, Moyer, & Naylor, 2000), and these criteria were discussed in more detail in Chapter 3.

Some general clinical attributes of neurotoxic disease

Psychology can be defined as the study of behavior, but it has also been described historically as the study of individual differences. Both attributes have relevance for medicine generally and neurobehavioral toxicology specifically. At the risk of cliché, there are few generalities that will apply to all patients. Having said that, there are some attributes that are more commonly seen with some types of disorders than with others, and the nature of neurotoxicants predicts some generalities. Chapter 1 reviewed some basic considerations regarding mechanisms of toxicity in the nervous system. For instance, we indicated that damage to the nervous system can be reversible, or it can be irreversible when cells die as a result of apoptosis or oncosis. For such death to occur, the cell's encoded death program must be activated (apoptosis) or the cell must be separated from its energy source, as might occur, for example, in the case of oxygen deprivation (oncosis). Apoptosis could occur as a result of direct activation by a chemical substance or secondarily, e.g., via the actions of a metabolite. The source might be extrinsic to the cell or intrinsic (McDonald & Windebank 2000). Regardless of the toxic mechanism involved, clinical recovery is possible if the patient is removed in time from the source of toxicity. A thorough history is, therefore, a critical part of the clinical evaluation. Has the patient experienced periods of loss of consciousness? Has there been opportunity for exposure to a potentially harmful substance? If so, what were the likely duration, dose, and frequency of that exposure? Also, what is the nature of the particular agent to which the patient has been exposed? What can it do? Are there other conditions possibly present that might lead to similar symptoms, e.g., oxygen deprivation as a result of sleep apnea? What is the likelihood that some of these conditions are the secondary result of chemical exposure?

Schaumburg & Spencer (1987) have emphasized that neurotoxic disease is seldom focal. Even when focal (e.g., localized to the basal ganglia), it is rarely asymptomatic. The signs and symptoms of neurotoxic damage are usually similar to metabolic, degenerative, or nutritional illnesses. Second, with consideration of individual differences in genetic and physical susceptibility, there is most often a consistent pattern of disease that relates directly to the quantitative aspects of exposure. Relatedly, neurotoxic illness most often occurs with exposure or following a very brief latency period (usually no more than a few weeks), and the illness generally improves following removal from exposure. There are exceptions, e.g., where damage has been extensive and more or less permanent or in some cases of cumulative exposure to specified medications or other substances. The emphasis on individual differences is apparent in the next point as well, which is that the same toxicant can produce a different clinical picture depending on the exposure level. Laboratory tests for the presence of a toxin are often of limited diagnostic value, either because of the absence of tests for many toxicants or the time frame in which the testing is done. With regard to the last point, the patient might present for clinical evaluation long after the actual toxicant has cleared the body. In general, localization to specific neurons is likely to occur in the case of exposure to a given substance. From a behavioral viewpoint, certain patterns of impairment can also be predicted. There are exceptions to these rules, however, and a specific chemical formula may not reliably predict its neurotoxic potential. In addition, the neurotoxic potential of a given agent may be potentiated by other chemicals, some of which may be considered harmless alone (Schaumburg & Spencer, 1987).

As should be readily apparent, there are few generalizations about neurotoxic disease that will apply in every clinical instance. On the other hand, there are a number of clinical manifestations that will simply not fit a neurotoxic etiology. Because of the variability involved, however, every clinical case will need to be evaluated individually with careful attention to findings from examination, the personal history, and integration of findings with what is known scientifically about a suspected cause for the patient's complaints.

Other considerations

Determining abnormality

Depending on the extent of the clinical neurobehavioral evaluation, one outcome is a relatively detailed description of the patient's behavioral functioning. The basic types of examinations associated with the neurological and the neuropsychological evaluations (see Chapters 5 and 6) are highly sensitive. They are not always specific, however, and a host of behavioral anomalies will be included in the findings of each. Whether or not these anomalies will be considered to reflect an abnormal condition will be a matter of careful analysis. Some criteria are necessary to aid the clinician in his or her analysis and conclusions that will be drawn concerning the abnormality of the findings.

The two primary models used to determine abnormality are (1) statistical and (2) qualitative (Berent, 1986). In the statistical approach, the definition of normality is determined by what most people do in a specified referent population. Many human functions are distributed normally (e.g., intelligence), while some show a skewed distribution (e.g., hand preference). Once the nature of the referent population has been determined, it is fairly easy to set a threshold, below which a given behavior will be considered abnormal (see Figure 5.1). *Normality*, in turn, can be described as scores or observations that occur within a specified range, e.g., a standard score between 85 and 115 as used in most measures of intellect. This range reflects the approximately 68% of scores in the referent sample that fall between +1 standard deviation (SD) and –1 SD from the mean of 100. The method is not entirely objective, however, as some subjectivity is employed in determining criterion scores. It seems unlikely, for example, that the more than 15% of the population whose scores are below –1 SD from the mean are low functioning because of pathology. In fact, every test score carries with it some specifiable error of measurement, ±5 points in the case of most intelligence tests. Because of this, a threshold of –2 SD is used to define deficiency in terms of measured intellect, and the range of scores that fall between –1 and –2 SD is considered to reflect borderline functioning. Also, it appears illogical to term someone abnormal in terms of their intellect if they happen to score above the +1 SD point on the curve, and these individuals are usually termed 'bright' or 'very bright' if above +2 SD or, simply, 'above average.' The statistical approach is attractive to many because of its quantitative and objective nature.

There are drawbacks to a simple statistical model of normality. What is considered normal in such a model is determined by behaviors and abilities exhibited by most people. There is, therefore, no easy way to deal with deviance that might occur on a large scale, a society, for example, that engages in practices of genocide, other behaviors that individuals who live outside of that milieu might consider to be abnormal, or illnesses that affect a large proportion of the normative sample. Of course, history is full of such examples. The statistical model does provide an effective means for objectively quantifying an individual's (or a group's) level of functioning at a point in time. On this basis alone, the model can be tremendously valuable, especially when there is a need to follow the clinical course in an individual over time, e.g., determining progression in a patient with suspected neurodegenerative disease or documenting improved functioning following an acute injury to the nervous system. However, the model does not inherently speak to cause or value.

Qualitative approaches to determining abnormality are of two types: those that list specific, positive criteria to define normality and those that specify pathognomonic symptoms considered to be abnormal. Like the statistical approach, the qualitative models also have weaknesses. For instance, specified qualitative criteria are often vague and not easily standardized or operationalized. The criteria might be derived through empirical research but are often determined subjectively and usually reflect time-limited societal values. There is a common-sense attraction to a qualitative approach, nevertheless. It is the approach that most people use to decide for themselves if they are experiencing a problem. Three basic questions to aid in addressing abnormality through a qualitative model relate to the individual's efficiency, comfort, and conformity. With regard to the first of these three aspects, a clinician might ask the following: 'Is the patient able to perform his or her expected personal, interpersonal, and societal roles at levels of efficiency that are either consistent with their past history or with normally expected changes in their personal situation?' For instance, a person who cannot work for a period following the loss of a loved one would most likely be reflecting a normal reaction within the context of that personal situation. With regard to the idea of comfort, the question might be as follows: 'Is the person reporting physical or emotional pain that is beyond that to be expected in the given situation?' The grief reaction just mentioned, for instance, is one where some emotional pain would be expected. The clinician must work with the patient to decide if the pain is beyond what would be expected normally in terms of severity or in terms of duration. Finally, and with regard to the concept of conformity, does the person exhibit behaviors that are considered extremely unusual, or even bizarre, for the context in which they are occurring? A bizarre costume at a masquerade ball is usual for that event. Wearing that same costume might not be usual for the workplace. Obviously, there is considerable subjectivity involved in addressing these qualitative considerations. Nevertheless, a positive answer to one or more of these questions can be used to signal the need for further clinical inquiry. While it should be obvious, positive answers to questions like these do not in themselves document pathology. The entirety of the clinical evaluation will be needed before a proper diagnosis can be rendered. It is surprising, however, the number of times a diagnosis is made on the basis of such information alone.

Despite the problems with these approaches, each type, statistical and qualitative, has significant value. The statistical model, for instance, is especially effective in allowing for an objective and often quantitative definition of conditions, with the added benefit of helping to grade the level of severity in a specified disorder. The qualitative model can be incorporated into the clinical process by including knowledge specific to the disorders in question, in reference to disease parameters such as onset, duration, symptom type, and progressive course. The most effective way to deal with the problem of determining abnormality, then, involves the inclusion of both approaches in the clinical enterprise.

Combining statistical and qualitative approaches to determine abnormality is not always easy. With regard to neurobehavioral toxicology specifically, the effects of exposure to a toxicant on a given individual often occur in a group context. That is, an entire family or community might exhibit similar reactions, a 'cluster' of symptoms and signs. A statistical model in such an example would necessitate identification of and comparison with an appropriate normal referent group in order to identify abnormality. This is a challenging task because while the affected community's 'normal' functioning might now be changed in response to the exposure, many aspects of the community's functions also will have been determined by non-toxicant factors. These might include historical educational attainment, income, and other aspects of socio-economic status; local and unique values and experiences, and other aspects of shared culture. In using a statistical model alone, a given patient when compared statistically with his or her community norms might appear to be normal when, in fact, he or she is not. On the other hand, comparing the patient's functioning to normative data obtained from a remote referent group might lead to a picture of abnormality when, in fact, the function is 'normal' for the person's own community and explainable on a non-toxicant basis. The obvious demand, of course, is to choose carefully and correctly a referent group that reflects as much as possible the non-toxicant factors and, in research, to control for all relevant confounders. In addition, however, the qualitative approach can be brought into the diagnostic process and combined with the statistical model in order to produce a more accurate picture. The pattern of strengths and weaknesses reflected in the clinical examination, for instance, may be revealing in terms of the presence or absence of a disease-like picture. The clinical pattern of findings should be compared with what is known about the suspected disorder. For instance, is it a pattern that suggests focal or generalized dysfunction, a decline from previous levels of function, areas of weakness that are known to be adversely affected by the suspected toxicant, and other areas of strength that are known to remain unaffected by the exposure? All of this should occur within a context of objectivity to the fullest extent possible and in a manner consistent with evidence-based healthcare. Importantly, it is insufficient to identify a non-sensible pattern of findings among a group of individuals, concluding that the disparate areas of weakness reflect a common cause.

Patient motivation and attention

There are a number of factors that can influence the patient's presentation in the clinical process. There are times when such factors may directly reflect pathology, but often they represent normal variations in behavior that may be unrelated to the working diagnosis even though they may serve to confound the clinical presentation, even obscure what would otherwise be a sensible clinical picture. Two factors that deserve specific mention are motivation and attention. The clinician should become knowledgeable about and sensitive to the potential effects of these behaviors on various parts of the examination.

Normal attention may vary from moment to moment for a variety of reasons. The explanations range from the individual's mental approach to a particular test to momentary distractions caused by external events or even thoughts unrelated to the task at hand. These normal variations can have a profound effect on tests that require focused and sustained attention for successful completion, e.g., tests of learning and memory.

With regard to motivation, while some things like the neurological reflex examination are unlikely to be influenced by patient effort, most of the tests and procedures used by the neurologist and neuropsychologist are volitional in nature. This means that accurate performance depends not only on the person's ability to complete the tasks presented, but it also depends on the person's cooperation and effort. The individual's motivation, therefore, is extremely important, and motivation can even explain a given finding in part or in whole. A variety of factors can influence a person's motivation in the examination. These factors include such things as how much rest the person has had before coming to the examination, how attentive he or she might be on a given occasion, whether they are hungry or thirsty, the nature of rapport the individual might have with the examiner, their mood on a given day, and being involved in litigation (Berent & Swartz, 1999; Berent Trask, 2000).

Malingering and *factitious disorders* can also influence the patient's motivation (American Psychiatric Association, 1994). In both malingering and factitious disorder, the physical or psychological symptoms are intentionally produced for the purpose of assuming a sick role in the latter or to achieve some other personal goal (e.g., to avoid work or to secure an insurance settlement) in the former (American Psychiatric Association, 1994). *Secondary gain* is another concept that can influence a patient's approach to the clinical evaluation. It refers simply to the recognition that every event, including illness, carries with it both negative and positive consequences. While being ill is seen by most as an undesirable state, the ill person may still experience some rewards as a consequence of that illness. For instance, the illness might be accompanied by positive attention from others, relief from the need to work, or a period of rest. Most who have worked with ill patients recognize the power of secondary gain in delaying the patient's return to a normal routine, at times long after the primary illness has ended. There are a number of ways that have been devised in attempts to identify the effects of malingering and other motivational factors in the clinical examination. Some of these will be examined in the remaining chapters and sections of this book. Here, let it suffice to say that many of the tests and procedures employed in the clinical examination are not specific to brain dysfunction. The patient's effort and other extra-neurological factors must be considered within the process of establishing a differential diagnostic before arriving at a conclusion about what caused a low score or positive finding on a given test or procedure.

Psychopathology

Psychopathology represents an important consideration in the process of establishing a differential diagnosis. While confirmation of the presence of psychopathology is diagnostic, the presence of such disorders also represents a potential confound that can obscure an otherwise clinically sensible picture of disease. While the occurrence of anxiety, depression, or other instances of psychopathology can be a direct result of substance-induced intoxication, such behavioral manifestations can also be unrelated to the primary effects of toxicity. As mentioned in Chapter 1, for example, Post-traumatic Stress Disorder was reportedly a common occurrence in the victims of the sarin gas attacks that occurred in Japan in 1994 and 1995, and this disorder was seen as accounting for the majority of prolonged symptoms in the victims of those attacks (Yokoyama, Araki, Murata, Nishikitani, Okumura, Ishimatsu, & Takasu, 1998; Matsui, Ohbu, & Yamashina, 1996). Even when psycho-pathology is independent of substance-induced toxicity, these disorders can mimic the symptoms of toxicity. This is because many symptoms reported by patients are not specific to a given disease. These 'non-specific' symptoms might be associated with a number of different disease states, and they often occur as variations in normal behavior as well. A complaint of headache represents a good example of a non-specific symptom because headaches occur regularly in the general population among individuals with no underlying disease (e.g., see Chapter 6).

The information obtained from interview, the patient's historical records, and results of examination are all important in helping to elucidate the relationship between the patient's problem and a possible toxic etiology. In one clinical case, for example, a patient[1] reported that he had never been depressed before being exposed to benzene. His past school and military records, however, revealed behavioral difficulties beginning in early adolescence and continuing to the present, with specific diagnoses of depression on several occasions. When confronted with this documentation, the patient was willing to discuss a variety of current stressful events in his life that were unrelated to exposure but which served to explain his current depression. Of course, actual or perceived exposure to a potential toxicant can serve to exacerbate pre-existing conditions such as anxiety or depression. Also, it can be accompanied by behavioral reactions that have not been previously experienced by the patient. The idea that illness can be accompanied by disturbing emotions is not new. Bonhoeffer (1912) wrote on this topic early in the 20th century (Berent, 1986), and it was his influence, in fact, that led to the use of terms such as 'reaction' to reflect the intimate relationship than can exist between an emotional response such as depression and a physical disorder (Berent, 1986). When confronted with a patient in whom a pre-existing history of disturbance has been documented, the clinician will need to determine not only the presence of pre-existing psychopathology, but also the nature of that prior disturbance, and then compare that information with the patient's current clinical presentation. In the particular case mentioned, previously administered psychometrics, i.e., serial MMPI (Minnesota Multiphasic Personality Inventory) examinations, revealed that the patient's depression was actually less severe following his exposure to benzene than in the past and otherwise unchanged in terms of symptoms. These facts, together with his interview descriptions of numerous current interpersonal stresses, contributed to the conclusion that his current depression was not the direct result of toxic exposure.

Since the early work on classification by Kraepelin (1909), the various manifestations of psychopathology have been classified as one of a specified number of types. The categories specified traditionally have most often included the following: neuroses (usually anxiety disorders and reactive depressions), psychoses (major disorders of thought or affect), psychosomatic disorders, conduct disorders (e.g., psychopathy), developmental disorders, below normal intelligence (at times included with the developmental disorders), and disorders that result from neurological disorders or disease (Berent, 1986; Berent & Swartz, 1999). Specific diagnoses are coded in practice using one or more of the current systems, e.g., the World Health Organization's International Classification of Diseases (2001) or the American Psychiatric Association's diagnostic manual (1994). There is an increasing interest in developing coding systems that emphasize health as well as disease models and which represent the full spectrum of human behaviors, e.g., the World Health Organization's ICF (2001).

Presence of third parties during a clinical evaluation

It is not unusual to receive a request for someone other than the patient to sit in on part or all of a clinical evaluation. There are times, and in portions of the evaluation, when such a request may be relatively benign and acceptable. The presence of a parent with his or her very young child, for instance, may be acceptable and even helpful to the aims of the evaluation. At other times, the situation is less desirable. When a person is sent by an attorney for a litigation-related medical or psychological examination, for instance, there are times when the opposing attorney may wish to be present or may want to have the procedure electronically recorded. Whether or not the clinician agrees to such requests, there are consequences to the process that come from a departure from standard practice, and the clinician needs to understand and consider consequences to the clinical process in arriving at his or her conclusions.

The clinical interview and history is accomplished in face-to-face inter-action between the patient and clinician, with professional assistance in a limited and carefully prescribed manner and only towards a planned, clinical outcome. Establishing rapport with the patient is one of the first objectives in the interview. Not only does good rapport foster an environment that is maximally conducive to optimal performance on any tests and procedures that might later be administered, but also it alleviates anxiety and leaves the patient more able to share information than might otherwise be the case. The patient might well behave differently when another person is present than when with the clinician alone. In addition to the other possible effects of an observer's presence, there may be a history of interaction between those parties that is unknown to the clinician but which may elicit certain behaviors while inhibiting others.

One of the authors once interviewed a patient in the presence of his wife. When the patient answered negatively to a question about his desire to go on a planned vacation, the spouse interjected with the statement, 'you know you love to travel'. In response, the patient changed his initial answer. In addition to the possibility of intrusions to effective communication such as in the example given, it should be readily apparent that many important topic areas would likely be unapproachable in the presence of others. Of course, in those parts of a clinical examination when partial or complete disrobing might be required, the difficulties of third-party observation should be obvious.

The simple presence of a third party can affect a person's motivation or otherwise influence performance in interview or testing. These effects are due largely to *social facilitation*, a phenomenon that has been studied extensively (Bond & Titus, 1983). Pertinent here is the observation that the effect of social facilitation varies as a function of the number of persons present, i.e., the more people present, the greater the effect on the individual's perform-ance. Observation via electronic means such as video or audio recording devices may also affect an individual's motivation. Also, ethical concerns may well be raised by the use of such devices. For instance, the protection of test materials in the neuropsychological examination from unnecessary familiarization may be compromised through such recording, weakening a specific test's validity in future professional use (Anastasi, 1976). In addition, the use of personal information in contexts or ways not originally intended cannot be controlled by the clinician once such recordings have been made. Responsibility for the interpretation and use of data derived from clinical evaluation is an ethical requirement imposed on clinicians by most professional societies (see, for example, standards of the American Psychological Association, 1985, 1992). There is also the need to inform the patient of the intended recording and to secure the patient's permission to do so before proceeding. This introduces another variable into the clinician–patient relationship that may influence the patient's behavior in ways that will be difficult to determine.

The interview and test environment must be free from any unnecessary distractions. This basic requirement has been discussed in many documents concerned with proper psychological and neuropsychological evaluation, and these publications specified a number of factors to attend to in eliminating potential distractions (Anastasi, 1976; American Psychological Association, 1985; Wechsler, 1997). Some of those factors included testing in a quiet, well-lit and well-ventilated room. Wechsler (1991, 1997) and Iverson & Binder (2000) underscored that a non-standard test administration might well invalidate the test results. The presence of third parties or devices would represent such non-standard administration.

The most effective solution to these and other potential problems that accompany the inclusion of third parties or recording devices during the clinical evaluation is to exclude them, thereby maintaining the evaluation setting in as standard a manner as possible.

Effects of litigation

It is common for clinicians involved in the area of neurobehavioral toxicology to become involved in a patient's personal injury or other litigation. This may occur on the basis of a direct referral for an independent medical or psychological examination, as a request to testify in a matter involving a patient seen clinically independent of litigation, or as an expert consultant in the clinician's area of specialization. Regardless of the source of referral, the general rule is to treat all patients in as standard a manner as possible. With the patient's consent, the clinician can answer questions posed as a part of the litigation process or as part of other extra- or quasi-clinical situations (e.g., work-related competency evaluations), as the clinician and patient choose or as the situation legally or ethically demands. As mentioned above, it is important that the clinician remain as objective as possible in all aspects of the evaluation. This need for objectivity also extends to giving testimony. If asked to provide information regarding a case seen solely for clinical purposes, the clinician is usually required only to state what was done and the nature of the findings. When serving as an expert witness, however, the demand to provide information is greater, usually extending to reviews of the relevant literature, the elucidation of a rationale for the use of specific tests and procedures, and facts about the clinician's qualifications. In all instances, a correct approach is to listen to the questions asked, to respond to those questions with detail sufficient for understanding, and to remain objective.

Regardless of the role played in the litigation process, there is likely to be an effect on the clinician's relationship with the patient. When a patient[2] appears for an independent medical examination, for example, his or her attitude will be affected by whether or not the referral is from his or her own attorney or from the opposing counsel. In the latter instance, the patient may reflect hostility or defensiveness, while in the former, there may be the expectation that the clinician will arrive at some diagnostic statement that is favorable to the plaintiff. In either circumstance, the clinician will need to attend to these *mental sets* in the process of building rapport with the patient. It is usually effective to discuss the structure of the examination with the patient, e.g., what tests and procedures will be employed, how long the examination will take, and the nature of possible outcomes. The clinician should be sensitive to particular attitudes or expectations the patient might manifest in the course of interview or examination, translate these into words, discuss them with the patient, and correct any misconceptions or unrealistic expectations that might surface. The overall objective of these interactions with the patient is to provide an examination as free of non-clinically related issues (e.g., litigation-related concerns) as can be achieved, and as standard an examination as possible. The clinician may at times be more or less successful in reaching these goals. To whatever extent these extra-clinical factors affect the examination process, they should be noted and considered in the final diagnostic formulation. Nevertheless, it is important to remember that being in litigation can in itself be stressful, and such stress, when present, becomes a part of the patient's clinical presentation.

There are other aspects that are uniquely associated with patients involved in litigation, and these should also be kept in mind by the clinician. For instance, individuals involved in litigation have been found to differ from the general population in terms of the base rates of reported symptoms (Lees-Haley, 1992). The effects of motivation on neuropsychological tests have been found to vary as a function of the extent of volition involved in the specific test as well as the potential gain to the individual as a result of litigation (Cullum, Heaton, & Grant, 1991). Another consideration is *malingering*. Malingering is a conscious attempt to falsify or exaggerate symptoms for the purpose of personal gain. It can be contrasted to other conditions that also have the capacity to produce 'false' or exaggerated symptoms but which are not the product of conscious intent, e.g., *somatization disorder, conversion disorder* (American Psychiatric Association, 1994). Also, in contrast to malingering, other conditions may be consciously controlled but promise no obvious gain to the person, e.g., *factitious disorder* (American Psychiatric Association, 1994). It is difficult in the clinical examination to determine that a person is malingering, or to differentiate between the various conditions that might contribute to misleading symptoms. There are tests that have been devised for this purpose, but there are limitations on their effectiveness as well. For instance, tests of malingering are usually based on the premise that the overly simple demands for success on these measures leave malingering, or a related phenomenon, as the most likely explanation for failure to complete them successfully. In the adversarial process of litigation, however, the 'secret' about how these tests work could easily be communicated to the patient by someone, essentially destroying any validity the measure might have in identifying malingering. While malingering may be difficult for the clinician to determine, it is known to occur more often when people are in litigation than in the population more generally (Berent & Trask, 2000). Estimates of its occurrence range from a little over 7% to over 30% for people involved in potential benefit-contingent situations (Binder, 1993; Trueblood & Schmidt, 1993). The clinician will need to be sensitive to the greater than usual likelihood of these effects on examination results in the context of litigation and attempt to account for them in the analysis and conclusions.

Summary

This chapter provided an overview of concepts we believe to be important to the clinical process in neurobehavioural toxicology. The chapter is intended to provide a bridge between the research process discussed in Chapter 3 and clinical practice, and to emphasize the intimate relationship we see as existing between the two. We emphasized the differences and commonalties between the two fields, Neurology and Clinical Neuropsychology, and the complementary nature of these disciplines to one another. Neurobehavioral toxicology calls for a multidisciplinary effort, and this is true in clinical practice as well as in research.

In addition, we tried to convey the continuity we see as existing between research and the clinical process. While the immediate goal of research is to generate new and generalizable knowledge, the primary objective of the clinician is to identify dysfunction in the individual and to respond to it therapeutically. The clinical neurobehavioral enterprise, however, calls for interaction between the two, research and the clinical process. If for no other reason, this interaction is required because of the need for the clinician to remain current with regard to continuing advances in knowledge that characterizes science. There are analogies between research and the clinical process, and these were also discussed. Because the disciplines that are involved in this area have a foundation in the scientific model, that model has found expression in the clinical as well as the research process.

Notes

1 Details of the history have been modified to preserve the anonymity of the patient and his family.
2 The term 'plaintiff' is probably more accurate in the situation of performing an examination for litigation. This is because the clinician is not entering into a 'doctor–patient' relationship in the usual sense and will not be offering the person ongoing treatment. Also, it is worth mentioning that some have expressed a dislike for the term 'independent medical (or psychological) examination', claiming that it connotes an independence that is not warranted by the circumstances of referral, usually from the defence or plaintiff side in a legal matter.

References

American Psychological Association (1985). *Standards for educational and psychological testing*. Washington, DC: APA.

American Psychological Association (1992). *Ethical principles of psychologists and code of conduct*. Washington, DC: APA.

American Psychiatric Association (1994). *Diagnostic and statistical manual of mental disorders* (4th ed.). Washington, DC: APA.

Anastasi, A. (1976). *Psychological testing* (4th ed.). New York: Macmillan.

Baker, D. B., & Benjamin, L. T., Jr (2000). The affirmation of the scientist–practitioner. A look back at Boulder. *American Psychologist, 55,* 241–247.

Belar, C. D. (2000). Scientist–practitioner not equal to science–practice. Boulder is bolder. *American Psychologist, 55,* 249–250.

Berent, S. (1986). Psychopathology and other behavioral considerations for the clinical neuropsychologist. In S. Filskov and T. J. Boll (Eds.), *Handbook of clinical neuropsychology*, vol. 2. New York: Wiley.

Berent, S., Giordani, B., Foster, N., Minoshima, S., Lajiness-O'Neill, R., Koeppe, R., & Kuhl, D. E. (1999). Neuropsychological function and cerebral glucose utilization in isolated memory impairment and Alzheimer's disease. *Journal of Psychiatric Research, 33,* 7–16.

Berent, S., & Swartz, C. L. (1999). Essential psychometrics. In J. J. Sweet (Ed.), *Forensic neuropsychology: fundamentals and practice* (pp. 1–24). Lisse: Swets & Zeitlinger.

Berent, S., & Trask, C. L. (2000). Human neuropsychological testing and evaluation. In E. Massaro (Ed.), *Neurotoxicology handbook*, Vol. 2. Totowa: Humana.

Bieliauskas, L. (1997). Houston Conference on Specialty Training in Clinical Neuropsychology. Houston, TX.

Binder, L. M. (1993). Assessment of malingering after mild head trauma with the Portland Digit Recognition Test. *Journal of Clinical and Experimental Neuropsychology, 15,* 170–182; erratum, *15,* 852.

Bond, C. F., Jr, & Titus, L. J. (1983). Social facilitation: a meta-analysis of 241 studies. *Psychological Bulletin, 94,* 265–292.

Bonhoeffer, K. (1912). Die psychoser in gefolge von akuter: Allgemein erkrankongen und inneren enkrankungen. In G. Aschaffenbury (Ed.), *Handboch der psychiatrie.* Leipzig: Deuticke.

Cullum, C. M., Heaton, R. K., & Grant, I. (1991). Psychogenic factors influencing neuropsychological performance: somatoform disorders, factitious disorders, and malingering. In H. O. Doer and A. S. Carlin (Eds.), *Forensic neuropsychology: legal and scientific bases* (pp. 141–171). New York: Guilford.

Festinger, L. (1957). *A theory of cognitive dissonance*. Stanford: Stanford University Press.

Festinger, L. (1962). Cognitive dissonance. *Scientific American, 207*, 93–98.

Guyatt, G. H., Haynes, R. B., Jaeschke, R. Z., Cook, D. J., Green, L., Naylor, C. D., Wilson, M. C., & Richardson, W. S. (2000). Users' guides to the medical literature: XXV. Evidence-based medicine: principles for applying the users' guides to patient care. Evidence-Based Medicine Working Group. *Journal of the American Medical Association, 284*, 1290–1296.

Iverson, G. L., & Binder, L. M. (2000). Detecting exaggeration and malingering in neuropsychological assessment. *Journal of Head Trauma Rehabilitation, 15*, 829–858.

Kraepelin, E. (1909). *Psychiatry*. Leipzig: Barth.

Lees-Haley, P. R. (1992). Neuropsychological complaint base rates of personal injury claimants. *Forensic Reports, 5*, 385–391.

Matsui, Y., Ohbu, S., & Yamashina, A. (1996). Hospital deployment in mass sarin poisoning incident of the Tokyo subway system – an experience at St. Luke's International Hospital, Tokyo. *Japan-Hospitals, 15*, 67–71.

McDonald, E. S., & Windebank, A. J. (2000). Mechanisms of neurotoxic injury and cell death. In J. W. Albers and S. Berent (Eds.), *Clinical neurobehavioral toxicology* (pp. 525–540). Philadelphia: W. B. Saunders.

Richardson, W. S., Wilson, M. C., Williams, J. W., Jr, Moyer, V. A., & Naylor, C. D. (2000). Users' guides to the medical literature: XXIV. how to use an article on the clinical manifestations of disease. Evidence-Based Medicine Working Group. *Journal of the American Medical Association, 284*, 869–875.

Schaumburg, H. H., & Spencer, P. S. (1987). Recognizing neurotoxic disease. *Neurology, 37*, 276–278.

Trueblood, W., & Schmidt, M. (1993). Malingering and other validity considerations in the neuropsychological evaluation of mild head injury. *Journal of Clinical and Experimental Neuropsychology, 15*, 578–590.

Wechsler, D. (1991). *Manual for the Wechsler intelligence scale for children* (3rd ed.). San Antonio: Psychological Corporation.

Wechsler, D. (1997). *WAIS-III: Wechsler adult intelligence scale. Administration and scoring manual* (3rd ed.). San Antonio: Psychological Corporation/Harcourt Brace.

Whipple, G. M. (1914). *Manual of mental and physical tests*. Baltimore: Warwick & York.

Woodworth, R. S., & Schlosberg, H. (1964). *Experimental psychology*. New York: Rinehart & Winston.

World Health Organization (2001). *International classification of functioning, disability and health (ICF)*. Geneva: WHO.

Yokoyama, K., Araki, S., Murata, K., Nishikitani, M., Okumura, T., Ishimatsu, S., & Takasu, N. (1998). Chronic neurobehavioral and central and autonomic nervous system effects of Tokyo subway sarin poisoning. *Journal of Physiology (Paris), 92*, 317–323.

5 The neuropsychological approach

Introduction

In this chapter, and the two that follow, we present the basic clinical methodologies that characterize the two fields of Clinical Neuropsychology and Clinical Neurology, as well as the tests and procedures relied upon in conducting these efforts and that are most relevant to clinical neurobehavioral toxicology. A consistent theme in the present work is that the diagnostic process proceeds independently of causal attribution. A diagnosis of dementia, for example, depends only on objective verification of certain diagnostic criteria; a process that remains independent of any causal explanation until the clinician undertakes the task of establishing the etiology. Even then, *cause* can be a relative concept since it involves multiple levels. For instance, the clinician may be able to distinguish between forms of dementia that result from multiple cerebral infarctions and those due to progressive neurodegeneration (e.g., 'probable Alzheimer disease'). While these finer distinctions address part of the question as to what 'caused' the patient to become demented, they do not tell the entire story of causation. For instance, what 'causes' Alzheimer disease? The answer at this time and with the present state of knowledge is unknown (see Chapter 1). The distinction between *diagnosis* and *cause* presents the clinician interested in neurobehavioral toxicology with a potential dilemma. The very name of this specialized area connotes a connection between neurobehavioral outcome and a toxicological antecedent. In fact, it is not unusual to see a patient who has been diagnosed using a term that denotes both the patient's diagnostic condition and the cause of that condition, e.g., 'toxic encephalopathy' (Albers, Wald, Garabrant, Trask, & Berent, 2000). Combining etiology with diagnosis is, in fact, common in Medicine and Psychology (e.g., 'reactive versus endogenous depression', 'febrile versus traumatic seizure', etc.), but care must be taken to arrive independently at conclusions about each component of the resulting 'diagnostic phrase'. That is, the clinician should first determine that the patient experienced a seizure and, then, independently, determine the specific type and cause of the seizure, recognizing that some diagnostic terminologies reflect the reality that no specific cause is known, e.g., 'idiopathic epilepsy'.

So, what are the implications of the foregoing discussion for the neuropsychologist who is interested in neurobehavioral toxicology or performing an evaluation of a problem potentially related to a neurotoxic etiology? The primary answer to this question is that the neuropsychologist should employ the methods and procedures of the profession in exactly the same manner as in any clinical case. The basic methodologies remain the same. The questions asked and the technical tools used to address those questions will vary with the extent of our knowledge about given clinical manifestations. In the following paragraphs, we present these basics of Psychology and the specialty of Clinical Neuropsychology. In Chapter 6, we present the basic approaches and methodologies used by the neurologist to evaluate the nervous system. Chapter 7 provides a critique of many of the tests and procedures that are relevant to one or the other, or both, of these fields. As mentioned above, there is considerable overlap between the two fields, such that all three of the chapters mentioned here contain information that is relevant to both.

Psychology and the specialty of Clinical Neuropsychology

Psychology can be defined in general as the scientific study of human and animal behavior. This study of behavior includes a search for commonalties within and between species, but it also involves the study of individual differences. Individual differences, in fact, probably characterize behavior more often than does commonality. The history of the scientific approach to the study of behavior has been discussed elsewhere (Berent & Trask, 2000). For now, let us emphasize that it was not until the 19th century that meaningful scientific methods were applied to the study of behavior. Once these methods became available, they could be applied to the study of clinical and other applied problems in addition to theoretical aspects of behavior. The development of 'tests' for the study of individual differences soon followed. Cattell has been credited with the first use of the term 'mental tests', and the first methodology for using a collection of tests to describe an individual's behavior can be credited to Binet and Henri (Hilgard, 1978). Since these earlier beginnings, the methods of psychological testing have been continually refined, achieving a place of importance in the study of individual differences and in their application to clinical problems. The present chapter addresses these methods and their specialized applications in the field of Neuropsychology.

Brain and behavior

As discussed elsewhere in the present book, the nervous system can be divided into central (CNS) and peripheral (PNS) components. Neuropsychology deals primarily with functions of the CNS, but it must also attend to the PNS. It does this at times by directly measuring behaviors that are mediated by the PNS, sometimes by working closely with other specialists such as neurologists with special expertise in neuromuscular function. Some behaviors, e.g., motor speed, strength, etc., are influenced by the CNS and the PNS, and the neuropsychological approach considers this in arriving at diagnostic conclusions. At times, the neuropsychologist will be left with no choice but to make a probabilistic statement about the likelihood that a given observation, or set of observations, reflects one system or the other, recognizing that a variety of specialized tests exist (e.g., nerve conduction studies) that can aid in making this distinction.

There are other ways in which the nervous system is divided as well, and these divisions become important in localizing an abnormality during the clinical diagnostic process. As discussed in Chapter 6, for instance, the nervous system can be conceptualized in terms of laterality as well as levels, i.e., supratentorial, posterior fossa, spinal, and peripheral. Neuropsychology can contribute importantly in the determination of abnormality. Neuropsychological test results, for example, can help localize an abnormality within the CNS, once it has been identified, by differentiating diffuse or generalized impairment from focal involvement, distinguishing probable acute or subacute from chronic disorders, and identifying progressive from resolving conditions. Psychopathology (e.g., major affective or thought disorders) and other psychological factors (e.g., motivation, coping style) are also addressed by neuropsychology. Since the symptoms of psychopathology often mimic neurological disease, the neuropsychologist may be looked to as the primary clinician to answer questions pertaining to the effects of such disorders on the patient's clinical presentation.

The brain regulates most human thoughts, feelings, and actions. Because of this, damage to the brain is very likely to be reflected in behavioral symptoms, e.g., expressive aphasia resulting from injury to Broca's area (Mohr, 1976), Parkinsonism as a result of dopaminergic neuronal system dysfunction (Yahr, 1989), and gait disturbance in bilateral frontal lobe disease (Gilman, 1989). The knowledge of predictable relationships between brain and behavior in many instances allows Psychology and Medicine to approach the problem of studying the brain through a combination of deductive reasoning ('tracing back' from behavior) and inductive problem-solving (proposing and testing hypotheses generated in the course of the clinical process). Because the brain is not easily accessible to direct observation, behavioral methods represent important and effective approaches to clinical problem-solving and diagnosis.

The neuropsychological approach provides a tool for inquiry that is aimed at enhancing our knowledge of brain–behavior relationships in addition to solving individual clinical problems. In addition, these psychological methods provide tools for understanding the meaning of information that comes from other approaches to studying the CNS. For example, positron emission tomography (PET), magnetic resonance imaging (MRI), and electroencephalography (EEG) allow us to image chemical, metabolic, electrochemical, and other functional and structural aspects of the nervous system. The data derived from such methods are of less than optimal value, however, unless there is some understanding of the relationship of such data to behavior, and to the suspected pathology in turn. A frequent referral to neuropsychology, for instance, contains a request to provide 'clinical corollary' to a previous positive finding on one or more of the listed procedures as well as on other medical tests not mentioned. The systematic and objective measurements contained in the neuropsychological method can be employed to complement other approaches to the study of the nervous system, providing practical meaning to test results that might otherwise lack functional significance. It has been shown, for example, that abnormally high brain cortisol levels are associated with decreased hippocampal volume as measured by MRI (Starkman, Gebarski, Berent, & Schteingart, 1992). The functional significance of these hippocampal changes (e.g., changes in memory), however, was discovered by exploring the relationships between these changes in brain structure and corresponding changes in neuropsychological test results (Starkman *et al.*, 1992).

There are challenges involving the effective use behavioral information to study the nervous system. Some problems are technical, such as how objectively and quantitatively to measure behavior. Human behavior is complex in its scope (e.g., multiple types of memory) as well as in its great variability between and within individuals. Some behaviors do not lend to direct observation (e.g., concept formation and other aspects of thinking), even though we know these processes are important to the individual's normal functioning. Behavior is also complex in its intra-active aspects, e.g., one aspect of behavior influencing the manifestation of another. The amount of effort directed to a task by a given individual, for example, will be influenced by that person's motivation at the time. Use of neuropsychological techniques within a scientific context depends on enquiry using scientifically meaningful questions within a methodologically acceptable paradigm. As discussed in previous chapters, a scientific orientation remains relevant in clinical as well as in research contexts. Consideration must be given as to the meaningfulness of data derived, drawing not only on knowledge regarding psychometric theory, but also on a wider scientific knowledge base. This knowledge base includes behavioral and medical theories of disease, normal and abnormal behavior, classification and other knowledge that is relevant to the task at hand.

The use of psychometrics (i.e., psychological and neuropsychological tests) is but one component of the neuropsychological evaluation. Among the most important concepts in neuropsychology is the recognition that test results alone are never specific to a given disease or disorder. As emphasized by Boll (2000), 'neuropsychology can never get ahead of its criteria'. That is, the meaningfulness of test findings must be established through the systematic efforts of scientific enquiry. This process allows for the comparison of test findings with criteria that are established through independent means. In meeting this demand, discovering the meaningfulness of neuropsychological test results is no different than for the results of any other test procedure used in medicine. To give an example, attempts to apply PET scanning to the diagnosis of dementia began roughly in the 1980s (Kuhl, Metter, & Riege, 1985). Although patterns of hypometabolic cerebral glucose utilization among demented patients was fairly quickly established using this imaging technique, it took over 15 years to document a claim for a reasonable level of specificity that certain metabolic patterns reflected a diagnosis of dementia (Minoshima, Frey, Koeppe, Foster, & Kuhl, 1995). Amongst other things, this documentation required multiple comparisons of PET data to a host of independently derived clinical and basic criteria. Still, the claim for specificity remains controversial, and it would be unlikely that PET findings alone would be sufficient to establish the diagnosis of dementia (American Academy of Neurology, 2001). This does not mean that PET findings have no value to the diagnostic process in dementia, any more than neuropsychological test results are of no value in making the diagnosis. Both contribute substantially to the diagnostic process in dementia as well as in a host of other neurological and behavioral disorders. This does mean that the conclusions drawn on the basis of these tests must be consistent with the prevailing scientific knowledge base concerning the disorders considered and the devices used. In neuropsychology, this translates into a multifactorial approach to the clinical problem that includes more than simply analyzing test results.

Clinical Neuropsychology and its relationship to neurobehavioral toxicology

As mentioned in Chapter 1, chemical transmission is the primary mode of communication between cells in the nervous system (Siegel, Agranoff, Albers, Fisher, & Uhler, 1999). This leaves the nervous system potentially vulnerable to damage from toxic substances that injure neurons or other nervous system cells or interfere with the transmission of chemical signals across synapses, whether these agents are endogenous or introduced via the environment. As will be discussed in more detail in Chapter 6, the nervous system is complex, leaving a large number of ways in which neurotoxic injury can occur. It remains the job of science to determine the types of injury and the conditions under which such injury can occur. Since, as already mentioned, the nervous system regulates behavior, chemical injury can often be expected to manifest in some aspect of behavioral change that lends itself to neuropsychological evaluation. Leukoencephalopathy, for instance, results from damage to cerebral white matter, primarily damage to myelin or cells import in its maintenance, and can be caused by a variety of toxic substances (Filley, Heaton, & Rosenberg, 1990; Filley & Kleinschmidt-DeMasters, 2001). The disorder may range from mild to severe, and the clinical manifestations will reflect the extent and location of damage, which is usually symmetrical and diffuse (Filley & Kleinschmidt-DeMasters, 2001). The resultant symptoms reflect a number of neuropsychological impairments and, especially when the disease is mild, these behavioral manifestations can be non-specific and difficult to define. Some of these non-specific symptoms include confusion, problems with attention, forgetfulness, depression, and other changes in personality. With regard to determining that symptoms such as those just listed are specific to neurotoxic injury, the nature of neuropsychological tests makes it extremely unlikely that isolated test results can allow for such conclusions. Any and all of the symptoms and associated clinical impairments just listed could result from a number of causes, as a group or individually. The neuropsychological test results do provide important behavioral descriptions concerning the individual. A first step, then, and one that neuropsychology may be particularly good at performing, is to document the presence and association of objective performance measures with the symptoms. Viewed in this way, the neuropsychological test results are analogous to *signs* in clinical medicine. These neuropsychological descriptions then can be used to define patterns of abnormalities that can be compared with independent criteria to reach diagnostic conclusions. In arriving at a diagnostic conclusion, the neuropsychologist will often need to rely on data beyond those generated by neuropsychological tests. Although not necessarily limited to, these additional data include the reported results of medical tests (brain imaging and laboratory tests), the findings of clinicians from other disciplines (social, occupational, psychiatric, medical, histories, findings of neurological dysfunction), information from interview and patient history (documentation of exposure, baseline functioning), as well as knowledge about the nature of various disorders. Such information will include the identification of expected symptoms, signs and their clinical course for a specified disorder. When used in this appropriate fashion, neuropsychological test results provide an important, at times necessary, and powerful tool for reaching clinical conclusions.

Neuropsychological evaluation

The neuropsychological evaluation consists of three general and somewhat overlapping components. Information that is critical to arriving at clinical conclusions derives from each of these components. On completing this process, the neuropsychologist analyzes the results, taking into consideration any information from ancillary tests or additional sources, and reports the conclusions. In approaching a question of possible exposure to toxicants, the process is identical to addressing any clinical question. The three basic components to the evaluation are:

- History (including a review of available past neuropsychological, medical, and other records).
- Clinical interview.
- Psychometric examination.

The history

Historical information is obtained directly from the patient and, with the patient's (or other appropriate) permission, also may be obtained from formal historical records as well as from others (e.g., family members) familiar with the patient's history. While interview of others with knowledge about the patient is not a general requirement of the neuropsychological evaluation, there are situations when this is important. Dealing with very young children is one such instance, for example. Another would involve interview of someone with advanced dementia. In some circumstances, a family member may be the only person to have experience with and be able to describe the patient's problems, or even the manifestation of symptoms. This might occur in a case of seizure disorder, for instance, when a person close to the patient may be the only witness to be able to describe the paroxysmal event (Sackellares & Berent, 1996). With regard to questions about neurotoxicity, information about exposures to medicines, nutritional supplements, or other potential toxicants might be revealed. In all cases, the source of the historical information should be carefully recorded and discrepancies noted.

To the extent possible, formal historical records relating to the patient should be obtained. These records may contain information that was overlooked by the patient, though more importantly, they may contain facts that were never within the patient's sphere of knowledge or facts that the patient did not recognize as important for the clinician to know. A record of a past surgery, for instance, might reveal a recorded instance of prolonged hypoxia, as well as the details of the incident. The same record could be important in reflecting a medical condition with implications for the patient's present neuropsychological functioning. What prompted the need for surgery in the first place? It might also reflect medications the patient had taken, as well as adverse events that might have occurred as a result of those medications. At times, one note in a record will refer to another note that was previously unknown to the neuropsychologist. While reading a physical therapy note, for example, a clinician noted reference to a past neuropsychological examination. The present examiner had not been aware of such an examination before reading this note. Although the patient had been asked about past examinations of this sort, he had not recognized the past examination as being of the type about which the clinician had inquired. With this new information, the examiner was able to obtain the important past records. Past medical records should be obtained as completely as possible, but other classes of record can be equally important. An attempt should be made to obtain past school transcripts, especially those that contain the results of achievement or aptitude tests. Occupational or military records may contain information regarding past job-related injuries or exposures to toxicants as well as details concerning the nature of those exposures.

Use of a standard history form

Most clinicians find it helpful to prepare a standard history form for use in the clinical interview. The patient can complete this form, in part or in whole, before the actual appointment, saving interview and testing time, as well as helping to ensure that all relevant areas are covered.[1] The form typically includes information in specified areas, including an occupational and exposure history. The clinician should document who completes the form, as others often accompany patients to the appointment. In all cases, the clinician should go over the completed form, to correct misreading, to clarify the author of a given response, and to follow-up responses recorded on the form with more detail when necessary. The use of such a form helps to structure the interview process, but care needs to be taken to ensure the opportunity for spontaneous contributions to the interview.

At a minimum, topics in the history should include the following:

- Personal identification and demographic information, including present and past occupational and marital status.
- List of chief complaints and the date of onset for each.
- Past medical and surgical histories, including all psychiatric and medical illnesses, injuries, and treatments.
- Current and past medications, prescribed and over-the-counter.
- Results of past medical tests and procedures, including neuro-psychological evaluations, and dates of service.
- Family history, including disorders and diseases, and the nature of the relationship to the patient.
- Information regarding immediate family members; including their relationship to patient (e.g., mother, father, brother, etc.); if deceased, age or age of death, illnesses or cause of death; children's sex, age, health, and school progress; spouse's age, occupation, health.
- Educational history, including where the patient attended school, the grades achieved and grade averages, the presence and nature of past learning problems, specialized vocational training.
- Present or past use of tobacco, alcohol, caffeine drinks, other substances, including illicit drug use (amounts and frequencies).
- Hobbies, vacations, exercise programs.
- Present and past occupational history, including military service, and details regarding job assignments, chemicals used, and exposures for each.
- Review of systems, which is designed to cover some of the primary symptoms associated with each of the major biological systems, e.g., shortness of breath, cravings for sweets, skin lesions, mood changes or depression, work or personal stresses, digestive problems, confusion, memory complaints, sleep problems, headaches, fainting spells, dizziness, muscle or joint pain, numbness or tingling, bladder or bowel dysfunction,

sexual dysfunction, marital discord, difficulty swallowing, etc. Positive answers to these questions are pursued during the interview.

Exposure history

Knowing that someone has been exposed to a given toxicant is considered a necessary prerequisite in identifying a toxicant-induced disorder. Such knowledge includes information not only about the specific agent involved, but also about the amount, duration, and other details of the exposure. In the research setting, this information is expected, or the investigator must argue the use of some very good analog, approximation, or surrogate measure of exposure. When the research occurs in an industrial setting, there may be very good exposure information as such settings are likely to maintain data from industrial hygiene monitoring. The same is true in medical settings where, for example, medications might be the subject of study or clinical evaluation. When the research is prospective, exposure details that are relevant to the substance being studied can be identified in advance. In many instances of clinical evaluation, however, the details of exposure, or even the knowledge that the person has been exposed, are absent. In research and in clinical practice, an exposure assessment is an important component of the evaluation. Even when exposure to a specific neurotoxicant has been identified, knowledge of other potential exposures is important. While quantification is ideal, many times the best that can be accomplished is to document that there was an opportunity for exposure. Preferably, the information about an opportunity for exposure also will include some estimate of the magnitude of exposure and that the exposure was of sufficient magnitude to cause the observed disorder.

Exposure assessment involves enquiry as part of the standard occupational, social, and medical histories. The occupational history includes details about where the person has worked, for how long, and with what potential exposures. This should include all past employment, including a history of military service. What was the person's job title and function? Were there requirements for use of a respirator or other protective equipment? Were these devices used correctly? Did others work with neurotoxicants that could result in inadvertent exposure to the patient? Were there ever incidents of acute exposure that resulted in clinical symptoms or signs or the need for medical attention? If so, where and how was the person treated and for how long?

The history should also enquire about hobbies and sports that the individual is currently involved in, or might have been in the past. Is the person a gardener? If so, does he or she work with pesticides, herbicides, or other chemicals? Is she or he involved in fishing, hunting, or target shooting? If yes to any of these questions, does he or she load their own ammunition or cast lead shot or sinkers? What kinds of solvents or other chemicals are used to clean guns and other equipment? What safety precautions does the person employ when working with potentially dangerous substances?

Of course, it is unlikely that a history obtained in this manner will result in an objective quantification of exposure. Nevertheless, the history does document opportunities for exposure, both for a specific substance that might be of immediate clinical interest as well as for substances that might compete with a suspected agent in explaining the clinical diagnosis.

Aside from a history of systemic disorders that hold the possibility of endogenous intoxication, a complete history of medication use is obtained. This should list medications the person is taking presently as well as those taken in the past, including over-the-counter medications, herbs, and dietary supplements that the patient may not consider 'medications'. Instances of adverse reactions to any of these medications should be explored and noted in order to determine possible past acute over-exposures.

The individual's personal habits in terms of non-medicinal drugs should be evaluated. This includes illicit as well as legalized substances – tobacco, alcohol, coffee, and other caffeinated products, as well as marijuana and other stimulant and depressant drugs. Given the hesitancy that accompanies disclosure about the use of such products, explore for less direct indications about the use of such drugs. For instance, ask about the person's sleeping habits and if anything helps them with their sleep, ask if they have ever been in trouble because of their use of any substances, or if their spouse or other people close to them has ever complained about any of their habits.

Aside from information obtained directly from the assessment, the history may also identify areas that would be important to explore further, such as the need to obtain additional and specific records related to the person's medical, social, or occupational histories.

The clinical interview

The interview includes a review of the patient's primary, or presenting, symptoms and elicitation of additional complaints the patient might have. The clinician also obtains information during the interview that, together with the history, might be relevant to the possible diagnoses that are being formulated, as well as information that will contribute to conclusions regarding the potential causes for the patient's complaints. Attention is also given to evaluating the patient's suitability for various treatment options should those become relevant later on. The difficulty, or ease, of establishing rapport with the patient, for instance, could have implications for how well the patient would accept psychotherapeutic intervention, should that be considered later as a treatment recommendation.

The interview takes place in a face-to-face situation. It affords the clinician the opportunity to observe the patient and, in so doing, to evaluate various aspects of the patient's behavior that can be later used to reach diagnostic conclusions. In this respect, the interview in neuropsychology can be seen as similar to the clinical examination in neurology. Through the process of the interview, the clinician has the opportunity to review the various behavioral domains that are known to be important to a complete evaluation of the patient's neuropsychological functioning (Table 5.1). While these same behavioral domains are evaluated in the psychometric portion of the examination, the observations made in the interview enable the clinician to experience the consequences of the patient's behavioral strengths and weaknesses in a setting that approximates everyday life (e.g., interpersonal interaction with the interviewer). Also, it is possible to identify discrepancies in the patient's behavior within the interview and, later, between interview and test performance.

The clinician formulates questions during the interview portion of the evaluation and seeks to answer these questions through the process of observation. The patient's orientation to his or her surroundings can be assessed with a question like, 'How did you get to today's appointment?' The clinician can respond to the patient's answer with a series of questions designed to encourage the patient to reflect his or her level of awareness. Such questions also test the patient's memory for recent events. Does the patient reflect adequate comprehension and other aspects of effective communication? Are the expected social, cultural, and interpersonal conventions reflected in the patient's interactions with the clinician? Small interventions can be inserted into the interview process in order to test hypotheses regarding the patient's language, cognition, psychomotor behavior, affect, coping style, and other behavioral domains listed in Table 5.1. The clinician should also observe the patient's posture, gait, and physical symmetry. Hearing and vision should not be overlooked. The various observations made during the interview will later aid in the clinical analysis, especially perhaps when there are major discrepancies between findings from interview and the results of formal tests. To give an example, a patient was found in interview to be at least normally conversant and socially appropriate. He was able to provide an excellent past medical, social and personal history that corresponded almost exactly to formal historical records. His short- and long-term memory appeared normal based on his description of recent and past events, again verified against formal records of those same events. Yet, on formal psychometric examination, he produced scores that were consistent with other patients seen by the clinician who were diagnosed with advanced Alzheimer disease and incapable of more than rudimentary self-care. A review of tests and procedures that were ancillary to the neuropsychological evaluation, e.g., neurological examination, EMG, MRI, found them to be normal. Clearly, the discrepancies noted in this case between interview and test findings required resolution before a final diagnostic statement could be made. In this particular case, further interview and selected testing revealed that the patient had been malingering in his test performance.

A semi-structured interview can be prepared and used during the interview process. This ensures that the clinician will cover all relevant aspects during the interview. At the same time, the semi-structured nature of the interaction allows for some free discourse that maximizes the likelihood that the

Table 5.1 General behavioral domains to observe and some specific questions to address during interview.

General mental status:
  Is the patient oriented to his or her surroundings in terms of time, place, and person?
  Does the patient reflect reasonable understanding about the purpose of the evaluation?
  What is the degree of knowledge concerning current events and important aspects of community and personal life?
  Is the patient able to pay reasonable attention to remain focused on the interaction with the interviewer?
  Are language, social convention, and other aspects of interpersonal interaction sufficiently normal to allow for meaningful communication?

General intellectual level:
  What is the patient's level of vocabulary in comparison with other patients seen?
  On what level does the patient appear to comprehend what is said?
  Does the patient's fund of general information appear to be average, above, or below average?
  Does the patient reflect adequate abstract reasoning?

Cognitive processes:
  Does the patient reflect a sufficient level of working memory to answer the interviewer's questions?
  What is the balance between communications that require the reporting of recent events in the patient's life and those that involve longer term, historical information?
  How do the reports of historical information compare with formal records the clinician has reviewed?
  Is the patient able to learn new information during the interview and able to retain such information for varying periods of time?
  Is the patient circumstantial in communicating with the interviewer? Is the patient tangential in this respect?

Language:
  What is the patient's level of reading recognition?
  Is the patient able to write cursively, legibly, free of the effects of tremor, and with acceptable line orientation to the page?
  Are thought processes intact as reflected in spoken and written communications?
  What is the patient's level of vocabulary? Is it consistent with the patient's history?
  Is the patient's speech coherent and impediment free?
  Does the patient reflect a normal verbal fluency?
  Are language-based communications normal in expressive and receptive areas?

Psychomotor abilities:
  Is the patient normal in areas of motor speed, steadiness, dexterity, coordination, and strength?
  Is ambulation normal? How about posture, muscle tone?

Affect and coping:
  Are emotions situationally appropriate? Are they appropriately modulated?
  Is there evidence for major affective or thought disorder or for other psychopathology?
  What is the patient's primary coping strategy: repressive, sensitizing?

---

unanticipated will also become known. While the use of a semi-structured interview affords the luxury of predicting the approximate time a given interview will take to complete, it is also important to allow patients to present the situation from their own points of view, even if this involves minimal verbal interaction with the clinician. Allow surprises to occur. An interview that was conducted with an almost mute, elderly male patient provides an example of how the unanticipated can sometimes reveal information that is critical to the clinical process. The interview was painfully slow, and the clinician felt as if the answer to each question had to be painstakingly extracted from the patient. Even though very little information about his history or symptoms had been obtained directly from the patient, the list of structured questions was nearing an end. At this point, the clinician stopped asking questions and allowed the patient to sit quietly. He appeared calm, but the interviewer noticed that the patient frequently tended to glance up and to the left, over the interviewer's right shoulder. His tendency to make these glances was so frequent and seemingly deliberate that the clinician turned to look in the direction of his glances. Turning back to the patient, the interviewer commented on these observations. Since the interviewer had seen nothing but the ceiling, the patient was asked directly what he had been looking at. To this, the patient responded that he was looking at the woman who tells him how to answer the interviewer's questions. Had the clinician not allowed the time for observation and non-structured interaction, the visual hallucinations the patient was experiencing might not have been discovered.

The psychometric examination

The three primary portions of the neuropsychological evaluation are information gathering. This information will be used to arrive at a clinical impression, but the process of arriving at these conclusions begins from the start of the evaluation. With this in mind, it can be said that a substantial part of the interview includes the initial development of the 'differential diagnosis.' This initial formulation identifies the kind of additional information that will be needed to evaluate items in the differential diagnosis, and it sets the stage for developing conclusions related to treatment recommendations and establishing causation. While the clinician often will form initial impressions regarding the patient's condition, the process of differential diagnosis results in a list of all of the conditions that could explain the patient's complaints and, eventually, the findings from other tests and procedures that might be obtained by the clinician. This part of the process is similar in both neurology and neuropsychology. In both fields, the possible conditions and explanations that apply to the case are used to formulate questions and the tests and procedures that generate the data needed to address these questions. The neuropsychologist determines which tests to include in the psychometric portion of the evaluation based on this process. The need for ancillary tests or information also is determined, e.g., past educational records to aid in establishing a baseline for the patient's intellectual abilities. As mentioned a number of times in the present book, the clinical process is systematic, and it is analogous to the steps in scientific inquiry. That is, the clinical questions are analogous to research hypotheses while the clinical tests and procedures are similar to the scientific experiment. One key difference between the two is that the scientific experiment provides information about a group of individuals, information that may or may not generalize to an individual. The clinical process, on the other hand, yields findings that speak to the individual case. Put another way, one aim of scientific research is to discover the probability of the occurrence of an event, while the clinical enterprise asks if a specified event probably occurred in a given individual.

Some important technical aspects of the psychometric examination will be discussed in greater detail below. While the analogy is not perfect, this aspect of the neuropsychological approach corresponds to a degree with the specialized tests and procedures used in neurology (see Chapter 6). A battery (i.e., collection) of neuropsychological typically tests sample multiple domains of functioning, including intelligence, academic skills (e.g., reading, spelling, arithmetic), attention, learning and memory, language, visuospatial processing, executive skills, sensory–motor, emotion and coping style (Table 5.1). The psychometric portion of the evaluation serves two major purposes. First, it provides an opportunity to obtain information that speaks to the differential diagnostic considerations that were defined initially in earlier portions of the evaluation. Second, it seeks to provide objective and systematic measurement of behavior that complements the information obtained by the clinician through other means and that can be used to test the clinician's hypotheses. The results of these tests, of course, might yield information that was not previously considered by the clinician. As a consequence, additional possibilities might be added to the differential diagnosis, and additional tests and procedures might be employed to address the new questions that result.

The domains of behavior listed above usually are measured routinely as part of the psychometric process. This is done because the nervous system has both interdependent portions as well as parts that function with some independence. A sufficiently comprehensive clinical evaluation usually requires the measurement of behaviors that are known to be mediated by these various and primary portions of the nervous system. Of course, potentially confounding variables will also be measured. It is important to know the patient's reading level, for instance, as this variable has important implications for the selection and interpretation of other tests in the battery. Other potential confounds include age, gender, handedness, motivation, education, pre-existing psychological or cognitive disorders, language or cultural differences, and certain medical conditions (Rozensky, Sweet, & Tovian, 1997).

Another constant that influences the selection of measures to be included in the test battery relates to the concept of 'redundancy'. Several measures with similar or overlapping demands for successful completion are included in the 'standard' battery. This is done for two primary reasons. First, the redundancy serves to strengthen the conclusion of abnormality when it occurs in a given test instance. Second, the redundant tests usually contain different demand characteristics, allowing the clinician to identify more precisely the specific impairment involved. An example of this last test characteristic is reflected in the Trails tests (Lezak, 1995; Berent & Swartz, 1999). A patient who has done well on Part A of this test has demonstrated normal abilities in the motor requirements of the test. Subsequent poor performance on Part B by the same patient, therefore, suggests a problem with the cognitive aspects of the test rather than a motor impairment. On the other hand, a patient who has performed poorly on both parts might have impairment in either the motor, or the cognitive, or in both functional areas. In the last case, a third measure would be sought; one with isolated motor or cognitive demands similar to that required in performing the Trails test. Of course, redundancy is also provided by way of serial testing. It is not unusual for a patient to have undergone previous psychometric evaluation, and the scores from such examinations should be sought and brought into the current analysis whenever possible. In addition to the principle of redundancy, an analysis of serial testing also addresses the nature of clinical course. Such information can be critical in arriving at a final diagnostic impression. The symptoms and signs that accompany most acute toxicant-induced disorders, for example, tend to improve over time (Schaumburg & Spencer, 1987). When a toxicant-induced disorder is part of the differential diagnosis, a finding of worsening performance across serial test sessions in the absence of ongoing exposure would be contrary to the expected clinical course of most neurotoxicant exposures. This clinical picture might be suggestive, however, of some other disorder in the list of differentials, e.g., progressive dementia from Alzheimer disease (Berent, Giordani, Foster, Minoshima, Lajiness-O'Neill, Koeppe, & Kuhl, 1999).

Beyond the more or less common battery that is administered to most patients, other tests are included to provide data that are relevant to the various diagnostic-related questions that the clinician posed during history and interview, i.e., the initial or preliminary differential diagnosis. We have used terms like 'initial', 'preliminary', and, in places, 'working diagnosis' to reflect the differential diagnosis as a process. Changes can be, and may be likely to be, made to the list of possible diagnoses at any point in this process. From this perspective, the psychometric portion of the neuropsychological evaluation can be viewed as a measurement of behavioral data that will help to answer the clinical questions and refine the differential diagnosis. As mentioned repeatedly, the clinical process is analogous to a scientific experiment. The neuropsychologist hypothesizes a certain test outcome based upon the given clinical question, and the examination results serve as data to accept or reject the individual hypotheses. At times, further questions may be raised even at late stages in the process. In response, the neuropsychologist may look to additional measures or may seek information from ancillary tests or consultations.

The neuropsychological method

Nature of neuropsychological data

The process of neuropsychological evaluation provides the data needed to document the existence and nature of impairment, to define the problem in terms of the nervous system, recommend further evaluation or treatment, and to discover the etiology if possible. There are some questions that can be answered through the neuropsychological process and others that cannot. It is not unusual, for example, for a clinical diagnosis to be established even though a specific etiology cannot be specified. In fact, the descriptive nature of neuropsychological test findings serves important clinical objectives even at those times when the neuropsychologist cannot make a formal diagnosis. These descriptions can have a multitude of clinical applications and can help to make the clinical presentation more sensible than might have been the case before the evaluation. As discussed in several places in this book, many symptoms are non-specific. It is common that some complaints made by a patient reflect the underlying disorder, whereas the patient's other symptoms do not. In keeping with the principle of 'proportionality' (Boll, 2000), there are some consequences of neurological disorder that are to be expected and others that are not. According to Boll, 'because individuals have brain damage does not mean that any neurocognitive performance that they produce must in some way be attributable to that brain damage.' Put another way, the picture of impairment should be consistent with the type of injury concluded.

In general, the neuropsychologist can deal only with observable events or those with objective behavioral analogs. The process occurs within a scientifically oriented, evidence-based model, and what can be said in a given case will be limited by the extent of available scientific fact. This is not to say that the clinician's background knowledge from past clinical experience cannot be brought into the analysis. It can, but the conclusions that are based on such experience should be clearly labeled as such to distinguish them from those based on a formal scientifically derived database. The ideal is to strive for the latter in making final conclusions.

Clinical evaluation of neuropsychological data

The neuropsychological process can be conceptualized as a methodology that includes the evaluation and the interpretation of the results from the evaluation. The method contains a series of steps that the neuropsychologist follows in reaching a final clinical impression (Berent & Trask, 2000). Each step can be viewed as a general question area that needs to be systematically addressed (Table 5.2). The clinical components of history, interview, and

Table 5.2. Clinical neuropsychological method and some questions to address during the neuropsychological evaluation.

Determine the presence or absence of abnormality

Identify the affected behavioral domains

Describe the pattern of strengths and weaknesses:
  Is the pattern consistent with neurological dysfunction?
  Does the pattern suggest focal or general neurological involvement?
  Is the pattern suggestive of acute, subacute, or chronic disorder?
  Is the pattern progressively worsening, static, or resolving?

Grade the level of severity

Determine the extent to which anxiety, depression, motivation, or other non-neurological disease factors are contributing to the observed clinical picture

Determine the implications of the findings for making clinical conclusions:
  What possible explanations (the differential diagnosis) might explain the problem?
  Do the findings support one or more specific diagnoses?
  Are recommendations for further evaluation or treatments suggested by the findings?
  Can a prognosis be stated?
  Can a statement about the cause of the patient's problem(s) be determined?

Describe the functional significance of the findings for the patient's daily life:
  What are the implications for self-care, management of finances, return to work, etc.?

---

psychometric examination can be viewed as procedures that the neuropsychologist uses to carry out the clinical work. These various clinical procedures are designed to generate data, which, in turn, serve three basic functions. First, they allow for the identification of problems relevant to the case at hand. Second, the identified problem areas are used to generate specific hypotheses and to determine the type of additional data that will be needed for the clinical analyses. Third, the data are used to answer questions regarding diagnosis, prognosis, and other clinically relevant concerns about the patient. As with any technical procedure, the process requires the disciplined and reasoned judgment of a properly trained person, a neuropsychologist in this instance, to be successful. The clinical process in Neuropsychology is similar to that employed in Neurology, with analogous steps employed by both disciplines (see Chapter 6). These similarities contribute to the compatibility between the two fields. The differences in approach between the two disciplines make them complementary.

The first step in this clinical process is to determine the presence or absence of abnormality. The clinician must have knowledge of normal and abnormal behavior in order to address this question area. Also, the neuropsychologist must have a good understanding of the psychometric characteristics of the measures to be used, since, in most instances, the results from neuropsychological tests will be examined in relationship to a reference group. The problem of individual differences underlies the approach to the question of normality. That is, people vary from one another along a continuum for any given behavior. As emphasized numerous times in this book, the factors leading to individual differences are many and complex. The neuropsychologist must consider these factors in interpreting the evaluation results.

Aside from determining abnormality by comparing scores to normative referent groups, impairment is often defined on the basis of decline in comparison with an actual past level of functioning. This type of conclusion can be made more easily when the patient has undergone serial testing over time than when such data are not available. When direct measurement of changes over time are not available, the clinician will look to historical data that reflect the person's past performance. As already alluded to, records of the patient's past educational performance represent one place such information can be found. There are varying levels in terms of the strength of such evidence, with past school grades, perhaps, being of less value than are the results of aptitude tests administered at the time. It has been shown that overall grade level attained correlates significantly (about $r = 0.70$) with Wechsler Full Scale IQ (Matarazzo, 1972). A history of special educational placement or grade failure can also be used to aid in the understanding of present test performance by an individual (Wilson & Stebbins, 1991).

Aspects of the current examination results can also be used to predict baseline levels (Berent & Trask, 2000). Certain behaviors, such as reading speed, are less sensitive to the impairing effects of mild to moderate brain injury than are other variables, like information processing (Boll, 2000). The relationship between more- and less-affected language variables has been used by some to estimate a patient's past performance (Nelson & O'Connell, 1978). When using such an approach, however, it is important first to determine if primary disturbances of language are a part of the patient's clinical picture. Recently acquired problems with language could potentially lead to an underestimate of the patient's past intellectual abilities (Stebbins, Gilley, Wilson, Bernard, & Fox, 1990). There have also been attempts to use demographic variables (e.g., factors associated with the patient's socio-economic status) to predict past ability level mathematically, but these have been met with mixed reviews (Barona, Reynolds, & Chastain, 1984).

Complaints (symptoms) may be communicated to a clinician either directly by the patient or by someone close to the patient, such as a family member or friend. The complaints are often based in some perceived change in behavior in one of several areas of the person's usual functioning. These functional areas may relate to the person's comfort (e.g., pain, unhappiness, worry), performance efficiency (e.g., inability to perform a particular job or family role), or to the appropriateness of their thoughts or actions (e.g., peculiar verbalizations and ritualistic acts). Not only do people differ from one another, but also a given person is never exactly the same from one period of time to another. Change characterizes life. People also vary in terms of self-concept and self-expectation, and there is often a discrepancy between self-expectations and the expectations of others applied to a person. Based on the considerations just mentioned, the clinician can expect to see many patients whose concerns are based either in normal variations between people or symptoms that arise from developmental or other expected life changes.

As people have become increasingly sophisticated about the nature of disorder and the various events that can potentially lead to disorder, the authors have experienced an increase in the tendency for patients to include suggestions as to possible causes for their complaints. Rather than presenting a list of symptoms and asking the clinician for an explanation, patients are as likely to describe some event that they believe may have harmed them, or may cause them harm in the future. One patient, for instance, noted that one of his parents died from complications of Alzheimer disease. Although he initially reported no dramatic memory difficulties that he was aware of, he was concerned that he might face the same fate as his parent and requested an evaluation in order to establish a baseline for later comparison. During the subsequent interview, the patient confided that he was experiencing difficulties with his memory. Formal examination, however, revealed totally normal functioning. His concerns had influenced his interpretation of normal variations in memory, leading him to conclude that his memory was abnormal. The examination allowed the clinician to reassure the patient, but he did appear to take some comfort in knowing that he could return periodically to re-evaluate his situation. Another patient reported that he had worked for about 2 years as a welder. Although his employment in that capacity had been many years before, he was convinced that exposure to welding fumes was now responsible for his perceived changes in his memory. The only difficulty with his memory, as it turned out, was attributable to the intrusive effects of his anxiety.

While this tendency to self-diagnose is interesting from a psychosocial viewpoint, it has little impact on the nature of the clinical neuropsychology evaluation. For all practical purposes, the suspicion of abnormality is raised whenever a patient makes a clinical complaint. In response to the patient's complaints, the clinician approaches the evaluation in an impartial manner. The various steps in the clinical process described here are followed, and a determination of normal or abnormal functioning is arrived at as objectively as possible. Despite those instances when presumed causes are presented by the patient together with the complaints, the determination of etiology remains a step that is separate from diagnosis and which is approached at the appropriate point after a decision has been made about the presence of impairment. It cannot be stated too strongly, perhaps, that the clinician's job includes reassuring the patient when the findings make that reassurance appropriate.

Patients are correct in being concerned about their health. Also, there is nothing wrong with the patients who express ideas about the cause of their perceived difficulties. The fact that the patient brings these concerns to the clinician can be viewed as reflecting a belief that the clinician will be able to do something more to resolve the problem than the patient can accomplish alone. The patient recognizes what the clinician knows well, that complaints alone do not provide the entire story. The complaints, as well as the causal speculations when they are present, can be viewed as questions by the patient to the clinician. To answer these questions, the clinician seeks to identify objective signs that substantiate and more fully elucidate the clinical nature of the patient's symptoms.

As already mentioned, the formal neuropsychological evaluation sometimes ends when the question of the presence or absence of abnormality has been answered. At this point, the clinician decides on appropriate responses to the patient's initial concerns and actions that may be further needed, e.g., reassurance of the patient through patient education, referral for counseling, referral to another specialist or some other appropriate action as indicated by the situation. When the answer to this question is positive, however, a series of additional questions follow. Some of the most often used questions are summarized in Table 5.2. The specific neuropsychological tests that will be administered to the patient will be determined to a great extent by the kind of data that will be needed to answer the questions.

Psychometrics: basic technical considerations

The psychometric examination represents a very important portion of the neuropsychological evaluation. Because of this, we will here review some basic technical considerations regarding neuropsychological testing in general. The term 'psychometrics' can be used to refer to the technical aspects of a behavioral measuring device, e.g., aspects such as the validity or reliability of a given test. Formal methods and standards exist for establishing the validity and reliability of a test (American Psychological Association, 1985). While not all of the procedures used in the neuropsychological examination will necessarily meet the field's requirements to establish validity and reliability (e.g., some self-report measures or self-rating scales), the clinical usefulness of instruments without such established technical information will be limited. The neuropsychologists who employ these devices will also need to be diligent in recognizing their limitations in any conclusions drawn from their use. In addition, a device that has not met these standards should not be referred to as a 'test' (the authors prefer the word 'task' to refer to such instruments), since 'test' connotes a specialized device that has been shown to meet such standards (Berent & Trask, 2000). A test, in the psychological and neuropsychological sense, is a device that samples some aspect of behavior and that has been shown through formal scientific-based methodology to meet certain technical standards that have been set by appropriate professional bodies (Anastasi, 1976; American Psychological Association, 1985; Berent & Trask, 2000).

Reliability

The term 'reliability' refers to the consistency of a test's results (American Psychological Association, 1985). Put another way, the term refers to the measurement precision of a test. In measuring behavior, the neuropsychologist will need to know that the scores derived from a given instrument are, in fact, reflecting the person being measured and not some variation in the measuring instrument itself. Of course, every measuring device carries with it some error. The reliability statement regarding a given test allows one, however, to know something about the extent of such error. This information can then be factored into the conclusions made on the basis of the test's results.

It is the test developer, rather than the test user, who has the responsibility for establishing the reliability of the test. The test user, on the other hand, does retain the responsibility for knowing the test's reliability as well as other technical aspects of the test being employed. The test publisher will generally include information about the standard error of measurement that is characteristic of a given test. The error of measurement for a commonly used intelligence test, for example, is plus or minus 5 points. Therefore, any observed score on this test will actually reflect a range of possible scores. Using the customary mean of 100 and standard deviation of 15 points for such tests of intelligence, the actual score for a patient scoring at this mean would fall between 95 and 105. This knowledge is important clinically because an apparent change from one test session to another may not represent a true, or clinically significant, change once the error of measurement has been considered. There are other factors that affect the reliability of measurements as well, and some of these will be discussed below.

The error score will vary depending on the level of preciseness required. For instance, a larger confidence interval would be needed in order to be 99% accurate (e.g., 13 points) as opposed to 68% accurate (e.g., 3 points). Thus, every test-based conclusion represents a probability statement. This is no different than for any other scientific-based enterprise, of course. Further, while the error-adjusted scores in neuropsychological testing are less than perfect, the approximately 10–26 point variations compare favorably with the error found in other tests used to measure physiological and other medical aspects of human functioning (e.g., MRI, PET) (Berent & Trask, 2000).

A test's reliability is determined through scientific enquiry and statistical analysis. The main statistical tool used to establish a test's reliability is correlation, and the resultant statistic can be generally referred to as the reliability coefficient. Reliability is of several types, each reflecting a different aspect of the test's internal consistency of measurement. A few of the major types of reliability are test–retest, alternate form, and split-half. Tests also vary with regard to the form of stimulus presentation. Various specific correlation methods have been developed to be used in establishing a test's reliability, depending on the type of reliability or test format. Cronbach's coefficient alpha (Cronbach, 1951) was designed for use with multiple-choice-formatted tests, for instance. Dichotomous items (e.g., true or false items) will call for a statistical test such as the Kuder–Richardson formula 20 (Kuder & Richardson, 1937), while split-half formatted tests might use the Spearman–Brown coefficient of correlation (Walker & Lev, 1953). Some types of tests do not lend well to establishing internal consistency. This is true, for example, of most tasks that require speed over accuracy for successful completion (such as the finger-tapping task used in the Halstead–Reitan Battery) (Reitan & Wolfson, 1993; Berent & Trask, 2000).

Test–retest analysis involves the statistical measurement of the relationship of the test to itself on multiple administrations. This information is important because retest with the same instrument is a common way to monitor disease progression and, at the same time, to develop a picture of clinical course. Whenever a test is readministered, however, one has to consider the phenomenon of 'practice effect'. Practice effect refers generally to the effect of one administration of a test on a subsequent administration of the test. In common use, however, the term most often refers to the fact that a person may profit on a subsequent administration of a test simply because of the past experience with the same, or similar, instrument. To some extent, this profit reflects memory of the test, but practice effect is really a more complex issue than can be explained by the mechanism of memory alone. Changing a novel situation to one that is more familiar as a result of past experience can also have a facilitating effect on performance. Also, the effects of prior experience with a test, or test situation, are not necessarily always positive in terms of scores earned on repeat administrations. Still, practice effect is a variable the neuropsychologist has to consider in interpreting test results. These effects also influence the establishment of reliability. The time interval between test and retest is important and will likely be recorded in the test manual. One attempt to deal with practice effects has been to develop alternate forms of the same test. While this does maintain some novelty in terms of the test items, there is still carry over from the prior test experience, even when alternate forms are used (Anastasi, 1976). Split-half reliability provides a basis for shortening or lengthening a test as well as an indication of the internal consistency of the test in its entirety. Of course, factors other than those just mentioned affect the reliability of a test. Some of these include item complexity, test length, and range of possible scores. Knowing the reliability of a test is very important, to the degree that the neuropsychological test battery will include only those tests with established reliability to the fullest extent possible.

Validity

In its simplest definition, 'validity' refers to the extent to which a test measures the theoretical construct it claims to measure. A test of anxiety, for instance, will need to carry some scientifically based evidence that it does, indeed, measure anxiety. A first step in establishing such a claim would be to show that the instrument is reliable. That is, reliability determines the limit to which a test can be valid. Reliability reflects a test's precision of measurement, whereas validity refers to the test's accuracy. Validity, according to the standards of the American Psychological Association (1985), determines the, 'appropriateness, meaningfulness, and usefulness of the specific inferences made from test scores'.

Like reliability, validity is established through formal mathematical methods, the results of which will be contained in the published test manual and in the scientific literature more generally. Some general reference books also contain reviews of tests that include comments on the technical aspects of these tests, e.g., *The mental measurements yearbook* (Mitchell, 1998) and *Tests in print* (Buros Institute of Mental Measurements, 1999). Information can be found also in the field's published standards concerning test development and use (American Psychological Association, 1985).

There are several types of validity. The simplest form is 'face validity'. Face validity refers to the apparent meaningfulness of a test item. Continuing with the example of 'anxiety', an item on a test purporting to measure anxiety might ask if the person ever feels tense when in a group of people. Such an item would appear to have good face validity because this reaction is one known to occur in people with some forms of anxiety. While seemingly straightforward, and the type of item that represents a good place to start in constructing a test of anxiety, an item with good face validity might not be included in the final version of a test. When formal statistical methods are brought into test development, an item with good face validity might prove to be lacking in its ability to reflect accurately the construct of interest, anxiety in the present example. Why? One must compare the response against some independent criterion known to reflect anxiety. This is usually accomplished using correlation methods. Say, for example, that a group of individuals with known anxiety disorders are administered a face-valid item. Most or all of them might say 'no' in responding to the question. Since this group has been chosen to represent anxiety independently of the test itself, their answers will determine a type of validity (i.e., 'criterion validity') that takes precedence over face validity.

Approaching the establishment of a test's validity in this objective way, items that seem to be unrelated to the construct (i.e., items with poor face validity) might be found to be valid indicators of the construct. In other words, the test developer might find that anxious people are more likely to say they like to ride bicycles than to say they become tense in crowds. This observation explains the puzzlement that is sometimes expressed by people who are unfamiliar with the nature of psychological tests when they ask why a particular test item is on the test (e.g., 'I like sports magazines') when it has no apparent relationship to the problem at hand. It also explains why for many tests, the score is more important than the specific answer given in terms of content (e.g., whether or not the person likes a particular type of magazine). Beware, by the way, of tests that purport to measure a particular construct based solely on the face validity of the test. Unfortunately, such practice is all too common.

While criterion validity is defined as the mathematical relationship between a test and some other independent criterion, this type of validity can be divided into subtypes. One of these subtypes is 'concurrent validity'. One way in which criterion validity is established is to correlate the results of a new test with the concurrent results of an already scientifically established test. The validity for many of the variously used tests of intelligence, for instance, was established in this way. Anastasi (1976) emphasized, however, that it is important to remember that tests that have been developed in this way are really approximations of the original. The practice of using this technique for determining the validity of a new test is commonly used, nevertheless, and viewed as acceptable by the field of Psychology (American Psychological Association, 1985) as long as there is some compelling reason to do so. For instance, the new measure may be shorter, culturally current, more economical to administer, or otherwise preferable to the original (Berent & Trask, 2000).

A second subtype of concurrent validity is 'predictive validity'. Predictive validity is determined by correlating the results of a test with some independent future criterion. Scores on an intelligence or aptitude test, for instance, might be studied in relation to outcome following a course of study. This type of validity will be limited by the criterion chosen, however. That is, the result of one's performance in a course of study is multiply determined. There is more involved in successfully completing an educational program than intelligence or aptitude. For this reason, there can never be a perfect prediction of one's future performance on the basis of one such test. The clinician will need to consider a host of factors, the test result being but one, in predicting future outcome.

'Content validity' represents yet another type of validity. Content validity reflects the comprehensive representativeness of a test's content in relation to the construct it claims to measure. The sample of behavior that is a test (Anastasi, 1976) will need to include sufficient behaviors to represent the construct. Put another way, the test will need to reflect the scientific understanding of the construct in order to reflect the criterion in the test's results. A test of memory, for example, will need to sample short- and long-term memory, verbal and non-verbal aspects, recognition and recall of learned material, and the like if it is to claim to measure memory comprehensively. Since many constructs that are relevant to clinical neuropsychological inquiry are complex, one way to deal with this issue is to use multiple tests, each designed to test some one aspect of the construct of interest. Expert judgment is an important component in establishing content validity.

Here, it might be worth noting that most of the constructs measured by neuropsychological tests are theoretical and not accessible to direct observation. As already mentioned, anxiety is one such construct. Other examples include depression, memory, and intelligence. Observable analogs must be found that are known to reflect these constructs if we are to use tests to make objective and meaningful statements about them. In this requirement, neuropsychology is no different than other fields that seek to measure aspects of human functioning. Many biochemical systems of interest to nuclear medicine, for instance, are not directly observable for clinical study. In response, nuclear medicine has developed chemical ligands that reflect characteristics that are similar to the chemical of interest. By studying the activities of the chemical analog, meaningful statements can be made about the agent of actual interest. In a similar fashion, aspects of an emotional state that are observable can be studied to understand something of the basic emotion. Anxiety, for instance, is not directly observable. We can, however, study the known aspects of anxiety, such as increases in heart rate, changes in skin conductance, increased agitation, changes in breathing, and the like. These observable aspects can then be used as criteria in the development of test instruments that are designed to study the underlying emotional state, in this case, anxiety.

Another validity related topic has to do with the practical utility of test findings. Cronbach (1988) suggested that a test should be evaluated in terms of its 'functional validity' by comparing this aspect of validity against the test's 'statistical validity' in order to determine its usefulness for predicting an individual's performance in everyday life. Others have referred to this as a test's 'ecological validity' (Wilson, 1993). It is important to know, for instance, to what extent a test of memory will predict how the patient will perform in a job, in taking medications, or in other activities outside of the test situation. From this perspective, it is important to know how the test results relate to real-life circumstances as well as to know the relationship of the test's scores to theoretical constructs.

The extent to which a test is found to correspond or fail to correspond to the specified construct is reflected in its 'convergent' and 'discriminant' validity (Campbell & Fiske, 1959). That is, the test should ideally show a strong relationship to criteria associated with the construct and weak relationships to extraneous concepts. The concepts of convergent and discriminant validity can be related to the sensitivity and specificity of a given test. Sensitivity and specificity are concepts that are routinely used in medicine to describe clinical tests (Kraemer, 1982). Sensitivity refers to the capacity of a test to detect dysfunction when it is present. Specificity, in contrast, reflects the capacity of a test uniquely to detect dysfunction when it is present and to fail accurately to do so when it is not. The two concepts are independent, and an ideal clinical diagnostic test is both sensitive and specific. Some neuropsychological tests are specific and not sensitive. Others are sensitive but not specific. IQ tests, for example, are specific in terms of the criteria against which they have been evaluated, i.e., independent indices of intellectual function. These tests, however, are not as sensitive to underlying neurological dysfunction as some other neuropsychological measures. Tests of information processing, on the other hand, are very sensitive, but they are not specific to any particular type of underlying dysfunction (Boll, 2000). To give an example, the Halstead Category test has been shown to be sensitive to dysfunction in frontal regions of the human brain (Reitan, 1955). This test is not specific to frontal brain dysfunction, however, as there can be a host of reasons why a person performs this test in less than an ideal fashion (Berent & Trask, 2000).

While the lack of specificity associated with neuropsychological tests could be viewed as a weakness, it is important to keep in mind that this characteristic results from the design of neuropsychological tests. That is, neuropsychological tests have been designed to measure behavior. They do this task very well. Behavior is multiply determined, and disruptions to behavior can occur for many reasons. As mentioned above, a neuropsychological test can never go beyond its criteria. It is the nature of dysfunction that is reflected in the results of neuropsychological testing. For this reason, no neuropsychological test will be able to detect neurotoxicant-induced disorder specifically. When used as an objective measurement of behavior within the context of differential diagnosis and the totality of the neuropsychological evaluation, however, the neuropsychological approach represents an effective tool that can make important contributions to all aspects of the clinical enterprise.

Other issues in test construction, selection, and administration

Standardization

A requirement in test development is that the test device be 'standardized.' A standard procedure for the administration of the test should be specified. The person who later administers the test will need to follow this procedure faithfully. Standardization applies to all aspects of the test and its administration. This includes the instructions that are given to the patient, the physical setting in which the testing occurs, the timing of stimulus presentations, examples given, how the patient's questions are responded to, and other aspects of the testing. The way in which tests are scored has also been standardized. This explains why considerable training is required before a person can become qualified to administer neuropsychological tests. The results of tests that have been administered by any other than properly qualified individuals should be viewed with suspicion. Some tests can be standardized more easily than can others. This includes paper-and-pencil inventories such as the MMPI (Minnesota Multiphasic Personality Inventory), which can be administered following familiarization with a relatively few basic and general rules of test administration. These basic considerations can be found in texts such as those by Anastasi (1976) or Cronbach (1984). Other tests, such as the Wechsler Intelligence Scales, require considerable training before an individual can become qualified in their administration or interpretation. Guidelines have been published that address the various requirements regarding the clinical use of neuropsychological tests. Two such publications are *The TCN guide to professional practice in clinical neuropsychology* (Adams & Rourke, 1992) and The Division 40 Guidelines regarding the use of personnel in test administration (Division 40 Task Force on Education, 1989).

Normative data

When tests are employed in research, their results are generally compared statistically with one or more control groups. In clinical practice, the meaningfulness of the test results is determined by comparison with a 'normative sample'. That is, the observed scores are compared with a representative population sample. These normative data, or 'norms', lend meaning to the obtained scores by informing the clinician how the patient performed in comparison with this referent group. These scores might be expressed as percentile rankings or some other standard score that indicates where the patient's score fell in relation to the referent sample. By using the standardized norms for intelligence tests, for example, a person earning a score of 100 is known to be functioning on this test at the mean, or at the 50th percentile in terms of the comparison group. While normative data are used primarily in the clinical setting, they are useful in research as well. For instance, a statistical difference between two groups in a research study may or may not reflect a clinically meaningful difference based upon a comparison of scores to existing clinical norms.

Normative data are developed through formal research wherein the test is administered to large, representative groups of subjects. Care should be taken to ensure that the group of subjects are indeed representative of the population to which their performance will be compared and of a size as to be statistically meaningful for comparison. The shape of the distribution of scores is important in making comparison between the sample and a given individual's score. The average performance that is expected for an individual is determined by the normative sample. The normal range of scores is determined by the sample variance. From the perspective of normative sampling, the adequacy of a test is intimately related to the adequacy of its test norms. The reference group will determine the shape of the distribution, as well as central tendency and variance. Although sample distributions differ (e.g., handedness reflects a skewed distribution), most human behavior, when of sufficient size, approximates the normal curve (Figure 5.1).

Some additional comments on the neuropsychological clinical approach

Developing the neuropsychological impression

We have discussed in this chapter the ways in which the neuropsychologist proceeds in developing a neuropsychological impression and, eventually, a

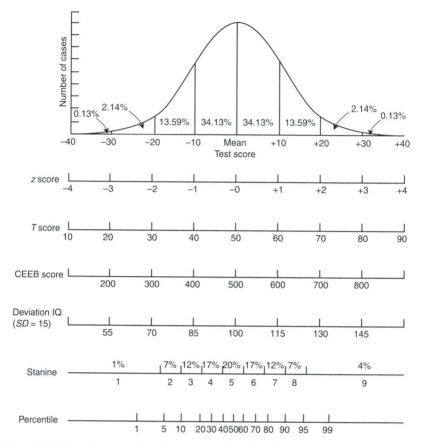

Figure 5.1 Normal curve depicting standard deviations, corresponding percentiles, and standard scores. Reprinted with permission: Pearson Education, Upper Saddle River, NJ, USA.

final diagnostic conclusion in a given clinical case. While other options may be open to the neuropsychologist, the methodological approach reflected in Table 5.2 seems a reasonable way to achieve this goal. The neuropsychologist is dependent in this process on the data he or she has obtained regarding a given clinical case. The information from the evaluation – including results from interview, history, and psychometric examination – provide these data, which are then used to formulate an initial impression regarding the patient's condition. As in Neurology (see Chapter 6 and Table 6.4 specifically), the neuropsychologist will also use these data to create a list of possible explanations for the patient's problem(s). This list represents a 'differential diagnosis', and items on the list may eventually be excluded as non-explanatory or included as explaining all or part of the problem. For example, an initial clinical impression of 'progressive dementia' will almost always include depression in the differential diagnosis (Zakzanis, Leach, & Kaplan, 1999). In those instances when the initial impression of 'progressive dementia' has been confirmed, depression might remain as an additional diagnosis.

The first step listed in Table 5.2 reflects the need to determine if there is evidence from the evaluation that the patient's problems are in fact abnormal. While the consideration of abnormality is discussed a number of times in the present volumes, this point is deserving of additional comment. Abnormality is not always easy to determine from a neurobehavioral viewpoint. One reason for this is the great variability in behavior amongst individuals. Because of this, the fact that a patient (or someone close to the patient) is complaining at all can be interpreted by the neuropsychologist as a reflection of possible abnormality. This is to be differentiated in the clinician's mind, however, from the formal indices of abnormality that might be present or absent in the evaluation results. Therefore, a conclusion of 'normal functioning' will occur in the context of the differential diagnosis. This is the basis for stating as we did earlier, that the patient's complaints should never be negated. At the same time, it is important to share with the patient the fact that by our standard criteria, no abnormality was found, adding that he or she should contact the clinician if the difficulties continue.

Localizing the abnormality

From a neuropsychological perspective, localizing the abnormality begins with the identification of abnormal functioning in specified domains. Without repeating our earlier discussions of behavioral domains, these various areas of behavior can become impaired differentially as a result of dysfunction in one or more biological systems. Because of this, it is important to describe the relative strengths and weaknesses across these domains. Areas of preserved strength can be as diagnostically revealing as are impairments, and the pattern reflected by these strengths and weaknesses are critical to an accurate neuropsychological diagnosis. The neuropsychological approach to localization proceeds from the more general to the more specific. Of course, one task for the neuropsychologist will be to determine if the abnormality suggests neurological dysfunction at all since factors other than neurological disorder (e.g., psychopathology) can explain many behavioral manifestations. Again, by determining the strengths and weaknesses in specific domains, along with the various behaviors that comprise these domains, the neuropsychologist reveals a pattern that may or may not be consistent with underlying neurological dysfunction or with specified neurological regions of dysfunction. The various neurological regions, or levels, are described in detail in Chapter 6 and outlined in Table 6.4, and most if not all of these levels are accompanied by functions that are amenable to behavioral measurement, i.e., psychometrics.

Identifying general diagnostic categories

In a generic sense, neuropsychological diagnoses can be thought of as falling into two categories. Usually, the word 'diagnosis' denotes a specific disorder, a neurological condition such as encephalopathy, or a psychiatric abnormality such as major depression. The neuropsychologist might make a diagnostic statement, however, that is confined to a description of the patient's functional state. That is, a neuropsychological diagnosis might at times be limited to descriptive conclusions about functional states, such as impaired memory, language, motor speed, or the like. In fact, such descriptions represent an important step in the process of arriving at a final and formal diagnosis (Table 5.2). At other times, however, the descriptive diagnostic statement is the best that can be accomplished. The reason for this rests with the nature of behavior itself, as well as the way in which abnormality is determined. We know, for example, that a sizable number of people complain of difficulties with their memory, and for whom no firm explanation for their memory difficulty is found. This may be the case even when formal neuropsychological testing confirms an abnormal memory. As was previously discussed in this book, the condition of memory impairment in otherwise normal individuals has been of scientific interest and study for many years. While we have the technology to document objectively the condition, we still do not know for certain if these cases reflect disease or disorder or simply an extreme of normal variation (Berent *et al.*, 1999).

Use of additional neurodiagnostic testing to arrive at a final neuropsychological diagnosis

We have emphasized in these volumes the multidisciplinary nature of neurobehavioral toxicology. From this perspective, the findings reported by other specialists often become important to the neuropsychologist in reaching his or her own diagnostic conclusions. These other specialists may employ regularly in their work tests and procedures that are not part of the neuropsychologist's regular procedures. Such information might range from findings from general physical examination to the results of electrophysiological studies. In addition to such information that comes from the benefit of working within the context of a team, there are other specialized tests that yield information that may be of critical help to the neuropsychologist.

The results of imaging and other neurodiagnostic tests can be critical to an accurate neuropsychological diagnosis. In many instances, in fact, published diagnostic criteria will call for evidence from such tests. We have mentioned elsewhere, for instance, that a diagnosis of leukoencephalopathy manifests in neuropsychological impairments that include problems with attention, forgetfulness, depression, and other personality changes (Filley & Kleinschmidt-DeMasters, 2001). Language is usually spared in this condition. A behavioral description by itself would obviously be insufficient to conclude such a diagnosis. Results from MRI or other neuro-imaging that reveals white matter lesions in a pattern consistent with these behavioral patterns, however, would lend diagnostic meaning to the behavioral findings. Many of the major tests relevant to neurobehavioral toxicology are critiqued in Chapter 7.

Summary and conclusion

Neuropsychology has a history of specialization in the area of testing and measurement, examining the relationship between brain disruption and observable behavioral changes. In particular, neuropsychological approaches to the assessment of environmental exposure can be used fruitfully in either the clinical or the research setting. Within the clinical arena, it is particularly important to evaluate a patient's complaints within a comprehensive context that considers the person's history as well as current functioning. Maintaining current knowledge about the clinical manifestations of toxicant-induced disorders will enable the clinician to determine the areas of neuropsychological functioning that will need to be evaluated in order to arrive at accurate conclusions about diagnosis and etiology. With regard to that portion of the evaluation that relies on psychometric test data, a comprehensive evaluation requires analyses of patterns of results, such as the degree of consistency between historical records and current performance, the relationship between results and normative data, and within the context of differential diagnosis. Selection of specific test batteries reflects coverage of the major domains of behaviour, as well as knowledge of the psychometric properties of the instruments chosen. The attribution of cause is a process to be separated from diagnosis, and it is often possible to arrive at a meaningful clinical impression without being able to determine its cause. The nature of causal attribution will be discussed in more detail in Chapter 8.

Notes

1   When allowing a patient to complete some part of the evaluation on her or his own (e.g., a history form), the clinician will need to verify who in fact has completed the task. It is not unusual for the patient to enlist the aid of others and, depending on the nature of the patient's impairments, such action may at times be appropriately necessary. Still, the clinician needs to know. One way to achieve this knowledge is to review directly with the patient all externally completed tasks during the clinical interview and to note on the form the circumstances of task completion.

References

Adams, K. M. & Rourke, B. P. (1992). *The TCN guide to professional practice in clinical neuropsychology*. Berwyn: Swets & Zeitlinger.

Albers, J. W., Wald, J. J., Garabrant, D. H., Trask, C. L., & Berent, S. (2000). Neurologic evaluation of workers previously diagnosed with solvent-induced toxic encephalopathy. *Journal of Occupational and Environmental Medicine*, *42*, 410–423.

American Academy of Neurology (2001). AAN guideline summary for point of care: Detection, diagnosis and management of dementia (available at: http://www.aan.com/public/practiceguidelines/md_summary.htm).

American Psychological Association (1985). *Standards for educational and psychological testing*. Washington, DC: APA.

Anastasi, A. (1976). *Psychological testing* (4th ed.). New York: Macmillan.

Barona, A., Reynolds, C. R., & Chastain, R. (1984). A demographically based index of premorbid intelligence for the WAIS-R. *Journal of Consulting and Clinical Psychology, 52*, 885–887.

Berent, S., Giordani, B., Foster, N., Minoshima, S., Lajiness-O'Neill, R., Koeppe, R., & Kuhl, D. E. (1999). Neuropsychological function and cerebral glucose utilization in isolated memory impairment and Alzheimer's disease. *Journal of Psychiatric Research, 33*, 7–16.

Berent, S. & Swartz, C. L. (1999). Essential psychometrics. In J. J. Sweet (Ed.), *Forensic neuropsychology: Fundamentals and practice* (pp. 1–24). Lisse: Swets & Zeitlinger.

Berent, S. & Trask, C. L. (2000). Human neuropsychological testing and evaluation. In E. Massaro (Ed.), *Neurotoxicology handbook*, Vol. 2. Totowa, NJ: Humana.

Boll, T. J. (2000). Measuring behavior. In J. W. Albers and S. Berent (Eds.), *Clinical neurobehavioral toxicology* (pp. 579–599). Philadelphia: W. B. Saunders.

Buros Institute of Mental Measurements (1999). *Tests in print*. Lincoln: Buros Institute of Mental Measurements, University of Nebraska.

Campbell, D. T. & Fiske, D. W. (1959). Convergent and discriminant validation by the multitrait–multimethod matrix. *Psychological Bulletin, 56*, 81–105.

Cronbach, L. J. (1951). Coefficient alpha and the internal consistency of tests. *Psychometrika, 16*, 297–334.

Cronbach, L. J. (1984). *Essentials of psychological testing*. New York: Harper & Row.

Cronbach, L. J. (1988). Five perspectives on validity argument. In H. Wainer and H. I. Braun (Eds.), *Test validity* (pp. 3–17). Hillsdale: Lawrence Erlbaum.

Division 40 Task Force on Education, A. a. C. (1989). Guidelines regarding the use of nondoctoral personnel in clinical neuropsychological assessment. *Clinical Neuropsychologist, 3*, 23–24.

Filley, C. M., Heaton, R. K., & Rosenberg, N. L. (1990). White matter dementia in chronic toluene abuse. *Neurology, 40*, 532–534.

Filley, C. M. & Kleinschmidt-DeMasters, B. K. (2001). Toxic leukoencephalopathy. *New England Journal of Medicine, 345*, 425–432.

Gilman, S. (1989). Gait disorders. In L. P. Rowland (Ed.), *Merritt's textbook of neurology* (8th ed.) (pp. 54–60). Philadelphia: Lea & Fibiger.

Hilgard, E. R. (1978). *American psychology in historical perspective: Addresses of the Presidents of the American Psychological Association*. Washington, DC: American Psychological Association.

Kraemer, H. C. (1982). Estimating false alarms and missed events from interobserver agreement: comment on Kaye. *Psychological Bulletin, 92*, 749–754.

Kuder, G. F. & Richardson, M. W. (1937). The theory of the estimation of test reliability. *Psychometrika, 2*, 151–160.

Kuhl, D. E., Metter, E. J., & Riege, W. H. (1985). Patterns of cerebral glucose utilization in depression, multiple infarct dementia, and Alzheimer's disease. *Research Publications – Association for Research in Nervous and Mental Disease, 63*, 211–226.

Lezak, M. D. (1995). *Neuropsychological assessment* (3rd ed.). New York: Oxford University Press.

Matarazzo, J. D. (1972). *Wechsler's measurment and appraisal of adult intelligence.* Baltimore: Williams & Wilkins.

Minoshima, S., Frey, K. A., Koeppe, R. A., Foster, N. L., & Kuhl, D. E. (1995). A diagnostic approach in Alzheimer's disease using three-dimensional stereotactic surface projections of fluorine-18-FDG PET. *Journal of Nuclear Medicine, 36,* 1238–1248.

Mitchell, J. V. J. (1998). *The mental measurements yearbook.* Lincoln: Buros Institute of Mental Measurements, University of Nebraska.

Mohr, J. P. (1976). Broca's area and Broca's aphasia. In H. Whitaker & H. A. Whitaker (Eds.), *Studies in neurolinguistics* (pp. 201–235). New York: Academic Press.

Nelson, H. E. & O'Connell, A. (1978). Dementia: the estimation of premorbid intelligence levels using the New Adult Reading Test. *Cortex, 14,* 234–244.

Reitan, R. M. (1955). Investigation of the validity of Halstead's measures of biological intelligence. *Archives of Neurology and Psychiatry, 73,* 28–35.

Reitan, R. M. & Wolfson, D. (1993). *The Halstead–Reitan neuropsychological test battery: Theory and clinical interpretation.* Tucson: Neuropsychology Press.

Rozensky, R. H., Sweet, J. J., & Tovian, S. M. (1997). *Psychological assessment in medical settings.* New York: Plenum.

Sackellares, J. C. & Berent, S. (1996). *Psychological disturbances in epilepsy.* Boston: Butterworth-Heinemann.

Schaumburg, H. H. & Spencer, P. S. (1987). Recognizing neurotoxic disease. *Neurology, 37,* 276–278.

Siegel, G. J., Agranoff, B. W., Albers, R. W., Fisher, S. K., & Uhler, M. D. (1999). *Basic neurochemistry: Molecular, cellular and medical aspects* (6th ed.) Philadelphia: Lippincott-Raven.

Starkman, M. N., Gebarski, S. S., Berent, S., & Schteingart, D. E. (1992). Hippocampal formation volume, memory dysfunction, and cortisol levels in patients with Cushing's syndrome. *Biological Psychiatry, 32,* 756–765.

Stebbins, G. T., Gilley, D. W., Wilson, R. S., Bernard, B. A., & Fox, J. H. (1990). Effects of language disturbances in premorbid estimates of IQ in mild dementia. *Clinical Neuropsychologist, 4,* 64–68.

Walker, H. M. & Lev, J. (1953). *Statistical inference.* New York: Holt.

Wilson, B. A. (1993). Ecological validity of neuropsychological assessment: do neuropsychological indexes predict performance in everyday activities? *Applied and Preventive Psychology, 2,* 209–215.

Wilson, R. S. & Stebbins, G. T. (1991). Estimating premorbid and preexisting neuropsychological deficits. In H. O. Doer & A. S. Carlin (Eds.), *Forensic neuropsychology: Legal and scientific bases* (pp. 89–98). New York: Guilford.

Yahr, M. D. (1989). Parkinsonism. In L. P. Rowland (Ed.), *Merritt's textbook of neurology* (8th ed.) (pp. 658–671). Philadelphia: Lea & Febiger.

Zakzanis, K. K., Leach, L., & Kaplan, E. (1999). *Neuropsychological differential diagnosis.* Lisse: Swets & Zeitlinger.

6   The neurologic approach

Introduction

Neurology is a medical subspecialty that deals with the human nervous system, in health and in disease. The neurologist uses a systematic approach to the evaluation of a patient with a suspected neurological disorder, including disorders caused by exposure to neurotoxicants (Albers & Berent, 1999; Albers, 2002). This approach, including the individual parts of the medical history and the neurologic examination, is described in the material that follows. This material assumes only limited familiarity with clinical medicine. The emphasis is on the clinical problem-solving process, because most diagnostic errors involve a failure to apply appropriately the diagnostic reasoning that characterizes the discipline of Neurology.

The neurologic approach

What is the 'neurologic approach' and how is it used to evaluate a patient with suspected neurotoxic disease? The second part of this question is easy to answer, because the neurologic examination is independent of the cause of the underlying problem. Therefore, the neurologic examination and the process of identifying and localizing a suspected neurologic lesion is essentially the same for all patients. For this reason, the material that follows is not specific to the evaluation of a patient with suspected neurotoxicity, but it is appropriate for the evaluation of any patient with symptoms potentially referable to the nervous system.

The neurologic approach uses the results derived from the patient's history and neurologic examination to identify and localize the presence of any abnormality within the nervous system. Next, the general forms of underlying pathophysiology capable of producing the abnormality are identified, followed by formulation of a differential diagnosis, a list of possible explanations for the patient's problem. The neurologist then develops a plan for further evaluation and treatment. The differential diagnosis frequently requires revision, depending on the results of any subsequent laboratory or neurodiagnostic testing or on the response to treatment. Additional examinations may include evaluation of blood, urine, cerebrospinal fluid, or tissue. Specific neurodiagnostic testing may include neuroimaging or electrophysiology evaluations of the brain, spinal cord, peripheral nerves, and muscle. The most important questions directed to the neurologist as part of the neurologic approach are (1) what is the explanation for the patient's problem, and (2) what can be done to correct or improve the problem. These questions are independent and the answer to either question can be known without knowing the answer to the other question.

It should not be surprising that the neurologist is frequently required to detect and treat nervous system dysfunction without any initial information related to an underlying cause or etiology. In other words, it is not necessary to know the cause of the problem to identify evidence of a neurologic impairment or to prescribe treatment. In fact, the underlying cause of the patent's problem is commonly irrelevant with regard to treatment decisions. Therefore, information about a potential neurotoxic exposure, while important, is no more necessary in identifying a neurotoxic syndrome than is information about a viral exposure in diagnosing herpes encephalitis. Identifying the ultimate cause of a problem remains an important goal for the neurologist.

Foundations of clinical neurology as they relate to neurobehavioral toxicology

The consideration of how to recognize neurotoxicity begins with an understanding of the response of the nervous systems to toxic exposure. There are countless substances that, when present in sufficient quantities and over sufficient periods of time, can interfere with or injure the nervous system. There is, however, no single, defined neurological response to chemical agents. The ultimate effect on the nervous system produced by any substance depends on many factors. These include the portal of body entry, the distribution in tissues, the ability to enter the nervous system, the site of attack, the specific vulnerability of a target site, the concentration at the target site, the duration of exposure, the rate of breakdown, the toxicity of metabolic products, and the efficiency of excretion (Albers, 2002). In addition, the dose and duration of exposure to any substance are important. 'Dose' refers to the concentration of the substance to which an individual is exposed. Dose is an important concept and fundamental to the disciplines of pharmacology and toxicology. For any given chemical, certain doses may be harmless or even have nutrient value, whereas higher doses elicit profound, long-lasting, or irreversible changes. Consider, for example, pyridoxine. This essential vitamin (B6) is necessary for life, yet, at high levels of exposure, pyridoxine is a neurotoxicant that produces a sensory neuronopathy. Duration of exposure also is a key consideration in determining whether a particular concentration of a substance will be neurotoxic. Another concept important in consideration is the possibility of a delayed-response following exposure to a neurotoxic substance. The longer the delay, the less likely the association will be readily identified. This is important because the cause of most 'neurodegenerative' disorders is unknown. Important examples of delayed neurotoxicity exist, but they are relative few in number (Albers, Kallenbach, Fine, Langolf, Wolfe, Donofrio, Alessi, Stolp-Smith, Bromberg, & the Mercury Workers Study Group, 1988) Nevertheless, the hypothesis of irreversible damage to a population of neurons, insufficient to produce clinical dysfunction but sufficient later to emerge following normal age-related attrition of the same cell population, has important application to some neurodegenerative disorders.

There are several well-recognized general patterns of response to nervous system injury, including injury caused by chemical agents. Most neurotoxicants injure the nervous system as part of a wider systemic response, thereby producing distinctive multisystem patterns of abnormality. For example, arsenic intoxication produces a peripheral neuropathy that sometimes resembles the Guillain–Barré syndrome, but it also causes multiorgan involvement characterized by anemia, gastritis, hepatitis, dermatitis, and Mees' lines in the nails (Donofrio, Wilbourn, Albers, Rogers, Salanga, & Greenberg, 1987). In contrast, some neurotoxicants selectively damage specific portions of the nervous system without causing other problems. For example, pyridoxine, when given in sufficient doses, causes selective degeneration of sensory neurons in the dorsal root ganglion, producing a sensory neuropathy or neuronopathy without producing other neurologic or systemic findings (Schaumburg, Kaplan, Windebank, Vick, Rasmus, Pleasure, & Brown, 1983; Albin, Albers, Greenberg, Townsend, Lynn, Burke, & Alessi, 1987). Similarly, methyl-4-phenyl-1,2,3,6-tetrahyrdopyridine (MPTP), a designer meperidine-analog inadvertently developed and distributed as a synthetic heroin, produces a form of Parkinsonism that results from selective injury to neurons in the zona compacta of the substantia nigra (Langston, Ballard, Tetrud, & Irwin, 1984).

The nervous system is arbitrarily divided into central and peripheral components, although there is substantial overlap in structure and function between the two components. The division has utility, however, in describing neurotoxic disorders and their evaluation. The central nervous system consists of those parts of the nervous system contained within the skull and the vertebral column. It initiates, receives, and integrates signals needed to maintain internal homeostasis, cognition, awareness, memory, language, personality, behavior, sleep and wakefulness, locomotion, sensation, vision, balance, and many other bodily functions. The peripheral nervous system consists of nerve cells and their processes that convey sensory, motor, and autonomic information to and from the central nervous system. Sensory receptors and free nerve endings in the skin, mucous membranes, and deep tissues initiate information for touch, joint position, muscle motion, pressure, vibration, temperature, and pain sensations. Afferent signals from these receptors are transmitted by sensory nerves to the central nervous system where they are processed, integrated, and stored. Motor nerves transmit information originating in the central nervous system to muscles. The information includes volitional and reflex signals that initiate movement and maintaining posture and balance. Autonomic nerves also convey information from the central nervous system to the periphery. Most autonomic information involves homeostasis, controlling activities that are not under direct volitional control, including activation of smooth muscle within blood vessels and the viscera, the heart, and endocrine glands.

Clinical Neurology

Clinical Neurology is based on information derived from a thorough medical history and the results of the neurologic examination (Dejong, 1979; Daube, Westmorland, Sandok, & Reagan, 1986). The medical history includes, among other items, inquiry about (1) chief complaints; (2) a history of present illness; (3) past medical problems; (4) exposure to medications, chemicals, alcohol, tobacco, or other drugs; (5) occupational history; (6) family history; (7) and systems review to identify symptoms not spontaneously volunteered (Gelb, 1995; Gilman, 1999). The neurologic examination is a highly structured portion of the medical evaluation that was developed and refined during the early to mid-1900s (Dejong, 1979). The examination derives from an understanding of the cellular and anatomic components of the nervous system, and from an understanding of the nervous system's response to injury. The examination is an extension of the general physical examination that includes, among other items, evaluation of (1) vital signs (blood pressure, respiration rate, pulse); (2) examination of the head and neck; (3) auscultation of the chest; (3) palpation of the abdomen; and (4) examination of the extremities and skin. The neurologic examination consists of five major components. These include evaluation of (1) mental status; (2) cranial nerves; (3) the motor system (strength, coordination, alternate motion rate, muscle tone and bulk, station, gait); (4) sensation (fine touch, pin, joint position, dual simultaneous stimulation); and (5) reflexes. Additional components of the neurologic examination that overlap with the general physical examination include evaluation of the musculoskeletal system, the neurovascular system, and response to provocative examinations such as hyperventilation and measurement of orthostatic blood pressure, if deemed indicated. The history and clinical examination take about 90 min to complete, depending on the complexity and number of complaints.

Normal or abnormal?

As in other specialties of Medicine, and in the biological sciences in general, the most difficult decision related to neurologic examination involves distinguishing normal from abnormal function. This determination is complicated by the wide variety of differences in human performance, as well as by the effects of education, motivation, learning, and training. Several portions of the neurologic examination, such as evaluation of coordination or alternate motion rate, are subjective and susceptible to patient effort and cooperation (Potvin, Tourtellotte, Pew, & Albers, 1973). Experienced clinicians understand the importance of motivation on test results, and they utilize a variety of redundant clinical tests to re-evaluate the same portion of the nervous system in order to reproduce a suspected abnormality. For example, in observing a patient attempt to identify objects placed in their hands when their eyes are closed, the manner in which the patient manipulates the object is more important in evaluating sensation than whether or not the object was identified correctly. Special effort is made to encourage maximal performance or to identify poor cooperation. On the other hand, many parts of the neurologic examination, such as the reflex examination, are objective and independent of patient effort, learning, or practice. Yet, even the objective portions of the examination are open to examiner interpretation (Tourtellotte & Syndulko, 1989). It is fortunate for the neurologist that all signs are not of equal importance. In fact, a hierarchy of findings exists relative to pathologic importance, with certain clinical findings having greater clinical importance than other findings. This permits the neurologist to identify consistency among identified abnormalities, and rank findings in terms of their likely importance. In addition, identification of patterns of abnormality is particularly helpful in localizing neurologic lesions.

When symptoms or signs suggest the presence of a neurological abnormality, there are numerous tests available to the neurologist to evaluate further for potential anatomical, chemical, electrophysiological, immunological, and genetic abnormalities. Physicians recognized by their peers as 'good clinicians' are typically those who understand how to utilize and interpret these neurodiagnostic tests. This ability requires knowledge about the sensitivity and specificity of individual examinations in the context of the overall evaluation. The art of medicine, as applied to neurology, reflects the neurologist's ability to interpret the results of the patient's history, clinical evaluation, and laboratory tests; to recognize the difference between physiological, psychologic, and pathologic abnormalities; to formulate a treatment program; to convey successfully the relevant information to the patient; and to involve the patient in the decision process throughout the entire process.

The material that follows describes that neurologic examination and the decision processes used to localize and identify the most likely pathology or pathophysiology. Information related to developing the differential diagnosis and establishing the cause of any identified problem is discussed in subsequent chapters.

Clinical neurologic evaluation

Textbooks have been devoted to descriptions of the neurologic examination (Dejong, 1979) and an exhaustive discussion of how to perform and interpret that examination is beyond the scope of this chapter. However, the basic principles involved in performing the examination are important in under-standing decisions related to the neurologic approach. The neurologic examination is one portion of the overall medical examination, and there is substantial overlap between the two examinations, with at least some portion of a general medical examination performed as part of every neurologic examination. As described, the neurologic evaluation of a patient with poten-tial neurotoxic exposure is identical to the evaluation performed on any patient with complaints potentially referable to the nervous system, independent of the cause of those complaints. Therefore, all information involving proper methodology relevant to the clinical neurologic examin-ation is pertinent to clinical neurobehavioural toxicology. Certainly, different portions of the evaluation are emphasized or de-emphasized depending on the patient's symptoms and other history, and identification of certain signs may result in a more detailed examination of that portion of the nervous system. The following description, while not exhaustive, describes components of a thorough, comprehensive neurologic examination.

Clinical history

The medical examination begins with a history obtained from the patient (Table 6.1). Exceptions include evaluation of patients who cannot provide information because of altered consciousness or emergent care, in which case relevant history is obtained from others or after the medical emergency is stabilized. Most of the information necessary to localize a neurologic lesion can be obtained from a careful history. Patients are asked to describe in detail each complaint because initial descriptions may reflect the patient's interpretation of the problem rather than a description of what he or she is experiencing. Even initial symptom descriptions should not be accepted at face value without clarification. For example, 'dizziness' may represent momentarily altered consciousness as in cardiac syncope, postural unsteadi-ness with orthostatic features, true vertigo, or even unsteady gait due to incoordination. 'Numbness' may represent tingling or paresthesias, loss of sensation, or even weakness.

History of the present illness

This initial portion of the history identifies what symptoms are important to the patient. For most neurologic problems, the chief complaints are used to localize the problem to one of several broad anatomical levels of the nervous system based on the description and distribution of each complaint. For each chief complaint, a history of present illness further examines the symptoms described by the patient. The temporal profile of the initial event is estab-lished in terms of onset, progression, severity, and frequency if intermittent. Associated relieving or provocative factors are identified. Regarding the onset of symptoms, special care is directed toward determining whether symptoms

Table 6.1 Medical history: information typically obtained by the clinician (Albers, 2002).

Chief complaint(s):
  Primary symptoms important to the patient

History of present illness, including onset, temporal profile, provoking or relieving factors
  Past medical and surgical histories:
  Specific illnesses (medical and psychological), operations, and serious injuries
  Known allergies, medication sensitivities
  Travel history
  Medications (current and past use), including blood transfusions
  Prior neurologic procedures and results (electromyography, encephalography, evoked potential studies, computed cranial tomography, magnetic resonance imaging, position emission tomography, single photon emission computed tomography, angiogram)

Family history:
  Describe a particular disease or cause of death for blood relatives

Social history:
  Marital status
  Children
  Education (years completed and grades)
  Tobacco and alcohol use (current and past)
  Use of drugs other than prescribed medications
  Hobbies and exposure to chemicals

Occupational history:
  Employment status
  Types of previous jobs (chronological list), including military history
  Special training or skills
  Occupational exposure to chemicals (direct or indirect)
  Job or hobbies involving repetitive or forceful hand exertions

Review of systems:
  General inquiry about additional symptoms not elicited above

---

appeared and progressed acutely (seconds to minutes), subacutely (hours to days), or chronically (weeks to months). This information has special importance in the preliminary identification of potential pathophysiological explanations for each symptom. The results of any diagnostic testing are reviewed.

Past medical history

The next portion of the history involves information with potential relevance to any medical or neurologic problem. This past medical history includes information about birth and development, previously diagnosed disorders, operations, allergies, injuries, and treatments, including previous and current medications. A review of prescribed and over-the-counter medications is important because all medications have the potential to produce adverse side-effects. Severe adverse responses are those most frequently described, and most patients are familiar with the potential for a severe allergic response to a recently prescribed medication, ranging from skin rash to anaphylaxis and death. Yet most patients and many physicians are slow to recognize the comparatively minor side-effects that occur frequently with prescription medications. The direct or indirect side-effects include many neurological symptoms such as headache, lightheadedness or dizziness, altered sleep patterns, impaired concentration, altered mood, and autonomic dysfunction.

Family, social, and occupational histories

Information about family, social, and occupation histories is obtained. The social history includes information related to illicit drug use. It also includes information related to potential toxic exposures in the home, such as pesticides and cleaning agents, and exposures associated with hobbies and other activities. Occupational history is particularly important in the evaluation of suspected neurotoxicity. This should include a review of all past employment, with special attention to the type of work performed and the duration, frequency, and amount of opportunity for exposure to toxic substances. Exposures may be indirect and related to substances used by other workers. On occasion, toxic substances may be brought into the home by other family members from their work place. Nevertheless, many exposures to neurotoxicants are unsuspected and go unrecognized. As important as the exposure history is to issues related to clinical neurobehavioral toxicology, the information is used only in establishing causation and not to establish the clinical diagnosis.

Review of systems

The review of systems is a direct enquiry about other potential symptoms that the patient may have forgotten or felt to be unimportant.

Review of previous evaluations

Finally, it often is possible to review previous medical records, including the results of previous diagnostic testing. Occasionally, the records contain information ignored or forgotten by the patient because it was seemingly unimportant.

Clinical examination

The neurologic examination is the most fundamental level of testing associated with the evaluation of a suspected neurologic disorder. The neurologic examination is an important part of the physical examination and is usually performed in combination with a general physical examination. While most of the information necessary to localize a neurologic lesion can be obtained from a careful history, the examination serves as an independent source of information. This is important when evaluating patients who are poor observers, have trouble communicating, or who provide incomplete or misleading information. The examination may also identify abnormalities not associated with symptoms. Examples include the presence of subtle cognitive abnormalities or identification of primitive or atavistic reflexes.

The purpose of the clinical examination is to document evidence of clinically evident abnormalities or impairments. These findings are referred to as 'signs'. The neurologist's initial goal is to determine whether or not there is clinical evidence of a neurologic impairment. If abnormal signs are present, the abnormalities are localized to broad regions of the nervous system, just as was done for the patient's symptoms. The examination includes substantial redundancy. This redundancy is used to establish internal consistency, and it is important in establishing the certainty of any suspected impairment. While the history is almost entirely subjective, the neurologic examination includes objective and subjective portions. For example, reflexes are considered objectively as they are independent of patient effort or influence, and whereas much of the sensory examination is subjective, it depends on the patient's cooperation and interpretation of sensory stimuli. Part of the neurologist's expertise involves an ability to interpret correctly responses observed during the neurologic examination.

Components of the general physical and neurologic examinations are shown in Tables 6.2 and 6.3. The standardized neurologic examination includes evaluation of mental status, cranial nerves, motor and sensory systems, reflexes, and several additional tests that are performed in response to particular complaints or findings.

Table 6.2 Components of the general medical examination (Albers, 2002).

Vital signs (resting and orthostatic blood pressure, pulse rate)
Head and neck (masses, bruits)
Pulmonary (auscultation of breath sounds)
Cardiac (heart sounds or murmur)
Abdomen (tenderness, masses, sounds)
Extremities (bulk, range of motion, masses)
Vascular (pulses)
Musculoskeletal (range of motion, straight leg raising)
Lymphatic (nodes)
Skin (rash, ischemic changes)

Table 6.3 Components of the neurological examination (Albers, 2002).

Mental status:
    General appearance (e.g., tense, hostile, agitated, uncooperative, inappropriate, tangential, hallucination, depressed)
    Level of alertness (lethargic, obtunded, coma)
    Cognition, including orientation, attentiveness, language (receptive and expressive), judgment, memory (immediate recall, intermediate, long-term), abstract reasoning (similarities, proverbs), arithmetic calculations, follow multiple step command
    Knowledge of current events
    Mini-Mental Status Examination (MMSE)

Cranial nerves:
    Olfaction, vision, pupillary size and response to light, ophthalmoscopy, visual fields, eye movements, ptosis, nystagmus (physiologic and optokinetic), facial sensation, facial symmetry, hearing, speech, and examination of jaw, palate, pharynx, neck, and tongue muscles

Motor:
    Station (eyes open and closed [Romberg])
    Gait (casual, tandem, arm swing, walk on toes and heels)
    Adventitious (involuntary) movements
        Tremor (resting, postural)
        Myoclonus
        Chorea
        Asterixis
        Tic
        Fasciculations
        Myokymia
    Coordination (finger-to-nose and heel-to-knee)
    Alternate motion rate
    Strength, bulk
    Tone (resistance to passive limb movement)

Sensory:
    Vibration, pin-pain, joint position, light touch, cold sensations
    Dual simultaneous stimulation
    Stereognosis
    Quantitative touch–pressure

Reflexes:
    Muscle stretch (jaw, biceps brachii, triceps, brachioradialis, quadriceps, hamstring, gastrocnemius)
    Pathologic (glabellar, snout, grasp, palmomental, Hoffmann, Chaddock, Babinski)

Additional provocative tests as indicated:
    Volitional hyperventilation, Tinel and Phalen signs, Adson maneuver

Mental status

The examination of mental status includes evaluation of cognition, orientation, attentiveness, language, judgment, memory (immediate recall, intermediate, long-term), abstract reasoning (similarities, proverbs), and arithmetic calculations. Standardized examinations exist, such as the Mini-Mental Status Examination (MMSE) (Folstein, Folstein, & McHugh, 1975; Crum, Anthony, Bassett, & Folstein, 1993), which are used to quantify the examination results. Nevertheless, the evaluation of mental status begins with the initial patient contact. While obtaining a history, the neurologist has the opportunity to evaluate most aspects of the mental status examination, including orientation, general mood, anxiety level, use of language, immediate recall and remote memory, suitability of behavior, social interaction, a general fund of knowledge, and judgment. The formal mental status examination is better able to identify evidence of mild impairment, and more detailed quantitative evaluation of cognition and mood requires psychometric testing. Signs of dysfunction involving mental status are referable to the cortex in the supratentorial level of the nervous system.

Cranial nerves

Evaluation of the twelve cranial nerves includes examination of olfaction, vision, pupillary size and response to light, ophthalmoscopy, visual fields, eye movements including documentation of abnormal nystagmus, facial sensation, facial symmetry, hearing, speech, and examination of the palate, neck muscles, and tongue. Ten of the twelve cranial nerves (all but cranial nerves I and II, the olfactory and optic nerves, respectively) originate in the posterior fossa. Therefore, examination of this portion of the nervous system has special importance in localizing posterior fossa abnormalities. Although a more precise origin is important to some neurologic problems within the context of clinical neurobehavioral toxicology, recognition that cranial nerve abnormalities may reflect a posterior fossa or peripheral nervous system localization is sufficient to solve most clinical diagnostic problems. This, at least in part, represents a lack of sensitivity of most diagnostic tests, such as imaging studies, to localize abnormalities to smaller, precise anatomic areas of the nervous system.

Motor system

Motor evaluation includes examination of gait and station (casual gait, tandem gait, and standing with eyes open and closed [Romberg test]). It also includes observation for abnormal involuntary movements such as asterixis, tics, dystonia, myoclonus, or tremor. Several forms of tremor exist. These include resting tremor, a form associated with Parkinsonism that is most apparent in the resting limb, disappearing momentarily during volitional movements. Sustension tremor is most apparent during sustained posture of the outstretched limb. Intention tremor is most prominent during volitional activation of the limb and is identified during the evaluation of coordination, such as during finger-to-nose and heel-to-knee tests. The motor examination also includes evaluation of alternate motion rate of the fingers, hands, and feet. Finger-to-nose coordination and the alternate motion rate testing are shown in Figure 6.1. Most skeletal muscles can be tested, and muscles are selected that are representative of different nerve root and individual peripheral nerve innervation. Distal muscles are involved to a greater extent than are proximal muscles in peripheral neuropathy. It is important, therefore, to evaluate intrinsic hand muscle strength. Evaluation of the first dorsal interosseous muscle in shown in Figure 6.2, and evaluation of the anterior tibialis (upper frame) and extensor digitorum brevis (lower frame) muscle is shown in Figure 6.3. Muscle bulk and tone are also evaluated as part of motor examination. Muscle tone is evaluated as resistance to passive movement of the limbs. Patient cooperation and effort is an important component of motor examination. A trained observer easily distinguishes the clasp-knife rigidity and slow, spastic alternate motion rate of an upper motor neuron impairment from the functional, give-away weakness pattern associated with poor effort or pain inhibition. Other motor tests based on knowledge of reciprocal activation are helpful in identifying poor volitional effort. For example, the patient with a functional leg paralysis will activate the paralysed limb when asked to lift the contralateral leg but generate no contralateral limb force when asked to lift the paralysed leg, thereby identifying absent effort.

Sensory system

Sensory evaluation includes selective tests of vibration, pin-pain, joint position, light touch, and cold sensations. Joint position is examined initially at distal joints of the index finger and the great toe (Figure 6.4, upper frame). Vibratory sensation is graded using a 128-Hz tuning fork. The base of the tuning fork is applied to the distal phalanx of the index finger or great toe (Figure 6.4, lower) by the examiner. Responses can be based on a forced choice response (vibrating or not vibrating), or the descending threshold can be compared with the examiner's threshold. If the response is abnormal, more proximal sites are evaluated. For patients with suspected functional sensory loss, the tuning fork may be applied to the mid-forehead or sternum, looking for unilateral abnormality (a non-physiological response). Pin-pain sensation is evaluated using a disposable safety pin. The sharp and dull sides are applied randomly for the patient to identify with the eyes closed. The sharp side is then applied sequentially, beginning at the dorsum of the great toe and ascending up the leg looking for evidence of a sensory gradient. The process is repeated for the hand and arm. Based on knowledge of individual sensory nerves and nerve roots (Figure 6.5), localized patterns of sensory loss

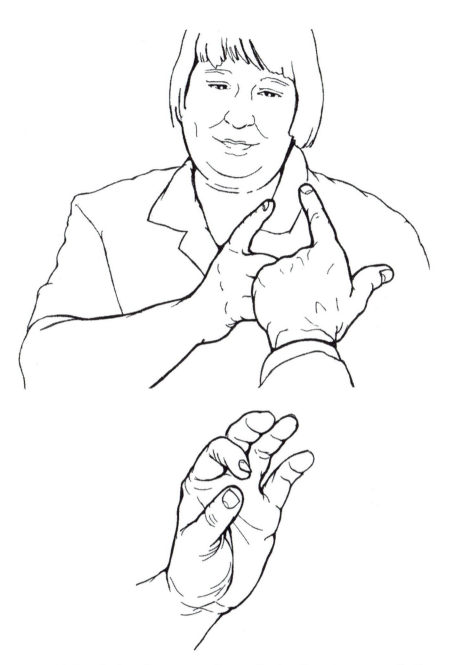

Figure 6.1 Examination of upper extremity coordination; finger-to-nose coordination testing (upper) and alternate motion rate testing (lower). Finger-to-nose coordination testing requires the patient to touch his or her nose repeatedly and then the examiner's finger, moving as rapidly and as accurately as possible. Alternate motion rate testing similarly requires rapid tapping of the index finger and thumb (or patting the hand or foot). In both types of test, the neurologist judges the rate and rhythm, content of movement, and accuracy.

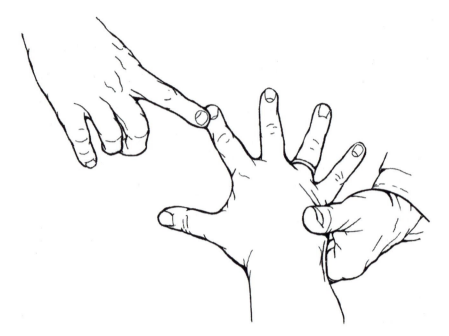

Figure 6.2 Examination of intrinsic hand muscles (first dorsal interosseous muscle). The examiner is evaluating the patient's ability to abduct the index finger.

can be investigated. If a spinal sensory level is suspected based on examination of the lower limbs, pin-pain sensation is evaluated over the trunk. The toe or finger is grasped on the sides to avoid pressure clues when the joint is flexed or extended. Using small excursions, the patient is asked to indicate whether the movement is 'up' or 'down'. Light touch is evaluated by asking the patient to indicate when they feel touch, using a cotton or tissue wisp, the examiner's finger, or a calibrated Von Frey hair. The latter is sometimes quantified by using a forced choice paradigm ('tell me whether I touch you during the first time interval or during the second time interval'). Cold sensation is evaluated by asking whether a cool object, such as the metal handle of the reflex hammer, feels warm or cold when applied to the skin. More discriminative sensory abilities are also evaluated, including the ability to identify objects placed in the hands, to distinguish dual simultaneous stimulation for unilateral stimuli, and to localize sensory stimuli.

Reflexes

Muscle stretch reflexes are examined at the jaw (masseter) and in the upper and lower extremities, usually including at minimum the biceps brachii, triceps, brachioradialis, quadriceps, and gastrocnemius-soleus reflexes (Achilles' or ankle reflex). The technique for obtaining the distal

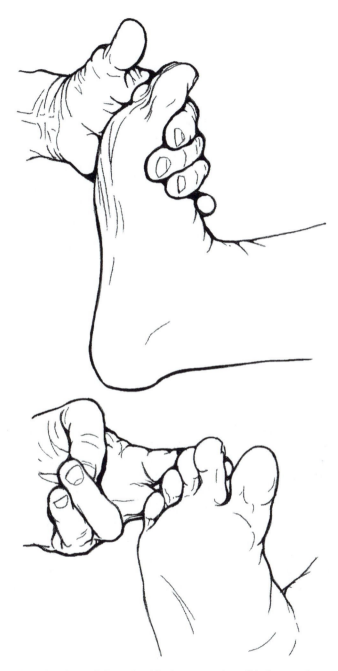

Figure 6.3 Examination of foot dorsiflexion (anterior tibialis muscle; upper) and examination of toe extension (extensor digitorum brevis; lower).

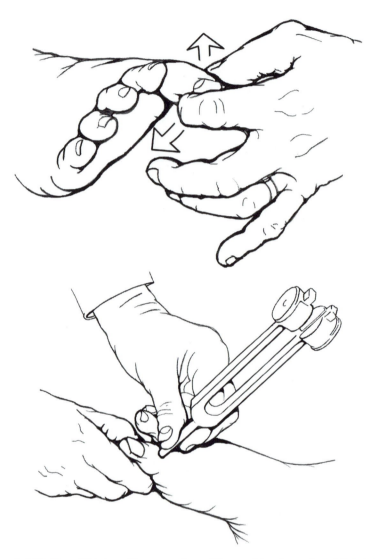

Figure 6.4 Testing of joint position sensation of the great toe (upper) and distal vibration sensation at the great toe (lower). Tests of joint position sensation require the patient to identify correctly small movements ('up' or 'down') of the selected joint, or to detect when movement of the joint in any direction is first perceived. Tests of vibration sensation required the patient to indicate when the vibration from a 128 Hz tuning fork can no longer be perceived ('descending threshold'), or to identify correctly when any vibration is perceived ('forced choice').

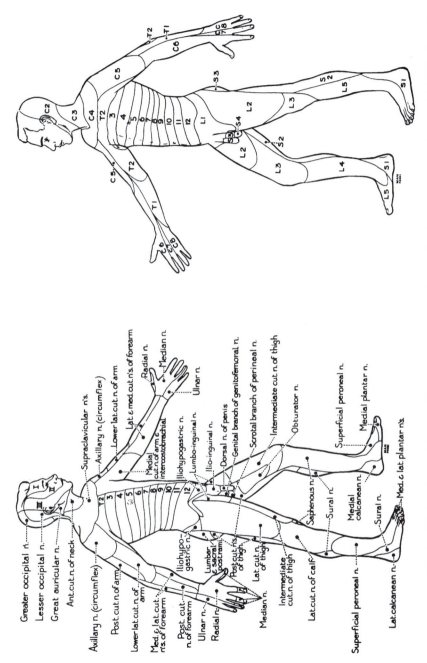

Figure 6.5 Cutaneous distribution of the peripheral nerves (left) and dermatomes (right). Reproduced with permission from Haymaker, W., & Woodhall, B. *Peripheral nerve injuries, principles of diagnosis*. Philadelphia, W. B. Saunders 1953.

brachioradialis reflex and gastrocnemius–soleus reflex is shown in Figure 6.6, in the upper and lower frames, respectively. The presence or absence of primitive or atavistic reflexes, such as snout, palmomental, grasp, Babinski, and Chaddock reflexes, is documented. The technique for testing for the palmomental and Babinski reflexes is shown in Figure 6.7, in the left and right frames, respectively.

Other

Additional provocative tests are sometimes administered, including observation during volitional hyperventilation or following positional maneuvers of the head (e.g., Barany maneuver) or limbs (Adson, Phalen, straight-leg raising). Peripheral nerves may be palpated to evaluate size, or percussed (Tinel sign) to evaluate sensitivity. The range of motion of the cervical and lumbosacral and shoulders, hips, or other joints is examined as part of the general musculoskeletal evaluation.

Grading an abnormal finding

The most important grading of abnormality on the neurologic examination is distinguishing normal from abnormal function. This information is used in the initial step of localizing the problem within the nervous system. The magnitude of abnormality can be graded for many components of the neurologic examination. The standard approach is to use a qualitative grading system of the magnitude of impairment consisting of five levels, from '0', which is no impairment, to '+ 4', which is maximal impairment or absent function. The three steps in between correspond to the subjective levels of mild, moderate, and severe abnormality. More quantitative levels exist for some measures, such as measurement of strength, sensation, or reflexes. The most commonly used scale for grading strength is based on the Medical Research Council (MRC) (1943) guidelines. The MRC scale is based on whether or not the limb has antigravity function. Unfortunately, this scale emphasizes the very weak limb and is therefore best at scoring severe impairments. Sensory functions such as light touch can be clinically quantified using different calibre Von Frey hairs. The individual hairs are sequentially applied to the skin and, based on their size, they deliver different amounts of pressure before they bend. Numerous devices are available to measure sensation more quantitatively (discussed in Chapter 7). Muscle stretch reflexes are graded on a five-level scale: 2+, which equals normal, 0, which equals absent, 1+, which equals diminished or present only with reinforcement (Jendrassik maneuver), 3+, which equals normal but brisk, and 4+, which equals abnormal with clonus.

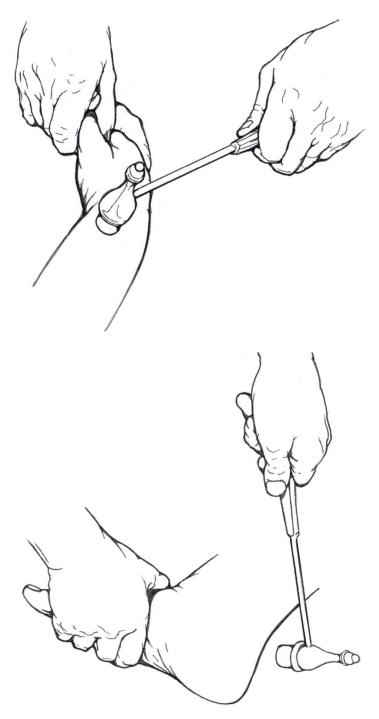

Figure 6.6 Eliciting muscle stretch reflexes: brachioradialis (upper) and gastrocnemius–soleus (lower). The involuntary reflex response is evaluated by the
neurologist after stretching the tendon (and therefore the muscle) using a
reflex hammer.

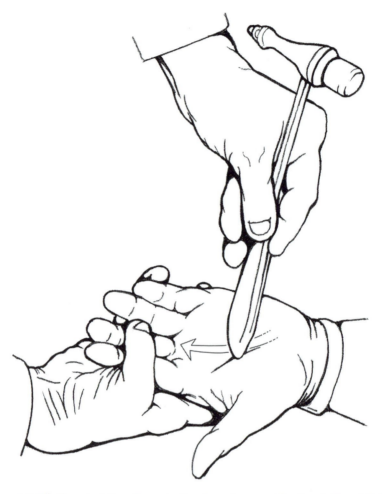

Figure 6.7 Eliciting atavistic reflexes: testing for palmomental reflex (left) and Babin-
    ski reflex (right). The palmomental reflex consists of an involuntary con-
    traction of the mentalis muscle (chin) in response to stimulation of the
    palm (in this case, using the handle of the reflex hammer). The Babinski
    response consists of involuntary movement of the great toe (extension in
    the case of a 'positive' or abnormal response) in response to an uncomfort-
    able stimulation of the plantar surface of the foot.

Summary

The neurologic examination is efficient, reliable, and reproducible with
demonstrated clinical validity and sensitivity when administered by a qualified
neurologist (McCombe, Fairbank, Cockersole, & Pynsent, 1989; Dyck, Kratz,
Lehman, Karnes, Melton, O'Brien, Litchy, Windebank, Smith, & Low, 1991;
Vogel, 1992; Cornblath, Chaudhry, Carter, Lee, Seysedadr, Miernicki, & Joh,

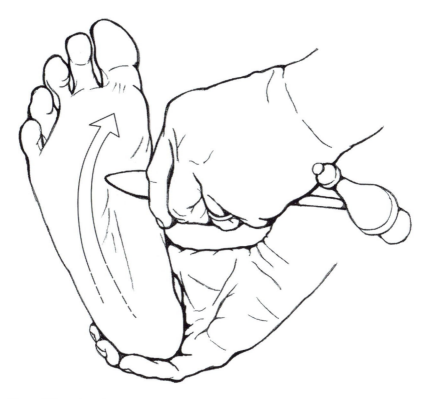

Figure 6.7 continued

1999) The results obtained from the complete neurologic examination allow the neurologist to recognize patterns of abnormalities localized to particular portions of the nervous system.

As described, the neurologist's most difficult task is identifying normal function, a task that forms the basis of most neurologic training. For example, in addition to the obvious importance of body size (height, weight, and body mass index) on the examination of strength, body size also influences the sensory examination. Whereas large individuals are stronger, increasing height and body mass index are associated with decreased sensitivity in the hands and feet. Other factors such as gender and age influence the results of the neurologic examination, and they are important considerations in defining abnormality (Albers, Brown, Sima, & Greene, 1996; Dyck, Litchy, Lehman, Hokanson, Low, & O'Brien, 1995). In the context of establishing clinical evidence of neurotoxicity, the sensitivity of the clinical neurologic examination in detecting an abnormality is important. Issues related to the sensitivity of the neurologic examination are beyond the scope of this chapter, but asymptomatic clinical abnormalities are frequently identified in patients being examined for reasons unrelated to the identified problem. Sensitivity has been addressed most extensively for evaluation of the peripheral nervous system (Dyck, Karnes, O'Brien, Litchy, Low, & Melton, 1992; Albers *et al.*, 1996). In that context, the ability to detect evidence of peripheral neuropathy among patients with disorders such as diabetes mellitus has been established for a variety of different measures. In general, there is substantial concordance between the different measures used to detect neuropathy (Albers *et al.*, 1996).

Developing the neurologic impression

The mechanism by which the neurologic impression is derived likely differs among neurologists (Eddy & Clanton, 1982; Barondess & Carpenter, 1994; Dyck, Grant, & Fealey, 1996). Ultimately, the final impression depends, as in any specialty, on the judgment of adequately trained and experienced clinicians, not on the results of single clinical or laboratory tests (Miller, Willard, Kline, Tarpley, Guillotte, Lawler, & Pendell, 1998). Symptoms obtained from the history and signs derived from the neurologic examination are used to develop an initial neurologic impression and eventually the differential diagnosis (Table 6.4). The differential diagnosis is the funda-

Table 6.4 Questions addressed by the neurologist in formulating a differential diagnosis.

Is there evidence of any neurological problem?

What is the general level of the suspected disorder?
 Supratentorial
 Posterior fossa
 Spinal cord
 Peripheral
 Multiple levels or diffuse

What is the location of the suspected disorder within the level selected?
 Left side, right side, midline, non-focal, diffusely located

What is the temporal profile of the onset and progression of the suspected disorder?:
 Acute (seconds to minutes), subacute (days to weeks), chronic (months to years)

What general diagnostic category is suggested by the temporal profile?:
 Vascular, traumatic, infections or inflammatory, degenerative, neoplastic, toxic, or metabolic

What possible explanations exist (differential diagnosis) to explain the suspected problem?

What tests would help to confirm, refute, or refine individual hypotheses in the differential diagnosis?
 Tests of blood and urine
 Electrophysiological evaluations
 Imaging studies
 Therapeutic (e.g., pharmacological) trial

What is the most likely final explanation (diagnosis) for the patient's problem?

What is the most likely cause of the identified problem?

---

mental component of any clinicopathologic exercise (Eddy & Clanton, 1982). In essence, it is simply a list of possible explanations for the patient's problem that are compatible with the presenting symptoms and signs (Kassirer, 1992; Pauker & Kopelman, 1992). The differential diagnosis may or may not include information related to the etiology (cause) of the patient's problem.

Localizing the lesion

The neurologic approach involves a systematic process by which the suspected neurologic abnormality is localized in the nervous system and the likely pathologic process identified. This is accomplished by following a didactic process consisting of several steps, each one reflecting the answer to a specific question (Mayo Clinic and Mayo Foundation, 1981; Gelb, 1995; Gilman, 1999). The purpose of this process is to localize the site of the lesion producing the clinical disorder in terms of broad general levels (supratentorial, posterior fossa, spinal cord, peripheral), and then to localize further the lesion within the identified level (left side, right side, midline, or non-focal and diffuse). For some problems, more precise localization within a given level follows. For example, in the case of a peripheral level abnormality involving the motor unit, additional localization could be to the anterior horn cell, nerve root, spinal nerve, peripheral nerve, neuromuscular junction, or muscle fiber. Information involving localization is of fundamental importance in terms of the clinical diagnostic process, and the ability to identify and localize a neurologic abnormality is used in all of the diagnostic examples included throughout this text. Of particular importance is the ability to recognize localizations that are unlikely to represent the adverse effects of a neurotoxicant. In fact, understanding the general principles of localization at times reflects information that has been the subject of some confusion. For example, many of the controversial issues involving the peripheral nervous system, as described in Chapter 14 of Volume II, are only controversial because of the limited understanding of characteristic distributions of symptoms and signs associated with neurotoxicants.

Level of abnormality

The first step involves localization of any suspected disorder to one or more of several broad levels within the nervous system (Daube *et al.*, 1986). These levels include the supratentorial (e.g., the cerebrum and related structures above the cerebellar tentorium), posterior fossa, spinal, and peripheral neuromuscular levels.

SUPRATENTORIAL LEVEL

Global supratentorial disorders usually produce abnormal function among tests of cognition, memory, mood, language, vision, motor function, or sensation. Unilateral supratentorial disorders produce contralateral symptoms and signs that include weakness (paresis), sensory loss, hyperreflexia, and emergence of primitive reflexes on one side of the body. These signs may include hemiparesis, hemisensory loss, and hemianopia with involvement of the face, trunk, and extremities. Sensory signs associated with supratentorial lesions typically produce abnormalities of discriminative function such as localization, two-point discrimination, and the ability to identify dual simultaneous stimulation to opposite sides of the body. Involvement of the dominant cerebral hemisphere also may produce language signs, such as expressive and receptive aphasia.

In the context of neurotoxic disorders, innumerable substances capable of injuring neurons and other cells are contained within the supratentorial level. Such injuries reveal themselves in several ways. For example, among the most common neurotoxic syndromes evaluated by the neurologist are those that produce encephalopathy. 'Encephalopathy' is the term used to describe diffuse dysfunction of the cerebrum, such as seen in association with prolonged hypoxia, hepatic dysfunction, uremia, hyperglycemia, or following exposure to neurotoxicants that directly injure cortical neurons. The resultant syndrome is in general not characteristic of the particular underlying cause, and therefore the symptoms and neurologic signs are relatively non-specific.

The general features of acute and chronic encephalopathy can be identified by considering the effects of exposure to ethyl alcohol (common alcohol) (Fraser & Arieff, 1985; Victor, 1989). Acute alcohol exposure has a dramatic dose–response central nervous system effect. The earliest manifestations include mild euphoria with relaxation and a lessening of inhibition. With increasing levels of exposure, intoxication or drunkenness becomes evident, with impaired coordination, unsteadiness, decreased reaction time, slurred speech, drowsiness, altered perceptions, and impaired intellectual and cognition functions. Examination shows altered judgment and disorientation, course nystagmus, and ataxia before more severe alteration of consciousness. At this level of acute alcohol exposure, the individual may be amnestic for events, with an impaired ability to form new memories. With increasing dose, the acute sedative properties of ethyl alcohol progress from somnolence to coma or even death. The acute effects of sublethal exposures resolve in hours after removal from additional exposure, as serum alcohol levels decline. There is no residual impairment other than amnesia for events occurring at high levels of intoxication.

Chronic alcohol exposure, usually in the form of daily repeat acute exposures to alcohol, is associated with variable degrees of permanent encephalopathy. However, the concept of a chronic, irreversible alcohol-induced encephalopathy is controversial because the effects of chronic alcohol exposure are difficult to distinguish from the malnutrition that almost always accompanies chronic alcoholism. Ignoring for a moment whether or not alcohol alone is capable of producing the syndrome, this form of chronic encephalopathy is characterized by supratentorial-level signs of dementia, with evidence of cerebral atrophy on imaging studies, and slowing of the background electroencephalogram. These combined anatomical and physiological abnormalities have limited diagnostic importance, however, other than to indicate the magnitude of the neurologic problem. Another syndrome associated with alcoholism and malnutrition is Wernicke–Korsakoff syndrome (Victor, Adams, & Collins, 1989). Wernicke's syndrome refers to the subacute onset of encephalopathy with impaired extra-ocular eye movements and peripheral neuropathy that is potentially reversible with administration of thiamine (Reuler, Girard, & Cooney, 1985; Victor *et al.*, 1989). Korsakoff's syndrome refers to a chronic residual amnestic state in which there is a relative inability to record new memories (Scully, Mark, & McNeely, 1986; Victor *et al.*, 1989).

Chronic exposure to alcohol produces neurochemical alterations in the central nervous system that result in one component of alcohol dependency. Abrupt withdrawal of alcohol after a period of prolonged exposure produces effects opposite to those associated with acute exposure. Namely, instead of sedation, relaxation, and somnolence, alcohol withdrawal produces agitation, tremulousness, hallucinosis, and generalized major motor seizures. The features of alcohol withdrawal are an indirect neurotoxic effect related to temporary, reversible neuropharmacological changes within the central nervous system. These changes reflect a response to chronic alcohol exposure, but they do not produce permanent injury. The acute withdrawal state can be 'treated' with additional exposure to alcohol. However, the neuropharmacological changes eventually reverse during prolonged abstinence, and the acute withdrawal effects disappear.

A disorder less controversial that chronic alcohol encephalopathy is the progressive encephalopathy associated with hepatic failure. This form of encephalopathy is characterized early in its course by increased irritability, confusion, and anxiety, followed in time by personality change, inappropriate behavior, impaired cognition, and disorientation. The neurologic examination, when performed at this level of involvement, typically demonstrates postural tremor, slowed coordination, and restlessness, usually in association with asterixis (an involuntary flap of the outstretch hands), dysarthria, akathisia, gross ataxia, and the appearance of primitive reflexes (palmomental, snout, suck, and grasp). With progression, delirium develops. Reflexes become hyperactive, and pathologic Babinski and Chaddock reflexes become evident, sometimes in association with myoclonus. At this level of impairment, there is a requirement for assistance in activities of daily living, including feeding and personal hygiene. Progression is associated with a decreased level of consciousness, and decerebrate posturing develops. If untreated, further progression terminates in death. Surprisingly, correction of the toxic–metabolic abnormalities, such as occurs after successful liver transplantation, frequently reverses even the most severe forms of acute hepatic encephalopathy.

POSTERIOR FOSSA LEVEL

The posterior fossa of the cranium contains the brainstem, cerebellum, and ten of the twelve pairs of cranial nerves (the olfactory and optic nerves are located in the supratentorial level). Unilateral posterior fossa lesions produce a combination of unique symptoms and signs that reflect involvement of exiting cranial nerves and transversing sensory and motor pathways before they cross to the other side in the medulla. One-sided lesions in the posterior fossa therefore produce ipsilateral abnormalities of the head and contralateral abnormalities of the trunk and extremities. There are several sensory and motor symptoms suggestive of posterior fossa involvement. These symptoms include diplopia (double vision), dysarthria (slurred speech), dysphagia (difficulty swallowing), dysphonia (impaired phonation), dysequilibrium, incoordination, and crossed motor and sensory impairments producing weakness or sensory loss of one side of the face and the opposite side of the body.

SPINAL CORD LEVEL

Neurologic lesions localized to the spinal cord are the only nervous system disorders that produce a level of abnormality, with intact function above and impaired function below that level. A unilateral spinal cord lesion produces a characteristic syndrome (Brown–Sequard syndrome) below the lesion consisting of ipsilateral weakness, hyperreflexia, pathologic reflexes (Babinski and Chaddock responses), and impaired vibration, touch, and joint position sensations in association with contralateral impairment of pain and temperature sensations.

PERIPHERAL LEVEL

The peripheral level includes the nerve roots, the brachial and lumbosacral plexus, the peripheral nerves including the peripheral component of the cranial nerves, the neuromuscular junction, and the muscles. Symptoms and signs of peripheral nervous system involvement depend on the component involved. Recognition of isolated peripheral nerve (mononeuropathy) or nerve root (radiculopathy) disorders requires knowledge of the distribution of sensory and motor innervation of individual nerves and isolated nerve roots. Generalized or diffuse dysfunction of peripheral nerves produces polyneuropathy. Most forms of polyneuropathy are characterized by dying-back, with the longest segments preferentially involved. This results in a symmetric stocking or stocking–glove distribution of sensory loss, distal weakness involving the feet before than hands, and distal decrease or loss of muscle stretch reflexes, beginning with the gastrocnemius–soleus (ankle) reflexes. Generalized dysfunction of muscles (myopathy) produces greater proximal than distal weakness preferentially involving the neck flexor, arm abductor, and hip flexor muscles with preservation of sensation and reflexes. Neuromuscular junction abnormalities produce fluctuating weakness and abnormal fatigability, with a predilection of extraocular, bulbar, and proximal limb muscle involvement.

The peripheral nervous system is, in general, a sensitive indicator of nervous system involvement from neurotoxic chemicals (Albers & Bromberg, 1995). Numerous neurotoxicants produce recognizable peripheral nervous system effects as part of their overall involvement when given in sufficient dose and over a sufficient period. The concept that the peripheral nervous system is sometimes involved as part of more generalized nervous system or systemic toxicity is important because the most objective and quantifiable evaluation techniques available to the neurologist measure peripheral nervous system performance. The characteristic peripheral nervous system abnormality following neurotoxic exposure is peripheral neuropathy. 'Neuropathy' is a general term that literally means 'sick nerve'. The term is used to denote damage to the peripheral nervous system. 'Mononeuropathy' indicates involvement of a single peripheral nerve. 'Mononeuropathy multiplex' indicates involvement of multiple individual nerves. 'Polyneuropathy' indicates diffuse or generalized involvement of most or all nerves. The terms 'neuropathy', 'peripheral neuropathy', and 'polyneuropathy' are used interchangeably in reference to generalized involvement of the peripheral nervous system. There are several different types of peripheral neuropathy, including those classified as sensory, motor, sensorimotor, and/or autonomic, depending on the predominant class of nerve fiber involved.

A clinical diagnosis of peripheral neuropathy is based on demonstration of a characteristic set of neurologic symptoms and signs. A diagnosis of confirmed peripheral neuropathy requires documentation of appropriate electrodiagnostic or neuropathologic abnormalities (Donofrio & Albers, 1990; Albers, 1993). The clinical signs include symmetric sensory loss or weakness that is most prominent distally, in the feet and hands. This distal distribution of abnormality reflects the underlying pathophysiology whereby most toxic or metabolic neuropathies are length dependent and characterized by a distal 'dying-back' neuropathy involving the longest axons (Spencer & Schaumburg, 1976; Dyck, 1982; Sterman, 1985). In any peripheral neuropathy that is clinically significant and that involves large myelinated fibers (the most common type of involvement), reflexes are diminished and usually absent at the ankles. Electrodiagnostic studies are used to provide objective evidence of peripheral abnormality, and electrodiagnostic test results also provide information about the underlying pathophysiology (Albers, 1993). These findings usually can be used to determine whether or not the neuropathy involves the cell body (neuronopathy), nerve roots (polyradiculopathy), or the axons (polyneuropathy). Test results also are used to determine whether or not there is evidence of primary demyelination or isolated axonal degeneration. Normal electrodiagnostic studies virtually exclude the likelihood of detecting a clinically significant peripheral neuropathy.

Location within the level

The second step involved in developing the neurologic impression addresses the location of dysfunction within the level selected. This relatively simple and straightforward question produces possible responses of lesions that are focal on the right or left side of the nervous system, lesions that are focal and involving midline structures, or lesions that are non-focal and diffusely located. Correct localization depends on an understanding of basic neuroanatomical principles.

Identifying general diagnostic categories

The answers to the first two localization questions can be derived entirely from information obtained from the neurologic examination, independent of any history. The next task involves identification of possible diagnostic categories using results from the first two questions plus information obtained from the history. Specifically, information describing the temporal profile of symptoms is used to predict possible pathologic mechanisms that could explain the patient's symptoms (Mayo Clinic and Mayo Foundation, 1981; Daube *et al.*, 1986; Gilman, 1999). This task is simplified by several basic generalizations about the nervous system's response to a variety of different injuries. These assumptions are as follows. In general, symptom onset can be categorized by the rate of onset to include those that develop acutely, with a temporal profile having onset over seconds to minutes, those that develop subacutely, over hours to days, or those that are chronic and develop slowly, over weeks to months. These three categories translate into vascular, inflammatory, and neoplastic or degenerative categories, respectively. Next, the distribution of signs into focal or diffuse locations allows further subdivision into additional categories.

How does this information translate into the neurologist's interpretation of the patient's history and neurologic examination? Based on the various considerations described above, the neurologist might summarize an initial impression of a slowly progressive left hemiparesis as having a progressive, right-sided (focal) supratentorial lesion, likely representing a neoplasm (new growth). Similarly, a patient with a 'stroke' producing diplopia, incoordination, and weakness of the right side of the face and left side of the body would be described as having an acute onset, right-sided, focal posterior fossa lesion, most consistent with a vascular etiology. A peripheral disorder associated with a neurotoxic exposure producing symmetrical stocking–glove weakness, sensory loss, and areflexia would be summarized as a subacute onset, symmetrical, distal greater than proximal, sensorimotor polyneuropathy. The description at this point usually does not include information about specific causes for the problem, other than listing broad diagnostic considerations. For example, a vascular disorder could be produced by emboli from a distant cardiac source, dissection of a major extracranial artery by local trauma, thrombosis from atherosclerotic vascular disease, or inflammation of blood vessels (vasculitis). All of these different events produce the same final pathology, namely occlusion of the vessel with resultant hypoxia or anoxia of tissues supplied by the blood vessel(s). Yet, none of the explanations includes the ultimate 'cause' of the problem (e.g., atherosclerotic vascular disease associated with oxidative stress or degenerative cardiac valve disease from a prior infection). In the context of this book, almost all neurotoxic disorders produce bilateral neurologic impairments, as opposed to focal or unilateral disorders. This is important, because a neurotoxic explanation is extremely unlikely if the results of the neurologic examination identify evidence of a focal or unilateral impairment, in which case other explanations should be explored. The course of the patient's symptoms is slightly less helpful. It is true that the temporal profile of most neurotoxic disorders is chronic, similar to most metabolic disorders. However, like metabolic disorders, there are exceptions, and neurotoxic syndromes may have acute or subacute presentations. On the other hand, progression over a period longer than a few weeks in the absence of further or ongoing exposure is atypical of most toxic disorders. These general categories are summarized in Table 6.5.

The neurologist's next task is to develop a preliminary list of possible explanations for the patient's symptoms and signs. This list of possible explanations is called the 'differential diagnosis'. The process by which the differential diagnosis is developed is addressed in the following sections, followed by a review of the different forms of neurodiagnostic testing and the accepted process of establishing the specific cause for an identified problem.

Establishing a differential diagnosis

The neurologist's most important task is establishing the diagnosis for the patient's problem. Exactly how this is done is based on a combination of knowledge, training, and experience. However, several aspects of the diagnostic process are easily described. This process is supplementary to but

Table 6.5 General diagnostic categories based on the neuroanatomic localization and temporal profile (Daube *et al.*, 1986; Gelb, 1995).

Localization	Temporal profile		
	Acute	*Subacute*	*Chronic*
Focal	Vascular (e.g., infarction or hemorrhage)	Inflammatory (e.g., abscess)	Neoplastic (e.g., 'new growth')
Diffuse	Vascular (e.g, subarachnoid hemorrhage	Inflammatory (e.g., encephalitis)	Degenerative
	Toxic/metabolic	Toxic/metabolic	Toxic/metabolic

not independent of the process of establishing the presence of a neurologic impairment. This does not mean, however, that a problem can be diagnosed only when a neurologic impairment is identified, as some neurologic diagnoses can be established with confidence in the absence of a neurologic impairment. For example, diagnoses such as migraine headache, seizure disorder, or sleep apnea do not produce abnormal findings on the clinical neurologic examination, yet they can be identified in most cases based on the patient's history and supportive information such as neurodiagnostic testing. The differential diagnosis is simply an inventory of explanations that are capable of explaining the patient's symptoms and signs. This conventional, commonsense approach of developing a differential diagnosis begins by localizing and characterizing the neurologic impairment using results of the history and neurologic examination (Miller *et al.*, 1998).

Use of neurologic symptoms

The process of developing a differential diagnosis begins with the description of chief complaints. The list of possible explanations for those symptoms is modified, as the results of the neurologic examination become available. Occasionally, the patient's symptoms are sufficiently characteristic to be considered 'cardinal' or diagnostic of one specific diagnosis, but this is uncommon. For example, a recurrent unilateral, pulsatile headache that is preceded by a visual aura, has an abrupt onset, and is associated with nausea and vomiting is characteristic of migraine. If the patient did not have a normal neurologic examination between episodes, the differential diagnosis would not include migraine because other disorders such as structural lesions may produce similar symptoms (Stang, Yanagihara, Swanson, & Beard, 1992).

Specificity of symptoms

How specific are neurologic symptoms for use in identifying a certain neurologic diagnosis? Transient neurologic symptoms are quite prevalent in the general population and rarely useful in establishing a diagnosis. Most transient symptoms are considered 'non-specific' because they have little pathologic importance. This is because most transient symptoms reflect normal physiologic variation. For example, momentary lightheadedness or dizziness after standing could represent abnormal postural hypotension due to dysautonomia, but usually this symptom represents a normal physiological response to assuming an upright posture, reflecting a momentary drop in blood pressure that rapidly equilibrates. A similar sensation results from rapid head movement, another normal physiologic response of no pathologic importance.

Fleeting numbness and tingling of a limb is commonly related to limb position, such as when awaking from sleep or after sitting in a crossed-leg position. This sensation reflects local limb ischemia or physiologic nerve compression that is not associated with nerve injury. Similar symptoms of transient numbness and tingling occur in association with hyperventilation. The respiratory alkalosis associated with hyperventilation influences binding of serum calcium, and the resultant hypocalcemia is associated with paresthesias. These normal physiologic events produce symptoms that are for the most part ignored by most individuals unless attention is drawn to them or concern develops that they indicate an abnormality.

In general, fleeting or intermittent symptoms are unlikely to reflect a serious neurologic impairment. There are exceptions, of course, the most obvious being seizure, transient ischemic attack (TIA) related to focal vascular insufficiency, altered consciousness associated with cardiac insufficiency (syncope), and transient weakness due to impaired neuromuscular transmission. Description of the patient's symptoms is an important first step in the neurologic evaluation. However, many explanations may exist for a given symptom, particularly those described as 'non-specific' and those not associated with abnormal neurologic findings.

Use of neurologic signs

Identification of neurologic signs is important in defining the neurologic impairment and in establishing a differential diagnosis. When combined with the patient's symptoms, the resultant information, independent of any ancillary testing, usually produces a differential diagnosis that contains the correct explanation for the patient's problem.

Objective and subjective 'signs'

Symptoms are always 'subjective'. Neurologic 'signs' identified during the examination are generally considered as being 'objective'. Unfortunately, objectivity in this context is a relative concept and few components of the neurologic examination are independent of patient effort and cooperation.

There are several exceptions. Few would argue that the reflex examination is not objective and independent of patient influence. Muscle stretch reflexes vary slightly in response to anxiety, but patient motivation or effort does not directly influence them. An important diagnostic finding in most patients with clinically important peripheral neuropathy is identifying absent reflexes in distal extremities. This observation depends only on the skill of the examining neurologist. However, even absent reflexes can be misleading unless further qualified, because absent reflexes may reappear with facilitation, as during the Jendrastic maneuver. When reflexes can be elicited by facilitation, the finding assumes less clinical importance than true areflexia. Documentation of normal ankle reflexes by one examiner and absent ankle reflexes by another likely reflects failure by the second examiner to obtain the reflexes properly, because reflex variability is a minor consideration,

It is true that some signs are more susceptible to examiner interpretation than are other signs. For example, the accurate evaluation of muscle strength requires a cooperative, motivated patient. However, even in the absence of complete cooperation, a skilled examiner can usually evaluate strength accurately. Like the reflex examination, demonstrating full strength for even a moment indicates an intact function in most situations, assuming that impaired neuromuscular transmission or an upper motor neuron lesion can be excluded based on the results of other clinical testing. The experienced examiner does not simply attempt to overcome the patient in examining strength. Instead, the patient is asked to overcome the examiner by applying increasingly greater force. In testing the triceps muscle, for example, the neurologist secures the forearm at 45° to the arm and instructs the patient to 'push' the examiner away. The examiner must provide increasing resistance using his mechanical advantage to resist the patient's efforts. Examination of patients with weakness associated with peripheral nervous system dysfunction of muscle or nerve demonstrates smooth release, as opposed to the sudden collapse of the limb. The latter is characteristic of decreased volitional effort or pain inhibition. 'Clasp-knife' weakness suggestive of upper motor neuron abnormality rarely occurs in isolation. Instead, the presence of pronator drift, increased resistance of limb movement to passive manipulation, impaired alternate motion rate, increased reflexes, and the presence of pathologic reflexes all support an upper motor neuron disorder. The alternate motion rate is another test that depends on maximal patient effort, and a non-specific reduced rate in the absence of other evidence of basal ganglia dysfunction would be of limited importance. Similarly, examination of coordination and gait require good patient effort, and slow deliberate responses do not always indicate neurologic dysfunction.

The sensory examination is primarily subjective, depending on patient cooperation and effort. Report of a 'dull' sensation following application of a sharp pin to the skin is a subjective response, whereas jumping in response to application of the pin would be an objective indication the pin was painful. Isolated or poorly reproducible findings that do not honour known boundaries of nerve or nerve root distribution are of limited importance.

The clinical sensory examination has substantial redundancy, making it possible to confirm subtle or suspect abnormalities. The patient who is unable to perceive light touch, yet who correctly performs dual simultaneous stimulation, would have findings that are internally inconsistent and require resolution. This is because the more difficult task demonstrates normal performance, whereas the simpler task is performed incorrectly. Similarly, an inability to identify objects placed in the hands with the eyes closed (astereognosis) yet having an intact ability to manipulate the objects could not be explained by a peripheral nervous system disorder. Redundancy also exists across tests that seem to evaluate different types of neurologic function. This occurs because portions of the nervous system are common to both evaluations. Impaired joint position sensation in the toes and ankles could not be reconciled with a normal stance with eyes closed, because the latter requires precise information about joint position and both tests evaluate in part function of large myelinated nerve fibers. Markedly abnormal vibration, fine touch, and joint position sensations and a positive Romberg sign could not be attributed to a peripheral neuropathy in the presence of normal ankle reflexes. This is because the same nerve fibers involved in these sensations comprise the afferent loop of the reflex arc. Similarly, the inability to feel light touch with eyes closed, yet correctly moving the finger touched by the examiner during examination of coordination (also performed with the eyes closed), would represent an inconsistency in the patient's response and is not a sign of abnormality. These are a few of examples of the redundancy in the neurologic examination. Internal consistency and concordance of clinical findings are important concepts in determining whether or not the examination is abnormal.

Specificity of neurologic signs

Just as few neurologic symptoms are specific for any diagnosis, few signs are pathognomonic of any given disorder (Eddy & Clanton, 1982). There are a few exceptions. Waxing and waning of neurologic signs over weeks to months in association with persistent double vision and eye movement abnormalities indicating an internuclear ophthalmoplegia strongly suggests the diagnosis of multiple sclerosis (McFarland & Dhib Jalbut, 1989). Subacute onset of a generalized movement disorder in a young adult noted to have Kaiser-Fleischer rings on ophthalmologic examination strongly suggests a diagnosis of Wilson's disease (Scully, 1984). Mees' lines in the nails of a patient who presents with a distal neuropathy suggests arsenic intoxication (Lerman, Ali, & Green, 1980; Donofrio *et al.*, 1987) (Figure 6.8).

More often, however, neurologic signs are used to localize the neurologic lesion rather than to establish a specific diagnosis or cause of the neurologic problem. Evidence of impaired cognition with disorientation, abnormal postural tremor, slowed coordination, akathisia, and prominent primitive reflexes suggest a clinical diagnosis of encephalopathy. Encephalopathy, however, is not indicative of any specific etiology. If these same signs appeared in combination with evidence of midline cerebellar degeneration and a distal sensorimotor polyneuropathy, the possibility of hepatic-related neurologic dysfunction would become a major consideration in the resultant differential diagnosis (Victor, 1989).

Finally, abnormal signs do not always indicate pathology. Abnormalities are frequently found in clinically normal, asymptomatic individuals, independent of any identifiable disease. Isolated signs are commonly found in association with advancing age, and some primitive or atavistic reflexes such as palmomental, snout, or suck reflexes exist in a substantial proportion of normal subjects with advancing age (Jacobs & Gossman, 1980). Identification of these reflexes should not be taken as indicative of any specific disease. Ankle reflexes, whose absence is considered among the most sensitive

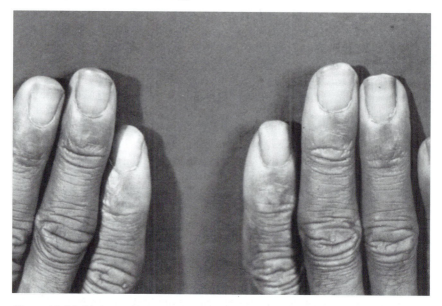

Figure 6.8 Multiple Mees' lines in a patient with multiple episodes of arsenic intoxication. The Mees' lines are the white horizontal lines that transverse the
entire nail.

indicators of peripheral neuropathy, are decreased or absent in 5% of healthy
subjects older than 50 years (Dyck *et al.*, 1995; O'Brien & Dyck, 1995). This
greatly limits the value of such findings when used to indicate peripheral
neuropathy in this population of patients.

Even absent reflexes may not suggest any underlying pathology. Some individuals, particular athletic males, have diffuse areflexia with no other
abnormal findings and no evidence of any underlying pathology. Healthy
subjects retain their ability to walk on toes and heels regardless of age, excessive weight, or lack of physical fitness. However, the ability to arise from a
kneeled position is lost in more than 5% of people 60 years and older (Dyck
et al., 1995). It is clear that abnormalities limited to tests requiring the
patient's full cooperation and interpretation, such as tests of sensation, must
be used cautiously. Furthermore, a sensory abnormality in a cooperative
patient must be interpreted in the context of normal for that patient.
Decreased touch sensation in a person with highly callused hands or
decreased distal touch and vibration sensations in an overweight individual
occur commonly in the absence of an underlying peripheral nerve disorder
(Dyck *et al.*, 1995; Stetson, Albers, Silverstein, & Wolfe, 1992).

Preliminary differential diagnosis

The process of developing and refining the differential diagnosis is based on
the scientific method as an iterative hypothesis-generating–hypothesis-testing

procedure. The purpose of this iterative process is to identify the correct diagnosis by eliminating competing explanations until only one likely diagnosis remains or the disorder remains undiagnosed (Miller *et al.*, 1998). Of course, the remaining item in an incomplete differential diagnosis does not necessarily represent the correct diagnosis. The neurologist frequently detects systemic illnesses that produce neurologic abnormalities as well as normal patterns of physiological or psychological variation that mimic neurologic disease. There are logical algorithms that imitate this diagnostic procedure, but the process also depends on clinical judgments based on extensive neurobiological and clinical knowledge, training, and experience (Miller *et al.*, 1998). The challenge presented by the differential diagnosis process is that of selecting the most probable cause of the condition in question, a challenge complicated by the limited ability of humans to calculate statistical probabilities mentally (Eddy & Clanton, 1982).

At this point in the diagnostic process, it is common to request additional diagnostic or laboratory tests to refine the differential diagnosis into a final impression. Quite often, the results of the initial diagnostic testing will fall below some threshold of diagnostic credibility that results in rejection of one or more of the leading diagnostic possibilities. Sometimes a test result suggests possibilities not initially considered or suggested the need for additional testing. The process is intended to filter out all but the most likely diagnosis (Eddy & Clanton, 1982). Even at this seemingly final point in the diagnostic process, the ultimate cause of the patient's problem may remain unknown. Ironically, numerous neurologic disorders can be identified with confidence and treated successfully without knowledge about the actual cause of the problem. For many disorders, the cause remains uncertain even though the underlying pathophysiology is at least partially understood.

Neurodiagnostic testing

There usually are several items included in differential diagnosis that have different etiologies, prognosis, and treatment. The initial differential diagnosis invariably includes some items that are more likely than others to account for the patient's symptoms and signs than are others. The neurologist is responsible for refining the differential diagnosis in an iterative process until the correct explanation for the patient's problem is identified. Revising the differential diagnosis commonly involves selecting from among different laboratory, psychometric, electrodiagnostic, and imaging studies. The different forms of relevant neurodiagnostic tests are described briefly below and further critiqued in Chapter 7. A detailed description of the EMG examination can be found in Chapter 9 in Volume II. Specific laboratory testing (e.g., blood, urine, or tissue levels of a particular substance) is beyond the scope of this chapter and is not addressed.

Psychometric tests as viewed by the neurologist

When an abnormality of cognition or mood is suspected, the neurologist uses the results of standardized neuropsychological evaluations, performed in consultation with a clinical neuropsychologist, to define better the suspected disorder. Formal neuropsychological testing is important in quantifying cognitive and mood impairments, and these measures are especially important in evaluating non-specific complaints such as decreased memory or impaired concentration. With regard to altered mood, the neuropsychological evaluation may identify abnormal anxiety states, motivational factors, or psychopathology.

Selected psychomotor or psychosensory tests occasionally supplement the neurologic and neuropsychological examinations. These measures are sometimes used to identify subtle abnormalities in neurologic function, particularly when a specific abnormality such as diminished sensation, impaired coordination, or abnormal tremor is suspected. Few of these specialized measures have had widespread application in standardized form, and their sensitivity and specificity have limited evaluation.

Electrodiagnostic evaluations

There are standardized electrophysiological tests used to investigate neurologic function, and several have widespread application as part of the clinical neurologic evaluation (Table 6.6).

Electroencephalography (EEG)

The EEG records electrical activity from the scalp of electrical signals generated by neural tissue in the brain. The EEG study is non-invasive and is not uncomfortable. The entire EEG examination takes about 1 hour to complete. The EEG waveforms are inspected visually and interpreted subjectively. Interpretation includes evaluation of the waveform amplitude, frequency, coherence, symmetry, and responsiveness. Clinical EEG has extensive application in the evaluation of several problems, including the evaluation of seizure disorders and, to a lesser extent, the evaluation of encephalopathy. Certain clinical problems produce characteristic EEG abnormalities. In the evaluation of suspected neurotoxicity, however, the EEG abnormalities are of unknown sensitivity and limited specificity, as discussed further in Chapter 7 (Aminoff & Albers, 1999).

OTHER

Several other electrodiagnostic studies exist that are related to the EEG evaluation. Some have an established application, whereas others and have a potential but unproven clinical utility. These include quantitative EEG

Table 6.6 Physiologic, electrophysiologic, and neuropathology tests useful in evaluating the central (CNS), peripheral (PNS), and autonomic (ANS) nervous systems (Albers, 2002).

Level	Category	Associated tests
CNS:		
	Psychometric	Intellect
		Cognition
		Psychomotor:
		speed
		steadiness
		Affect
	Electrophysiology	Electroencephalography (EEG)
		Evoked potential (EP) studies:
		visual (VEP)
		auditory (AEP)
		somatosensory (SSEP)
	Neuropathology	Brain biopsy
		Meningeal biopsy
PNS:		
	Psychometric	Quantitative sensory testing (QST)
		Posturography
	Electrophysiology	Electromyography
		Nerve conduction studies:
		sensory
		motor
		F-wave response
		reflex responses
		repetitive stimulation
		Needle electromyography:
		conventional
		single fiber
	Neuropathology	Nerve biopsy
		Muscle biopsy
ANS:		
	Physiological	Q-SART
		Postural blood pressure
	Electrophysiology	Sympathetic skin response (SPR)
		R-R interval analyses

(QEEG) and EEG brain mapping, visual-evoked responses (VER), brain stem auditory evoked responses (BAER), somatosensory-evoked potentials (SSEP), and event-related potentials (e.g., P-300). These studies are critiqued separately in Chapter 7.

Electromyography (EMG)

'Electromyography' refers to nerve conduction studies and the needle electromyography examination. The EMG examination evaluates the physiological function of the peripheral nervous system. The most important application is to patients with suspected disorders of anterior horn cells, nerve roots, peripheral nerves, neuromuscular transmission, or muscle. The EMG examination is well standardized, with established sensitivity, specificity, and reproducibility. Board certification examinations provide standards of threshold levels of competence. EMG has special application for disorders potentially caused by neurotoxicants, particularly those that produce neuropathy. EMG results are used to classify the neuropathies into broad categories, narrowing the differential diagnosis. Because of their precision, EMG studies are increasingly important to clinical pharmaceutical studies, including their role in identifying potential neurotoxicity. The methodology employed in EMG evaluations is discussed in more detail in Chapter 9 of Volume II.

By way of summary, the EMG examination has several components. These include sensory and motor nerve conduction studies, evaluation of late responses (F-waves) and reflex responses (H reflex, blink reflex), needle EMG testing, and ancillary studies such as sympathetic skin responses used to evaluate some autonomic nervous system functions. The particular EMG protocol selected by the electromyographer depends on symptoms, clinical signs, and the diagnostic problem being investigated. Nerve conduction studies and the needle EMG examination address slightly different parts of the nervous system (Albers, 1993). In the context of neurotoxicology, nerve conduction studies have particular utility in the evaluation of neuropathy and disorders of neuromuscular transmission. Needle examination has special application in the investigation of myopathy. The complete electrodiagnostic examination plays an important role in identifying competing explanations for the patient's problem, the majority of which are unrelated to neurotoxicant exposure.

NERVE CONDUCTION STUDIES

Nerve conduction studies are non-invasive means of evaluating electrochemical signals generated by peripheral nerve or muscle in response to percutaneous electrical stimuli. The sensation produced by the stimulating electrode resembles a static electricity 'carpet shock'. Supramaximal stimuli, sufficient to depolarize all the fibers in a given nerve, generate signals in the form of sensory and motor responses that can be recorded from the surface of the extremities and head using surface electrodes. Important characteristics of these signals include amplitude and conduction velocity of the largest myelinated nerve fibers. Distal latencies are measured in the nerve terminal, where conduction is slower than along the more proximal portions of nerve. Conduction times over the entire length of a motor nerve are evaluated by F-wave latency. F-waves represent an antidromic motor nerve stimulation that travels from the periphery to the spinal cord, where a portion of the motor neuron pool is activated, sending an orthodromic motor response back along the same motor fibres initially activated. The F-wave latency represents a summation of the time necessary for the action potential to travel along the entire length of the motor nerve twice, to and from the spinal cord along a motor fiber. The long distance over which the measurement is made accentuates mild generalized slowing (Daube, 1987).

Conduction techniques are well standardized. Differences in published normal values reflect technical differences, limb temperature, age, and even patient size (Bolton & Carter, 1980; Rivner, Swift, Crout, & Rhodes, 1990; Stetson *et al.*, 1992; Trojaborg, Moon, Andersen, & Trojaborg, 1992). Improper electrode placement, inaccurate surface measurements, and a failure to monitor and control limb temperature influence the results. Limb temperature is a source of variability particularly important in the evaluation of neuropathy. Cooling decreases conduction velocity and increases amplitude, a combination of findings atypical for any pathologic process. Limb temperature should be monitored and cool limbs warmed if necessary to a surface temperature of approximately 32–36°C.

The most important nerve conduction measure relevant to neurotoxicological studies is amplitude. The response amplitude (sensory or motor) reflects the number of activated nerve or muscle fibres. Amplitude is influenced by many factors, including the distance between the stimulation site and the recording site. When the distance is short, amplitudes are larger than those recorded over longer distances. The difference in amplitude reflects normal physiology. The response is a summation of the electrical action potential from individual motor units or sensory axons (e.g., a 'compound' sensory or motor action potential). Axons differ in size, and larger axons conduct an action potential faster than do small axons. As the distance over which the action potentials travel increases, there is increased separation between the arrival time of the faster and the slower axons. The 'spreading out' of the response is referred to as temporal dispersion. Because action potentials are biphasic, separation of action potentials also produces phase cancellation, a process whereby the positive phase of a rapidly conducting action potential coincides with the negative phase of a more slowly conducting action potential. This cancellation accentuates amplitude and area differences that occur with increasing stimulation to recording distances. Temporal dispersion and phase cancellation play only a limited role in the evaluation of normal peripheral nerves under ordinary circumstances. However, these effects are accentuated by cool limp temperature. Temporal dispersion and phase cancellation are normal physiologic consequences of recording responses from axons of different sizes.

NEEDLE ELECTROMYOGRAPHY

The needle EMG examination is, by definition, invasive because the EMG electrode punctures the skin. However, it does not involve inordinate physical discomfort or risk. The two most common untoward effects are bleeding in individuals using anticoagulation medications or patients with bleeding disorders, and transmission of infectious disease (American Association of Electromyography and Electrodiagnosis, 1984; American Association of Electrodiagnostic Medicine, 1992; AAEM Professional Practice Committee, 1999). The risk of excessive bleeding among anticoagulated patients must be mitigated by the potential importance of the resultant EMG information. The risk of transmitting infectious disease is minimized by using sterile disposable-needle EMG electrodes.

The needle EMG examination is subjective. Measures include an estimate of insertional activity, identification of abnormal potentials not ordinarily present, and evaluation of motor unit action potential ('motor unit') recruitment and configuration. Normal insertional activity consists of a brief burst of electrical activity caused by placing the EMG electrode into the muscle. Abnormal signals, including fibrillation potentials and positive waves, appear as a consequence of denervation hypersensitivity, a consequence of increased acetylcholine receptor density that develops in denervated muscle fibers. Fibrillation potentials and positive waves are the most sensitive and most specific indicators of 'denervated' muscle, and they are easily identified.

The needle examination includes a subjective estimate of motor unit recruitment and configuration. 'Recruitment' is the term used to describe the sequential introduction of additional motor units into the interference pattern as force is voluntarily increased. Recruitment decreases when fewer motor units are available, for example, after loss of motor axons or anterior horn cells. The subjective estimate of motor unit recruitment is difficult. Motor unit size and configuration are estimated as the amplitude, duration, and polyphasia (number of phases [baseline crossings + 1] or reversals [turns]). The reinnervation of denervated fibers by surviving motor axons (collateral sprouting) associated with incomplete axonal lesions produces increased muscle fiber density with increased motor unit amplitude, duration, and polyphasia. Estimates of motor unit recruitment and configuration are subjective and dependent on the electromyographer's training and experience. This portion of the needle EMG examination is complementary to the comparatively less subjective measurements of fibrillation potential and positive waves. As a general rule, abnormalities limited to motor unit recruitment or configuration should be viewed cautiously, because they are subjective in nature and only rarely appear in isolation.

The EMG examination does not diagnose 'toxic neuropathy' in isolation. However, different forms of toxic neuropathy can be classified on the basis of electrophysiologic test results, such as outlined in Table 9.5 of Volume II; the categories are not exclusive. The classification scheme separates peripheral disorders into broad categories based on electrodiagnostic evidence of sensory or motor involvement combined with uniform or multifocal demyelination or pure axonal loss. This scheme is helpful to the clinician by reducing the number of potential forms of neuropathy that could explain the electrodiagnostic test results. Although the disorders listed in Table 9.5 of Volume II are limited to different types of toxic neuropathy, numerous other disorders, including inflammatory and hereditary forms of neuropathy, also provide plausible explanations for the electrodiagnostic findings in the appropriate setting. More extensive discussions of this classification scheme exist elsewhere (Donofrio & Albers, 1990).

REPETITIVE MOTOR NERVE STIMULATION

The electrical response to repetitive motor nerve stimulation can be used to evaluate neuromuscular transmission (Ozdemir & Young, 1976). When neuromuscular transmission is impaired, there is a decrement in the motor response at low stimulation rates (3 Hz) (Massey, 1990; Albers & Leonard, 1992). At this stimulation rate, normal subjects show no evidence of a decremental response. Acetylcholine is released from the nerve terminal when the nerve is depolarized. Acetylcholine molecules diffuse across the neuromuscular junction and interact with acetylcholine receptors (AChR) on the muscle membrane. This interaction results in a configurational change in sodium channels, producing an endplate potential. If the endplate potential is sufficiently large, a muscle action potential is generated and the muscle fiber contracts. Factors important to this response include, among other factors, sufficient availability of acetylcholine, appropriate inactivation of acetylcholine in the synaptic cleft, and intact AChR. Abnormality of any of these factors can impair neuromuscular transmission.

SINGLE FIBER ELECTROMYOGRAPHY (SFEMG)

Single fiber electromyography (SFEMG) is a method for extracellular recording of single muscle fiber action potentials (MFAPs) (Stalberg, Ekstedt, & Broman 1974; Sanders & Stalberg, 1996). MFAPs recorded from the same motor unit show a small variation in the timing of the action potentials. This variation, called 'jitter', reflects the small differences in the time required for the endplate potential to reach threshold before generating the MFAP. Large endplate potentials well above threshold show little variability in the timing of MFAP discharge and jitter values are small. Small endplate potentials, for example just above threshold, show substantial variability in the timing of MFAP discharge and jitter values are large. Neuromuscular transmission fails when the endplate potential falls below threshold and an MFAP is not generated. The decremental response recorded among patients with defective neuromuscular transmission during repetitive motor stimulation is related to blocking of individual MFAPs. Before actual failure of some fibers, jitter is abnormally increased, making SFEMG recording the most sensitive indication of defective neuromuscular transmission. SFEMG can be used to determine the density of muscle fiber for a single motor unit. The most important application of this measure is to identify evidence of previous denervation and reinnervation.

BLINK REFLEX

The blink reflex has a teleological protective eye function, and the reflex produces eyelid closure in response to stimulation of the face or eye. Blink reflex studies are evoked responses, and blink reflex studies are performed as part of the nerve conduction examination. Somewhat similar to the H reflex (electrical equivalent of the ankle reflex), blink reflexes include a central nervous system component that produces an efferent motor output. In the case of the blink reflex, the central component is polysynaptic and crosses the midline, producing ipsilateral and contralateral motor responses (Small & Borus, 1983). The reflex is initiated by percutaneous stimulation of the supraorbital nerve, a branch of the trigeminal nerve. The stimulating current is less that used for other nerve conduction studies because a supramaximal response is not required. The complete reflex arc consists of the trigeminal sensory afferent limb, neuronal brainstem relays in the pons and medulla, and a facial motor efferent motor pathway terminating in facial muscles. The blink reflex is recorded from the orbicularis oculi muscles using surface electrodes (Kimura, 1989). The electrically induced reflex is comprised of R1 and R2 components (Esteban, 1999). The R1 component has the shortest latency and is recorded ipsilateral to the side of stimulation. The R2 component has a longer latency than the R1 component and is recorded bilateral following stimulation of either side of the face.

ELECTRODIAGNOSTIC TESTS OF AUTONOMIC NERVOUS SYSTEM FUNCTION

Sympathetic skin potentials (SSPs) are responses recorded from sweat. Sweat glands receive autonomic innervation, and abnormalities of the autonomic nervous system result in abnormal SSPs (Shahani, Halperin, Bolu, & Cohen, 1984). Unlike most other form of nerve conduction studies, SSPs evaluate small nerve fiber function, not large fiber function. SSPs are differentially recorded from the surface of the skin between areas of high and low sweat gland densities. SSPs appear spontaneously, but they also occur in response to a variety of stimuli. In the EMG laboratory, SSPs are evoked using percutaneous electrical stimulation, startle, cough, Valsalva maneuver, or by simply by asking an emotionally charged question to produce an autonomic response to startle or surprise.

Neuroimaging

Standard techniques, including X-ray computed tomography (CT) and magnetic resonance imaging (MRI), are used routinely in clinical practice to image the nervous system (neuroimaging). The primary types of imaging employed involve images of the structural (e.g., CT, MRI) or the functional aspects of the nervous system (e.g., single photon emission computed tomography [SPECT], positron emission tomography [PET], functional MRI

[fMRI]) (see Chapter 7) (Cullum & Harris, 1996). Hybrid techniques are increasingly employed in clinical applications, e.g., PET combined with CT in the same scan (PET/CT) (Townsend, Beyer, & Blodgett, 2003). These new approaches to combining functional and structural images are still in their infancy with regard to clinical applications and will undoubtedly reflect improved technology over time. Presently, the most common applications involve identification of anatomic or structural problems. The term 'structural' is used to refer not only to identification of abnormal tissue, as in the case of neoplasm, but also to changes involving volume loss (e.g., cerebral atrophy), increased intra- or extracellular volume (e.g., vasogenic versus cytotoxic edema), abnormal ventricular size (e.g., hydrocephalus), inflammation (e.g., meningitis, cerebritis, encephalitis), demyelination or dysmyelination, or focal, multifocal, or diffuse ischemia of any cause, including vasculitis or hypoxia. Also, disorders that interfere with the blood–brain barrier permeability can be investigated and localized using MRI and CT imaging before and after intravenous injection of polar contrast agents (Frey, 2000). When the blood–brain barrier is impaired for any reason, contrast agents enter the surrounding tissue, altering the CT and MRI signals. Increasingly, validity is becoming established for the use of imaging studies to diagnose, or at least to aid in the diagnosis of, disease as well as to monitor the progress of treatment, e.g., in Alzheimer disease (Zakzanis, Graham, & Campbell, 2003). In the context of the clinical neurotoxicology evaluations, imaging studies are used most commonly to exclude other disorders. They are not screening examinations and their use usually is not justified unless there is a demonstrable neurologic impairment or strong suspicion of a structural defect. The latter situation might arise, for instance, when a pattern emerges from formal neuropsychological examination that is strongly suggestive of a localized (focal) neurologic impairment that has been progressive.

In general, there are no conventional CT or MRI imaging abnormalities specific to any given neurotoxicant. There are some imaging abnormalities, however, that can result in a neuroradiology diagnosis of 'toxic leukoencephalopathy' (Filley & Kleinschmidt-DeMasters, 2001). 'Leukoencephalopathy' is the term used to reflect abnormalities of myelin and more general changes in cerebral white matter, and the abnormalities are believed to manifest primarily in neurobehavioral alterations (Filley, Heaton, & Rosenberg, 1990; Filley & Kleinschmidt-DeMasters, 2001). While, as mentioned elsewhere (see Chapter 5, for instance), neurobehavioral symptoms of this type are non-specific, in general the pattern of symptoms and signs associated with leukoencephalopathy mirrors the distribution and severity of white matter abnormality. That is, neurobehavioral or neurologic abnormalities are bilateral and diffuse, with mild cases exhibiting confusion and inattention, memory impairment, and emotional disturbance, without abnormal language function (Filley & Kleinschmidt-DeMasters, 2001). Of course, the differential diagnosis associated with imaging evidence of a toxic leukoencephalopathy includes numerous conditions associated with many different causes.

One of the conditions initially attributed to 'toxic' leukoencephalopathy was chronic and massive exposure to toluene, in the form of 'huffing' (recreational toluene abuse) (Filley, *et al.*, 1990). That situation, possibly in association with unrecognized hypoxia, produced MRI imaging abnormalities of cerebral atrophy and white matter changes characteristic of leukoencephalopathy. Further, the degree of white matter abnormality on MRI significantly correlated with neuropsychological impairments. Nonetheless, other conditions exist that may produce indistinguishable MRI white matter abnormalities, including hereditary and autoimmune demyelinating diseases, progressive multifocal leukoencephalopathy, acquired immune deficiency syndrome (AIDS), vasculitis, normal pressure hydrocephalus, and exposure to leukotoxic therapies including cisplatin or irradiation. Attribution to a toxic etiology from imaging evidence of a leukoencephalopathy will necessitate meeting criteria, such as Hill (1965), in order to establish causation. While objective documentation of neurologic or neurobehavioral deficits (i.e., the results from neuropsychological evaluation) is necessary (Schaumburg & Spencer 1987), the diagnosis of a leukoencephalopathy also requires that the neuroradiological abnormalities be present (Filley & Kleinschmidt-DeMasters, 2001). In the identification of imaging abnormalities characteristic of leukoencephalopathy, the results of MRI are the most sensitive of the imaging techniques because of the ability of MRI to image myelin, distinguish between gray matter and white matter, and identify primary and secondary loss of myelin to an extend which considerably exceeds that of CT (Frey, 2000).

Whereas CT and MRI are the most capable of identifying tissue-type changes associated with volume loss (neurons or myelin), inflammation, hemorrhage, calcification, or ischemia, other imaging techniques are available that evaluate more specifically processes that influence brain activity. SPECT and PET produce brain images that approximate the underlying anatomic structure but, more importantly, these techniques yield functional information, including physiologic changes that occur as a consequence of synaptic transmission (Frey, 2000). A representative PET scan obtained from a patient with Alzheimer disease is shown in Figure 6.9. These specialized functional imaging techniques are of research interest with uncertain sensitivity or specificity in most instances. They have little general application or acceptance for establishing specific diagnoses, and they have no direct role at the present time in identifying neurotoxicity (Frey, 2000). For instance, Alzheimer disease is a disorder primarily of the cerebral gray matter, whereas leukoencephalopathy is a disorder of white matter. Both might result in metabolic alterations, but PET or SPECT would be unlikely to differentiate the distinction between the types of cell involved, whereas MRI is capable of making such a distinction. This situation is likely to change as new technology is developed, e.g., development of new and specific radiolabeled ligands for PET imaging (Goh & Ng, 2003). PET and SPECT both have potential to investigate and reveal important aspects of underlying disease processes that

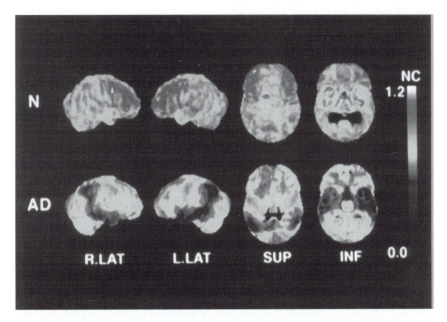

Figure 6.9 Representative position emission tomography (PET) scan obtained from a patient with Alzheimer's disease. In comparison with the normal PET scan shown, the patient's scan reflects relatively extensive, but regionalized, areas of hypometabolic glucose activity (darker areas on the rainbow scale relative to lighter areas). Characteristic of Alzheimer disease (AD), relative hypometabolism is most notable in parietal and temporal brain regions. Note, however, that frontal regions are also affected in this disorder. INF, inferior; L.LAT, left lateral; N, normal metabolic function; R.LAT, right lateral; SUP, superior.

adversely affect metabolism in the brain. Interestingly, all techniques of brain imaging have a degree of non-specificity for a given disease or disorder, especially in the context of neurobehavioral toxicology. As is the case for neuropsychological testing, specificity must be established for certain findings or patterns of findings. At the same time, all of these techniques reflect considerable sensitivity, sometimes to the point that abnormalities can be detected in normal as well as disordered individuals (Frey, 2000). Consider, for example, the frequent observation of non-specific findings of isolated or multifocal white matter hyperintensities, sometimes referred to as unidentified bright objects, on MRI studies among subjects with no known neurological disease (Soderlund, Nyberg, Adolfsson, Nilsson, & Launer, 2003). As in the case of leukoencephalopathy, combining techniques, e.g., findings from neuropsychological examination with MRI, can greatly increase the specificity over either technique alone, especially in the early course of a disease or when symptoms are mild (Berent, Giordani, Foster, Minoshima, Lajiness-O'Neill, Koeppe, & Kuhl, 1999). Further increases in specificity will be possible with enhanced standardization of procedures and protocols and normative patient data (Desmond & Annabel Chen, 2002). These enhancements will be especially important in the context of hybrid approaches that combine two or more imaging techniques together with behavioral variables, measurement and intervention.

Neuropathology

The neurologist frequently uses results obtained from examination of tissue biopsy in arriving at a particular diagnosis. It is not the purpose of this section to describe the methodologies and techniques special to neuropathology. The clinician does need to know, however, when pathological information may be helpful in establishing a final diagnosis, in addition to understanding the diagnostic limitations of the techniques. However, the information obtained from the neuropathological examination of selected tissues is comparable with the information derived from other laboratory test results. This contrasts to the results obtained from the electrophysiological examination, which are considered by most electromyographers to be an extension of the clinical examination. In general, the neuropathological investigation is only pursued after the differential diagnosis has been focused on a relatively small number of possible diagnoses.

In the context of clinical neurotoxicology, the neuropathological examination of selected tissue is most applicable to, but not limited to, disorders of the peripheral nervous system. Standard use of these techniques as diagnostic tools in the evaluation of peripheral neuropathy and myopathy became commonplace in the early 1970s in the USA. In the evaluation of peripheral neuropathy, the neuropathological techniques were refined and advocated by Dyck and associates at the Mayo Clinic. The text on peripheral neuropathy coauthored by Dyck includes information on nerve pathology, and it is generally considered one of the most comprehensive sources of information in the field (Dyck, Thomas, Griffin, Low, & Poduslo, 1993). The application of nerve biopsy in the classification of toxic neuropathies associated with occupational exposures was endorsed by others, including Schaumburg & Spencer (1976), at about the same time. Concerning muscle neuropathology, Engel, a neurologist who, like Dyck, also practiced at the Mayo Clinic, coauthored what is considered by most neurologists to be the premier text on the neuropathology of muscle (Engel & Franzini-Armstrong, 1994). Those interested in the scientific foundation of nerve or muscle pathology, or in the specific techniques used by these neuropathology specialities, are referred to these two texts and the references contained within.

The increased use of muscle biopsy (light microscopy, special staining techniques, and electron microscopy) has advanced our understanding of muscle diseases substantially in the past few decades. These advances have been particularly prominent in terms of developing insights into structure and function at the molecular level in parallel with increased understanding of the molecular genetics of many muscle diseases (Engel & Franzini-Armstrong, 1994). There is substantial information available about the many toxicants, including numerous medications, which produce generalized myopathy (as opposed to local myopathy that occurs with intramuscular injection of some substances) (Victor & Sieb, 1994). The pathological end-points resulting from the various myotoxicants are perhaps more numerous, or at least better understood, than those associated with toxic neuropathy. The pathological endpoints include necrosis of muscle fibers, selective fiber atrophy (e.g, type II muscle fiber atrophy associated with corticosteroids), acute loss of myosin (as in critical illness myopathy), impaired protein synthesis, abnormalities of microtubules, impaired energy generation (mitochondrial myopathies), increased lysosomal storage, and toxin-induced inflammation of muscle or connective tissue (myositis, fasciitis, microangiopathy) (Victor & Sieb, 1994). The pathologist may identify, for example, evidence of muscle cell lysis and necrosis with ongoing regeneration, fiber atrophy, abnormal response to specific stains or fiber-type grouping, abnormal mitochondria with ragged red muscle fibers, vacuolization, phagocytosis, accumulation of abnormal materials, inflammation, alteration of vascular structures, abnormal myofilaments, or fibrosis. The underlying mechanisms of muscle fiber necrosis have been established for some of these conditions and pathological findings. They include ischemia, inadequate delivery of nutrients, excessive energy use, metabolic poisoning (e.g., cyanide), potassium depletion, and a direct effect of the myotoxicant on the muscle cell structure (Victor & Sieb, 1994). Many substances known or believed to cause myopathy are listed in Table 11.2 in Volume II, as modified from Wald (2000).

For many central nervous system disorders, including Parkinson disease and Alzheimer disease, the formal definition of the disease includes the results of the neuropathological examination at the time of autopsy. For other disorders, such as vasculitis, tissue examination is the most definitive means of establishing a conclusive diagnosis. However, issues of sensitivity and specificity are important to the neuropathologist, particularly with regard to tissue biopsy. It is well established that the biopsy specimen does not always include all the information required to establish the appropriate diagnosis.

Conventional clinical pathology laboratory testing

The role of traditional laboratory measures as used by the clinician in the evaluation of suspected neurotoxic disorders relates primarily to identifying systemic disorders associated with neurologic dysfunction. For example, arsenic-induced toxic neuropathy is associated with anemia, pancytopenia, and abnormal liver function tests; and L-tryptophan intoxication is associated with an increased total eosinophil count and evidence of vasculitis (Donofrio *et al.*, 1987; Troy, 1991; Winkelmann, Connolly, Quimby, Gittling, & Lie, 1991; Kamb, Murphy, Jones, Caston, Nederlof, Horney, Swygert,

Falk, & Kilbourne, 1992). Some substances like arsenic and certain metals can be measured in the urine and other tissues (Poklis & Saady, 1990; Windebank, 1993). Unfortunately, the metabolism of most other chemicals is sufficiently rapid to make detection in body tissues difficult. In select situations, surrogates of exposure exist. For example, after acute organophosphate exposure, plasma butyryl (pseudo) cholinesterase and red blood cell AChE levels are reduced when measured soon after poisoning, although neither is directly related to neurotoxicity (Lotti, 1991; Richardson, 1995).

The evaluation of individual laboratory tests of blood and urine is beyond the scope of this chapter. It is important to recognize, however, that the role of random screening is limited and finding an abnormal value does not ensure that the cause has been established as competing explanations commonly exist. Consider, for example, the increased excretion of urinary arsenic or mercury associated with ingestion of some seafood. The commercial availability of numerous tests purporting to associate abnormal antibodies or borderline elevations of trace substances in response to some chemical exposure, for the most part, utilize measures of unknown reproducibility, sensitivity, or specificity. Frequently, control population information is unavailable or undefined. Until further evaluated, application of such measures has unknown utility.

Conclusion

The neurologic examination is a fundamental form of standardized clinical testing capable of detecting clinically important abnormalities in the nervous system. The neurologist routinely interprets symptoms and signs to determine the extent and clinical significance of neurologic dysfunction. The initial information derived from the neurologic evaluation consists of results from the clinical history and the neurologic examination. Most neurologists believe that this information forms virtually all of the information required to identify most neurologic disorders. Importantly, this information is used to develop the differential diagnosis, the first step in identifying the explanation for the patient's problem

References

AAEM Professional Practice Committee (1999). The scope of electrodiagnostic medicine. *Muscle and Nerve, 22*, S5–S12

Albers, J. W. (1993). Clinical neurophysiology of generalized polyneuropathy. *Journal Clinical Neurophysiology, 10*, 149–166.

Albers, J. W. (2002). Neurological assessment: the role of the clinician in clinical neurotoxicology. In R. Masschelein (Ed.), *Neurotoxicology handbook* (pp. 507–549). Totowa: Humana.

Albers, J. W., & Berent, S. (1999). Neurotoxicology. In R. W. Evans (Ed.), *Diagnostic testing in neurology* (pp. 257–271). Philadelphia: W. B. Saunders.

Albers, J. W., & Bromberg, M. B. (1995). Chemically induced toxic neuropathy. In

N. L. Rosenberg (Ed.), *Occupational and environmental neurology* (pp. 175–233). Boston: Butterworth-Heinemann.

Albers, J. W., Brown, M. B., Sima, A. A. F., & Greene, D. A. (1996). Nerve conduction measures in mild diabetic neuropathy: the effects of age, sex, type of diabetes, disease duration, and anthropometric factors. *Neurology, 46*, 85–91.

Albers, J. W., Kallenbach, L. R., Fine, L. J., Langolf, G. D., Wolfe, R. A., Donofrio, P. D., Alessi, A. G., Stolp-Smith, K. A., Bromberg, M. B., & the Mercury Workers Study Group (1988). Neurological abnormalities associated with remote occupational elemental mercury exposure. *Annals of Neurology, 24*, 651–659.

Albers, J. W., & Leonard, J. A., Jr (1992). Nerve conduction studies and electromyography. In A. Crockard, R. Hayward, & J. T. Hoff (Eds.), *Neurosurgery: The scientific basis of clinical practice* (pp. 735–757). Oxford: Blackwell.

Albin, R. L., Albers, J. W., Greenberg, H. S., Townsend, J. B., Lynn, R. B., Burke, J. M. J., & Alessi, A. G. (1987). Acute sensory neuropathy-neuronopathy from pyridoxine overdose. *Neurology, 37*, 1729–1732.

American Association of Electrodiagnostic Medicine (1992). Guidelines in electrodiagnostic medicine. *Muscle and Nerve, 15*, 229–253.

American Association of Electromyography and Electrodiagnosis (1984). *Guidelines in electrodiagnostic medicine*. Rochester: AAEE.

Aminoff, M. J., & Albers, J. W. (1999). Electrophysiologic techniques in the evaluation of patients with suspected neurotoxic disorders. In M. J. Aminoff (Ed.), *Electrodiagnosis in clinical neurology* (pp. 721–734). New York: Churchill Livingstone.

Barondess, J. A., & Carpenter, C. C. J. (1994). *Differential diagnosis*. Philadelphia: Lea & Febiger.

Berent, S., Giordani, B., Foster, N., Minoshima, S., Lajiness-O'Neill, R., Koeppe, R., & Kuhl, D. E. (1999). Neuropsychological function and cerebral glucose utilization in isolated memory impairment and Alzheimer's disease. *Journal of Psychiatric Research, 33*, 7–16.

Bolton, C. F., & Carter, K. M. (1980). Human sensory nerve compound action potential amplitudes: variation with sex and finger circumference. *Journal of Neurology, Neurosurgery and Psychiatry, 43*, 925–928.

Cornblath, D. R., Chaudhry, V., Carter, K., Lee, D., Seysedadr, M., Miernicki, M., & Joh, T. (1999). Total neuropathy score. Validation and reliability study. *Neurology, 53*, 1660–1664.

Crum, R. M., Anthony, J. C., Bassett, S. S., & Folstein, M. F. (1993). Population-based norms for the Mini-Mental State Examination by age and educational level. *Journal of the American Medical Association, 269*, 2386–2391.

Cullum, C. M. & Harris, J. G. (1996). Neuroimaging, neurophysiological, and neurobehavioral techniques. In E. D. Bigler (Ed.), *Neuroimaging II: Clinical applications* (pp. 11–24). New York: Plenum.

Daube, J. R. (1987). Electrophysiologic testing in diabetic neuropathy. In P. J. Dyck, P. K. Thomas, A. K. Asbury, A. I. Winegrad, & D. Porte, Jr (Eds.), *Diabetic neuropathy* (pp. 162–176). Philadelphia: W. B. Saunders.

Daube, J. R., Westmorland, B., Sandok, B. A., & Reagan, T. (1986). *Medical neurosciences. An approach to anatomy, pathology, and physiology by systems and levels* (2nd ed.). Boston: Little, Brown.

Dejong, R. N. (1979). *The neurologic examination* (4th ed.). New York: Harper & Row.

Desmond, J. E., & Annabel Chen, S. H. (2002). Ethical issues in the clinical application of fMRI: factors affecting the validity and interpretation of activations. *Brain and Cognition*, *50*, 482–497.

Donofrio, P. D., & Albers, J. W. (1990). Polyneuropathy: classification by nerve conduction studies and electromyography. *Muscle and Nerve*, *13*, 889–903.

Donofrio, P. D., Wilbourn, A. J., Albers, J. W., Rogers, L., Salanga, V., & Greenberg, H. S. (1987). Acute arsenic intoxication presenting as Guillain–Barré-like syndrome. *Muscle and Nerve*, *10*, 114–120.

Dyck, P. J. (1982). Current concepts in neurology. The causes, classification, and treatment of peripheral neuropathy. *New England Journal of Medicine*, *307*, 283–286.

Dyck, P. J., Grant, I. A., & Fealey, R. D. (1996). Ten steps in characterizing and diagnosing patients with peripheral neuropathy. *Neurology*, *47*, 10–17.

Dyck, P. J., Karnes, J. L., O'Brien, P. C., Litchy, W. J., Low, P. A., & Melton, L. J. (1992). The Rochester Diabetic Neuropathy Study: reassessment of tests and criteria for diagnosis and staged severity. *Neurology*, *42*, 1164–1170.

Dyck, P. J., Kratz, K. M., Lehman, K. A., Karnes, J. L., Melton, L. J., O'Brien, P. C., Litchy, W. J., Windebank, A. J., Smith, B. E., & Low, P. A. (1991). The Rochester Diabetic Neuropathy Study: design, criteria for types of neuropathy, selection bias, and reproducibility of neuropathic tests. *Neurology*, *41*, 799–807.

Dyck, P. J., Litchy, W. J., Lehman, K. A., Hokanson, J. L., Low, P. A., & O'Brien, P. C. (1995). Variables influencing neuropathic endpoints: the Rochester Diabetic Neuropathy Study of Healthy Subjects. *Neurology*, *45*, 1115–1121.

Dyck, P. J., Thomas, P. K., Griffin, J. W., Low, P. A., & Poduslo, J. F. (1993). *Peripheral neuropathy*. Philadelphia: W. B. Saunders.

Eddy, D. M., & Clanton, C. H. (1982). The art of diagnosis. Solving the clinicopathological exercise. *New England Journal of Medicine*, *306*, 1263–1268.

Engel, A. G. & Franzini-Armstrong, C. (1994). *Myology: basic and clinical* (2nd ed.). New York: McGraw-Hill.

Esteban, A. (1999). A neurophysiological approach to brainstem reflexes. Blink reflex. *Neurophysiologie Clinique*, *29*, 7–38.

Filley, C. M., Heaton, R. K., & Rosenberg, N. L. (1990). White matter dementia in chronic toluene abuse. *Neurology*, *40*, 532–534.

Filley, C. M., & Kleinschmidt-DeMasters, B. K. (2001). Toxic leukoencephalopathy. *New England Journal of Medicine*, *345*, 425–432.

Folstein, M. F., Folstein, S. E., & McHugh, P. R. (1975). 'Mini-mental state'. A practical method for grading the cognitive state of patients for the clinician. *Journal of Psychiatric Research*, *12*, 189–198.

Fraser, C. L., & Arieff, A. I. (1985). Hepatic encephalopathy. *New England Journal of Medicine*, *313*, 865–873.

Frey, K. A. (2000). Neuroimaging in neurotoxicology. In J. W. Albers and S. Berent (Eds.), *Clinical neurobehavioral neurotoxicology* (pp. 615–629). Philadelphia: W. B. Saunders.

Gelb, D. J. (1995). *Introduction to clinical neurology*. Boston: Butterworth-Heineman.

Gilman, S. (1999). *Clinical examination of the nervous system*. New York: McGraw-Hill.

Goh, A. S., & Ng, D. C. (2003). Clinical positron emission tomography imaging – current applications. *Annals of the Academy of Medicine (Singapore)*, *32*, 507–517.

Hill, A. B. (1965). The environment and disease: association or causation. *Proceedings of the Royal Society of Medicine*, *58*, 295–300.

Jacobs, L., & Gossman, D. (1980). Three primitive reflexes in normal adults. *Neurology*, *30*, 184–188.

Kamb, M. L., Murphy, J. J., Jones, J. L., Caston, J. C., Nederlof, K., Horney, L. F., Swygert, L. A., Falk, H., & Kilbourne, E. M. (1992). Eosinophilia-myalgia syndrome in L-tryptophan-exposed patients. *Journal of the American Medical Association*, *267*, 77–82.

Kassirer, J. P. (1992). Clinical problem-solving – a new feature in the Journal. *New England Journal of Medicine*, *326*, 60–61.

Kimura, J. (1989). The blink reflex. In *Electrodiagnosis in diseases of nerve and muscle: Principles and practice* (pp. 307–331). Philadelphia: F. A. Davis.

Langston, J. W., Ballard, P. A., Tetrud, J. W., & Irwin, I. (1984). Chronic parkinsonism in humans due to a product of meperidine-analog synthesis. *Science*, *11*, 160–165.

Lerman, B. B., Ali, N., & Green, D. (1980). Megaloblastic, dyserythropoietic anemia following arsenic ingestion. *Annals of Clinical and Laboratory Science*, *10*, 515–517.

Lotti, M. (1991). The pathogenesis of organophosphate polyneuropathy. *Critical Reviews in Toxicology*, *21*, 465–487.

Massey, J. M. (1990). Electromyography in disorders of neuromuscular transmission. *Seminars in Neurology*, *10*, 6–11.

Mayo Clinic and Mayo Foundation (1981). *Clinical examinations in neurology* (5th ed.). Philadelphia: W. B. Saunders.

McCombe, P. F., Fairbank, J. C. T., Cockersole, B. C., & Pynsent, P. B. (1989). Reproducibiity of physical signs in low-back pain. *Spine*, *14*, 908–918.

McFarland, H. F., & Dhib Jalbut, S. (1989). Multiple sclerosis: possible immunological mechanisms. *Clinical Immunology and Immunopathology*, *50*, S96–105.

Medical Research Council (1943). *Aids to the investigation of peripheral nerve injuries.* War Memorandum No. 7 (revd 2nd ed.). London: HMSO.

Miller, A. S., Willard, V., Kline, K., Tarpley, S., Guillotte, J., Lawler, F. H., & Pendell, G. M. (1998). Absence of longitudinal changes in rheumatologic parameters after silicone breast implantation: a prospective 13-year study. *Plastic and Reconstructive Surgery*, *102*, 2299–2303.

O'Brien, P. C., & Dyck, P. J. (1995). Procedures for setting normal values. *Neurology*, *45*, 17–23.

Ozdemir, C., & Young, R. R. (1976). The results to be expected from electrical testing in the diagnosis of myasthenia gravis. *Annals of the New York Academy of Sciences*, *274*, 203–225.

Pauker, S. G., & Kopelman, R. I. (1992). Clinical problem-solving. Trapped by an incidental finding. *New England Journal of Medicine*, *326*, 40–43.

Poklis, A., & Saady, J. J. (1990). Arsenic poisoning: acute or chronic? Suicide or murder? *American Journal of Forensic Medicine and Pathology*, *11*, 226–232.

Potvin, A. R., Tourtellotte, W. W., Pew, R. W., & Albers, J. W. (1973). Motivation and learning in the quantitative examination of neurological function. *Archives of Physical Medicine and Rehabilitation*, *54*, 432–440.

Reuler, J. B., Girard, D. E., & Cooney, T. G. (1985). Wernicke's encephalopathy. *New England Journal of Medicine*, *312*, 1035–1039.

Richardson, R. J. (1995). Assessment of the neurotoxic potential of chlorpyrifos relative to other organophosphorus compounds: a critical review of the literature. *Journal of Toxicology and Environmental Health*, *44*, 135–165.

Rivner, M. H., Swift, T. R., Crout, B. O., & Rhodes, K. P. (1990). Toward more rational nerve conduction interpretations: the effect of height. *Muscle and Nerve, 13*, 232–239.

Sanders, D. B., & Stalberg, E. V. (1996). AAEM Minimonograph #25: Single-fiber electromyography. *Muscle and Nerve, 19*, 1069–1083.

Schaumburg, H. H., Kaplan, J., Windebank, A. J., Vick, N., Rasmus, S., Pleasure, D., & Brown, M. J. (1983). Sensory neuropathy from pyridoxine abuse: a new mega-vitamin syndrome. *New England Journal of Medicine, 309*, 445–448.

Schaumburg, H. H., & Spencer, P. S. (1976). The neurology and neuropathology of occupational neuropathies. *Journal of Occupational Medicine, 18*, 739–742.

Schaumburg, H. H. & Spencer, P. S. (1987). Recognizing neurotoxic disease. *Neurology, 37*, 276–278.

Scully, R. E. (1984). Case records of MGH. *New England Journal of Medicine, 311*, 1170–1177.

Scully, R. E., Mark, E. J., & McNeely, B. U. (1986). Case records of the Massachusetts General Hospital. Case 33–1986. *New England Journal of Medicine, 315*, 503–508.

Shahani, B. T., Halperin, J. J., Bolu, P., & Cohen, J. (1984). Sympathetic skin responses – a method of assessing unmyelinated axon dysfunction in peripheral neuropathies. *Journal of Neurology, Neurosurgery and Psychiatry, 47*, 536–542.

Small, G. W., & Borus, J. F. (1983). Outbreak of illness in a school chorus. Toxic poisoning or mass hysteria? *New England Journal of Medicine, 308*, 632–635.

Soderlund, H., Nyberg, L., Adolfsson, R., Nilsson, L. G., & Launer, L. J. (2003). High prevalence of white matter hyperintensities in normal aging: relation to blood pressure and cognition. *Cortex, 39*, 1093–1105.

Spencer, P. S., & Schaumburg, H. H. (1976). Central peripheral distal axonopathy – the pathology of dying-back polyneuropathies. In H. Zimmrman (Ed.), *Progress in neuropathology*, Vol. III (pp. 253–250). New York: Grune & Grune-Stratton.

Stalberg, E., Ekstedt, J., & Broman, A. (1974). Neuromuscular transmission in myasthenia gravis studied with single fibre electromyography. *Journal of Neurology, Neurosurgery and Psychiatry, 37*, 540–547.

Stang, P. E., Yanagihara, T., Swanson, J. W., & Beard, C. M. (1992). Incidence of migraine headache: a population-based study in Olmsted County, Minnesota. *Neurology, 42*, 1657–1662.

Sterman, A. B. (1985). Toxic neuropathy (Editorial). *Mayo Clinic Proceedings, 60*, 59–61.

Stetson, D. S., Albers, J. W., Silverstein, B. A., & Wolfe, R. A. (1992). Effects of age, sex, and anthropometric factors on nerve conduction measures. *Muscle and Nerve, 15*, 1095–1104.

Tourtellotte, W. W., & Syndulko, K. (1989). Quantifying the neurologic examination: principles, constraints, and opportunities. In T. L. Munsat (Ed.), *Quantification of neurologic deficit* (pp. 7–16). Boston: Butterworths.

Townsend, D. W., Beyer, T., & Blodgett, T. M. (2003). PET/CT scanners: a hardware approach to image fusion. *Seminars in Nuclear Medicine, 33*, 193–204.

Trojaborg, W. T., Moon, A., Andersen, B. B., & Trojaberg, N. S. (1992). Sural nerve conduction parameters in normal subjects related to age, gender, temperature, and height: a reappraisal, *Muscle and Nerve, 15*, 666–671.

Troy, J. L. (1991). Eosinophilia-myalgia syndrome. *Mayo Clinic Proceedings, 66*, 535–538.

Victor, M. (1989). Neurologic disorders due to alcoholism and malnutrition. In R. J. Joynt (Ed.), *Clinical neurology* (pp. 1–94). Philadelphia: J. B. Lippincott.

Victor, M., Adams, R. D., & Collins, G. H. (1989). *The Wernicke–Korsakoff syndrome and related neurologic disorders due to alcholism and malnutrition.* Philadelphia: F. A. Davis.

Victor, M., & Sieb, J. P. (1994). Myopathies due to drugs, toxins, and nutritional deficiency. In A. G. Engel and C. Franzini-Armstrong (Eds.), *Myology. Basic and clinical* (2nd ed.) (pp. 1697–1725). New York: McGraw-Hill.

Vogel, H.-P. (1992). Influence of additional information on interrater reliability in the neurologic examination. *Neurology, 42,* 2076–2081.

Wald, J. J. (2000). The effects of toxins on muscle. In J. W. Albers and S. Berent (Eds.), *Neurology clinics. Clinical neurobehavioral toxicology* (pp 695–717). Philadelphia: W. B. Saunders.

Windebank, A. J. (1993). Metal neuropathy. In P. J. Dyck, P. K. Thomas, J. W. Griffin, P. A. Low, & J. F. Poduslo (Eds.), *Peripheral neuropathy* (pp. 1549–1570). Philadelphia: W. B. Saunders.

Winkelmann, R. K., Connolly, S. M., Quimby, S. R., Gittling, W. L., & Lie, J. T. (1991). Histopathologic features of the L-tryptophan-related eosinophilia-myalgia (fasciitis) syndrome. *Mayo Clinic Proceedings, 66,* 457–463.

Zakzanis, K. K., Graham, S. J., & Campbell, Z. (2003). A meta-analysis of structural and functional brain imaging in dementia of the Alzheimer's type: a neuroimaging profile. *Neuropsychology Review, 13,* 1–18.

7 Critique of relevant clinical tests

Introduction

The clinical evaluation of a person within the neurobehavioral toxicological context includes traditional clinical approaches, e.g., neurological and neuropsychological examinations. These applications began to be formalized near the end of the 19th century and developed out of clinical–pathological correlation that related the signs of clinical examination to observed neuropathological findings. While the two approaches, Neurology and Neuropsychology, reflect different historical roots, their histories overlap in many respects. Also, both fields rely on clinical examinations that are similar in many ways but different in others (see Chapters 5 and 6 for more detail regarding these two approaches). The neurologic examination is highly standardized and reproducible, with known sensitivity and specificity for many disorders. The neuropsychological examination includes history and interview and employs psychometric devices within a highly standardized context. In both Neurology and Neuropsychology, there are limitations to the efficacy of the direct clinical examination, and a variety of clinical tests have come to supplement the clinical examination (Albers, 1990; Junck, Albers, & Drury, 2000). In this chapter, we discuss and critique the tests that are most often employed in one or both of these clinical approaches.

It is generally assumed that most neurodiagnostic tests are more sensitive or specific than the clinical examinations. This assumption is not always correct. Most clinicians recognize that the sensitivity attributed to most 'new' tests appears 'too good to be true', and usually this proves to be the case. Likewise, the experienced clinician recognizes the lack of specificity inherent in many tests and procedures, and tempers the interpretation of results accordingly. The true value of any new test or procedure becomes clear only after extensive application and study. Therefore, the results derived from any diagnostic test are of limited value until the test itself has been evaluated. At a minimum, the sensitivity and specificity of the measure must be known within the context that it will be used before it can be meaningfully applied clinically. Reproducibility and knowledge of the rates of 'false-positive' and 'false-negative' findings are important, as is information about the effects of experience (i.e., practice effects) for any quantitative test measuring a neurological variable. Tests do not necessarily have to be specific to be clinically useful, but knowledge about technical factors such as specificity, and lack of specificity, is critical to the proper use of diagnostic tests. Neuropsychological tests, for example, are non-specific for many of their intended uses. That is, a test of intelligence is specific by definition to 'intelligence', but it is non-specific to any of the multiple substrates of intelligence, e.g., educational attainment, motivation, neurological dysfunction, and so on. Nevertheless, by knowing the validity, reliability, and extent of practice effect, such a measure can contribute importantly to diagnostic conclusions. It is imperative, therefore, that the clinician be informed not only about the availability of tests in order to select appropriate measures, but also about the quality of the information derived from a given test so as to interpret the results properly.

Many neurodiagnostic tests are available to the clinician. These include measures of cognition, affect, and psychomotor performance; electro-physiological evaluation of the central and peripheral nervous systems; imagery of anatomic structure and metabolism, and histopathological examination of nerve, muscle, and other tissues. Ancillary laboratory studies are available to evaluate the concentration of specific substances or their metabolites in blood, urine, hair, nails, and cerebrospinal fluid. The high specificity of some neurodiagnostic tests relative to the clinical examination allows use of the results to refine the differential diagnosis, eliminating some items from consideration or adding new items that had not been considered. However, all neurodiagnostic tests have limitations.

The major limitation of all neurodiagnostic studies involves misapplication or misinterpretation of test results. For example, minor deviations from normal may or may not have clinical relevance. Indiscriminate use of neurodiagnostic tests in suspected occupational or environmental disorders is inconsistent with their intended application. This is because few neurodiagnostic tests are capable of establishing the cause of a neurologic problem, and claims to the contrary should be viewed suspiciously. Few neurotoxic disorders have sufficiently characteristic or cardinal neuropathologic or electrophysiologic features to make test results diagnostic of a single problem. For those tests with high specificity for a given neurologic disorder, the disorder typically has more than one possible cause. For example, detecting an elevated acetylcholine receptor antibody (AChR Ab) level is almost pathognomonic for myasthenia gravis, an idiopathic immune-mediated disease of the neuromuscular junction. Yet, a disorder with clinical, physiological, and immunological features indistinguishable from idiopathic myasthenia is associated with exposure to penicillamine. The only distinguishing feature between the two disorders is resolution of penicillamine-induced myasthenia within months of discontinuing penicillamine.

Finally, most of the neurodiagnostic tests discussed below had their origin in the evaluation of individual patients. Application to groups of subjects is common in epidemiological studies. However, reports of subclinical group differences identified in cross-sectional studies of suspected neurotoxic disorders should be interpreted cautiously because of numerous confounders that influence such data (see Chapter 3).

Psychometric examination (neuropsychological testing)

The word 'psychometric' refers to the measurement of psychological attributes, and the psychometric examination is that part of the neuropsychological evaluation that employs formal tests and related procedures to quantify objectively the individual's behavior in a number of key areas (Table 5.1). The overall neuropsychological evaluation and its psychometric component were discussed in more detail in Chapter 5. As reflected in that chapter, the use of psychometrics represents a powerful tool that can be applied by the clinician to characterize objectively and systematically an individual's functional strengths and weaknesses and to use in developing the differential diagnosis and other aspects of the clinical process. When properly applied, a neuropsychological test provides for the collection of behavioral data that can be applied to clinically relevant questions (see Chapters 3 and 4). A critical question in determining the presence of dementia, for instance, is to determine objectively the patient's current level of cognitive functioning. While the identification of memory or other cognitive impairment may be obvious from clinical observation in many instances, a systematic, standardized, and objective approach is most often required to document formally such impairments. This is true especially when the manifestation of impairment is mild (American Academy of Neurology, 2001). We are emphasizing the clinical applications of these tests and procedures, but the standardized approach required in the use of neuropsychological tests make them valuable for research, prospective and retrospective, as well as for clinical applications.

Neuropsychological testing has become in many people's minds synonymous with the practice of neuropsychology. As emphasized in Chapter 5, however, the psychometric examination is but one part of the overall neuropsychological evaluation. As disciplines other than Psychology have come to discover the value of psychometrics to their own clinical work, individuals in these fields have come to view neuropsychological tests as another additional test to complement their own clinical examination. This attitude is not dramatically different from that of the neuropsychologist, who views these tests as that part of the evaluation that objectively addresses the clinical hypotheses and initial differential diagnoses that were formulated on the basis of the psychologist's clinical interview and history.

To complete the psychometric part of the evaluation, however, specific and appropriate tests must be chosen (Boll, 2000; Berent & Trask, 2000; Lezak, 1995). These tests must then be administered by a properly trained and supervised individual and the results interpreted by an appropriately trained and credentialed professional (Division 40 Task Force on Education, 1989). These and other technical requirements make neuropsychological testing labor intensive. In actuality, this labor intensity is no greater than that associated with many other tests discussed in this chapter. The seemingly simple nature of neuropsychological testing, however, has led at times to the application of these tests by persons not properly trained in their administration, interpretation, or even the criteria to use in deciding on a given test. The user of neuropsychological test results, therefore, should take care to ensure that the results and interpretations of those results were arrived at properly before applying them clinically. The best way to accomplish this is to ensure that a properly licenced psychologist with specialty board certification in neuropsychology report the results in a manner consistent with published professional standards (American Psychological Association, 1985).

As discussed in Chapter 5, a collection of specific tests is referred to as a 'test battery'. By historical precedent, psychologists have tended to assign names to the various batteries they employ. These names have been based on a variety of considerations. Sometimes, the name of a specific battery has been based on historical importance, e.g., 'The Halstead–Reitan Neuropsychological Test Battery' (Reitan & Wolfson, 1993). At other times, the name was chosen because of the subject area in which a given professional might be working. Someone interested in psychiatric disturbance, for instance, might refer to the collection of tests being employed as the 'Anxiety Battery'. Some test batteries have been developed with the intent they be used specifically to evaluate a given clinical area. One such area is neurotoxicology, and a number of batteries have been described as having some special relevance to this topic, e.g., the 'Individual Neuropsychological Test for Neurotoxicity', and 'World Health Organization Neurobehavioral Core Test Battery'. As emphasized by Boll (2000), none of these batteries has been validated with specific independent neurological or chemical criteria to claim that they specifically identify impairments as a result of exposure to chemicals. It is important to note, therefore, that while neuropsychological tests are sensitive measures of behavior, they are not specific to any given disease or disorder. The data derived from psychometric examination are useful clinically to the extent that they are considered within a framework of differential diagnosis and with consideration of information obtained from clinical interview, history, and other clinical tests and reports.

An important limitation of the neuropsychological examination is the lack of specificity, both in terms of the particular clinical diagnosis and the ultimate cause of the problem. Neuropsychological tests present an excellent approach to the measurement of behavior. The results of these tests provide the clinician with objective and quantified data that can be combined with other aspects of the clinical evaluation to arrive at diagnostic and other clinical conclusions. These test data in isolation, however, can never be more specific to pathophysiology than are the behaviors they measure. Since neuropsychological tests are not specific to neurologic dysfunction, other factors in addition to brain function must be considered in arriving at a conclusion about what caused a low score on a given test. As discussed in

Chapter 5, two factors to consider are the person's attention and motivation at the time of the testing. A person's attention, for example, might vary from moment to moment for a variety of reasons. These reasons might include the individual's mental approach to a particular test, or type of test, momentary distractions caused by external events, or even thoughts the person might be having at that instant. The influence of motivation is important because these tests are volitional in nature. As a result, accurate performance on the test depends not only on the person's ability to complete the tasks presented, but also on the person's cooperation and effort. The individual's motivation, therefore, is extremely important in the neuropsychological examination, and motivation can even explain a given test score in part or in whole. A variety of factors can influence a person's motivation in taking a series of tests. These factors might include how much rest the person had before entering the test situation, the person's attentiveness on a given occasion, whether they are hungry or thirsty, the extent and nature of rapport established by the examiner, general mood, and being involved in litigation (Berent & Trask, 2000). Malingering, of course, can also be a motivational factor, but the patient need not be consciously attempting to do poorly on a test to obtain a low score because of poor motivation. Depression, anxiety, thought disturbance, and a variety of other psychological or psychiatric disturbances can adversely affect a person's motivation and, as a consequence and without conscious intent, test performance.

Despite these areas of potential and actual relative weaknesses, neuropsychological testing, when properly employed, represents a valuable component to the clinical evaluation in neurobehavioral toxicology. In many instances, these tests and procedures are critical to differentiating amongst the many possible contributions to a clinical picture in order to arrive at a final diagnosis. While a given test score is not specific to disease or disorder, validity can at times be established for a pattern of scores, within a test battery, or in terms of changes from one examination to the next. These patterns can then be used as criteria to define some clinically relevant entity, e.g., impaired mental status. Even at those times that neuropsychological tests do not speak to the etiology of a patient's disorder, the results can provide an important functional description of the person's present condition. This information can then be used as a basis for an effective clinical management plan.

Neuroimaging

The development and refinement of procedures that apply principles from Physics, Chemistry, Engineering, and other basic science disciplines to image the nervous system has been explosive over the last two decades. The introduction of these tests has had a profound impact on research and clinical practices. Less than 30 years ago, a book such as ours would have made no more than a brief mention of the majority of these techniques. Some of the techniques did not exist at all. Today, imaging is commonplace, and as a result, the literature on this topic has expanded enormously. Since we will not be able to provide extensive detail about the various imaging techniques discussed here and throughout these volumes, the reader may wish to consult one or more of the numerous texts concerned directly with the topic. A few suggested references include E.D. Bigler's two-volume work on neuroimaging (Bigler, 1996a, 1996b), R.B. Buxton's text on functional magnetic resonance imaging (MRI) (Buxton, 2002), and R.L. Van Heertum's and R.S. Tikofsky's book on functional position emission tomography (PET) and single position emission computed tomography (SPECT) imaging (Van Heertum & Tikofsky, 2000). For more information on the early history of the development of brain imaging, see the reviews by Oldendorf (1980) and Eisenberg (1992).

Techniques for practical imaging of the brain were for many years limited to angiography and pneumoencephalography. Methods and devices for brain imaging, however, have made progressive and substantial advances since the introduction of computed tomography (CT or CAT) in the mid-1970s (Housenfield, 1972) and magnetic resonance (MR) in the early 1980s (Doyle, Gore, Pennock, Bydder, Orr, Steiner, Young, Burl, Clow, Gilderdale, Bailes, & Walters, 1981; Young, Hall, Pallis, Legg, Bydder, & Steiner, 1981). The development of the various techniques to image the brain was described by Ungerleider (1995) as 'explosive', and the ability to image aspects of the nervous system with these methodologies has provided a collection of tools that were never before available. Advances in the field of neuroimaging have had a profound impact on the clinical practices of both Medicine and Psychology in general and Neurology and Neuropsychology specifically. While there is still much to learn about these techniques and the interpretations of the data they produce, neuroimaging has become the gold standard for answering a host of clinical as well as research-related questions. In many instances, this includes the determination of the presence and location of lesions in the nervous system, the nature of pathology, the detection of asymptomatic lesions, as well as confirmation of initial clinical diagnoses more generally (Frey, 2000).

In addition to CT (Lee & Rao, 1997), some techniques often used for brain imaging include MRI (Budinger & Lauterbur, 1984; Lee & Rao, 1997), functional magnetic resonance imaging (fMRI) (Bandettini, Wong, Hinks, Tikofsky, & Hyde, 1992; Kim & Ugurbil, 1997), PET (Reivich, Kuhl, Wolf, Greenberg, Phelps, Ido, Casella, Fowler, Hoffman, Alavi, Sou, & Sokoloff, 1979; Phelps, Mazziotta, & Schelbert, 1986; Frey, 1999), and SPECT (Sorenson & Phelps, 1987). The data derived from these various techniques reflect primarily structural or functional aspects of the nervous system, depending on the nature of the device. Both CT and MRI, for instance, produce data that are especially useful in the identification of structural aspects of the nervous system. Each, CT and MRI, has special characteristics that leave them favored in specified situations. MRI, with its superior resolution over CT, is often favored in studies where certain abnormalities of the nervous system are suspected, such as differentiating between gray matter and white matter, identify primary and secondary loss of myelin, or identifying mild cerebral atrophy; but CT is seen as being superior to MRI in specific instances, such as demonstrating hemorrhage or calcification (Frey, 2000). PET, SPECT, and fMRI are capable of imaging functional aspects of the nervous system through measurement of physical or chemical aspects of neurotransmission. These capabilities make these techniques extremely valuable in clinical cases where changes, especially early in the course of disease, in motor, sensory, or higher cognitive processes are suspected, e.g., Huntington disease (Young, Penney, Starosta-Rubinstein, Markel, Berent, Giordani, Ehrenkauter, Jewett, & Hichwa 1986).

The phenomenon upon which MRI rests was first described in the mid-1940s (Bloch, Hansen, & Packard, 1946; Purcell, Taurry, & Pound, 1946). To create an image, MRI uses the principle that protons have a magnetic moment when they are arranged randomly, i.e., when these nuclei are at rest and the only influence on them is the Earth's magnetic field. By systematically exposing these protons to a magnetic field of specified strength (e.g., 0.02–1.5 tesla), they become aligned with this field. The magnetic moment is displaced by a radiowave. When allowed to return to their original state, the movement of the nuclei is measured in relation to several parameters. These measurements then are used to reconstruct an image of whatever structure these nuclei represent (i.e., some portion of the brain) (Young *et al.*, 1981; Freer, 1994).

fMRI is a relatively new but promising technique for brain imaging (Bandettini *et al.*, 1992). Like PET, fMRI produces a functional picture of the brain. It can be used to study brain activation in response to the systematic presentation of various stimuli. A potential advantage to the use of fMRI over PET lies in its greater magnitude of spatial resolution. This superior resolution might be critical when there is a need to image relatively small neuronal structures, i.e., structures that may be no larger than 2–4 mm in size. Nevertheless, a resolution capacity of 2 mm may be limited when the physiological mechanism of interest is even smaller (Ungerleider, 1995). As pointed out by Ungerleider, one should recognize that PET, which provides measures of blood flow and metabolism, and fMRI, which quantifies blood oxygenation, both reflect only indirect measures of neuronal activity. The relationship between functional images and neuroanatomy is also indirect and limited by the effectiveness of the model of structural mapping that is employed. In meeting the challenge of mapping, fMRI may have an advantage over PET since structural and functional data can be collected at one time. An added step of indexing to a different machine is required to achieve similar information with PET. We noted earlier that developments in neuroimaging have been fast paced. As a result, it is difficult to make absolute statements about the ultimate capabilities or limitations of these techniques. Magnetic resonance spectroscopy (MRS), for instance, is a relatively new technique that uses MRI to define brain regions (and specified regions in other organ systems) and then measures the concentration of specific biochemical compounds in these regions, providing information about structure as well as brain metabolism similar to PET (Novotny, Fulbright, Pearl, Gibson, & Rothman, 2003). Also, advances in PET technology have greatly enhanced spatial resolution over what was capable only a few years before, allowing the possibility for imaging on a molecular level (Jacobs, *et al.*, 2003).

MRI and CT primarily provide structural information by measuring the density of protons in MRI, and through indirect measurement of density by quantification of X-ray stopping power with CT (Frackowiak, 1986). In contrast, the image produced by PET is functional. PET measures an aspect of metabolism that is determined by the radiolabeled ligand used, and the resulting image reflects only a coincidental correspondence to structure. Although its theoretical history is older, the use of PET to produce practical images of the nervous system resulted from the work of Sokoloff and his colleagues (Sokoloff, Reivich, Kennedy, Des Rosiers, Patlak, Pettigrew, Sakurada, & Shirohara, 1977) and their development of the radioactive deoxyglucose method for the measurement of local cerebral glucose utilization. The methodology of PET rests on an autoradiographic technique that uses a radiolabeled ligand such as $[^{14}C]$ or $[^{18}F]$ deoxyglucose. Deoxyglucose mimics glucose in cell transport but differs in that deoxyglucose does not undergo glycolysis. A multicompartment model is used to translate the ligand's uptake and metabolism within the target structure. A theoretical model is then applied to the data to produce an image of greater and lesser metabolic activity in terms of relative brain location (Sokoloff *et al.*, 1977; Frackowiak, Lenzi, Jones, & Heather, 1980; Sokoloff, 1983; Freer, 1994).

SPECT is similar to PET in that it also involves the systematic delivery of a radiotracer. An image of the brain is created that reflects the distribution of the tracer in relation to its assimilation by tissue through which it passes (Frey, 2000). A number of different radionuclides can be employed as tracers for use with SPECT, but they are limited by their ability to pass through the body and to be detected externally. The nuclide must be of sufficient half-life to result in an acceptably safe level of radiation exposure to the patient (Frey, 2000). While the two techniques, SPECT and PET, share many similarities, PET is in most instances seen as superior to SPECT because of its greater detection sensitivity as well as in the availability of a greater range of radiotracers. Both techniques are limited by the fact that they involve exposure of the patient to radiation. While the amount of exposure is small, repeat scanning, as is often required to render a firm clinical conclusion, can result in substantially higher doses.

From a clinical viewpoint, standard clinical imaging techniques are most useful for identifying anatomic or structural abnormalities in the central nervous system. With regard more specifically to neurotoxicology evaluations, imaging studies are typically used to exclude other disorders in the process of forming a final impression. These examinations are not intended for general screening, and their use is seldom justified unless there is a demonstrable neurologic impairment or strong suspicion of a defect that could be revealed by the procedure. This is because, as in any disorder producing neuronal death, the abnormalities may not be immediately apparent, but develop sequentially after the initial injury. CT and MRI imaging studies are obtained in response to a clinical suspicion that a structural abnormality exists, and indiscriminate use as screening evaluations is never justified. Nevertheless, imaging studies are often important in the evaluation of patients with central nervous system disorders potentially related to exposure to neurotoxicants.

When there is suspicion of neurotoxicity, it is important to identify procedures capable of providing objective evidence of neuronal loss as well as to identify disorders other than neurotoxic exposure to account for the neurological and neuropsychological findings. Both CT and MRI are capable of identifying structural abnormalities in the nervous system. Also, both are sensitive to disorders that lead to cerebral atrophy. These test attributes are important for neurotoxicological evaluations because, depending on the location and extent of involvement, any neurotoxicant that produces neuronal death has the potential to produce symmetrical atrophy that can be identified by these imaging studies.

In contrast to findings of symmetrical atrophy, unilateral abnormalities cannot be attributed to toxic exposure. Structural imaging studies of patients with acute encephalopathy are unremarkable unless there is a pre-existing abnormality. When chronic encephalopathy is of sufficient magnitude, the abnormalities on imaging studies will reflect the magnitude of neuronal loss. Depending on the magnitude, duration, and site of damage, a spectrum of imaging abnormalities exist (Kinkel, Jacobs, & Kinkel, 1980; Tippin, Adams, & Smoker, 1984; Young, 1984; Varnell, Stimac, & Fligner, 1987; Eisenberg, Gary, Aldrich, Saydjari, Turner, Foulkes, Jane, Marmarou, Marshall, & Young 1990; Latchaw & Truwit, 1995; Van der Knaap, Jakobs, & Valk, 1996; D'Arceuil, De Crespigny, Rother, Seri, Moseley, Stevenson, & Rhihe 1998; Cakirer, Karaarslan, & Arslan, 2003). Some brain structures may be selectively vulnerable to global insults, as might occur in hypoxic injury of any cause. The selective vulnerability of such structures most likely results from relative differences between brain regions in terms of metabolic rates. Nevertheless, the neuroimages in such cases will reflect a symmetrical distribution. Bradley, Brant-Zawadzki, & Cambray-Forker (2001), for instance, described MRI findings in a middle-aged woman diagnosed with hypoxic ischemic encephalopathy. Her MRI findings included T2-weighted and fluid-attenuated inversion recovery images that reflected diffuse and abnormally high signals from the basal ganglia bilaterally, with subtle hyperintensity involving the thalamus, also bilateral. In another case reported by this same group, a diagnosis of 'anoxic ischemic insult' was accompanied by MRI findings of diffuse cerebral atrophy, with abnormal T1- and T2-weighted hyperintense signals within the lenticular nuclei and basal ganglia bilaterally. These symmetrical and diffuse images of hypoxic insult to the brain can be distinguished easily on imaging studies from damage that results from focal neurological insult as might occur in infarction or the defined areas of abnormality in space-occupying lesions.

With regard to functional imaging studies, both SPECT and PET may demonstrate abnormality in response to neurotoxic injury, and even those neurotoxicants that are highly selective for one specific cell type (e.g., 1-methyl-4-phenyl-1,2,3,6-tetrahydropyridine [MPTP] and neuronal damage in the zona compacta of the substantia nigra) can produce discernable PET abnormalities (Calne, Eisen, & McGeer, 1986; Calne & Snow, 1993). PET has proven clinical efficacy when used with other tests and procedures in the evaluation of movement disorders, dementia, and in the localization of brain tumours and seizure foci (American Academy of Neurology, 1991). However, there are still few controlled experimental studies of SPECT or PET, and sensitivity and specificity rates are rare (Society of Nuclear Brain Imaging Council, 1996). Reflecting the developing and as yet incomplete nature of our understanding of functional imaging in clinical diagnoses, perhaps, the Society of Nuclear Brain Imaging Council recently issued a note of caution regarding their use for clinical purposes. Specifically, the society noted that use of these studies to provide 'objective evidence' of impairment potentially leads to insupportable conclusions when used to link neurophysiological variables (such as blood flow or metabolism) to clinical dysfunction. With this in mind, it would appear to be inappropriate to interpret SPECT or PET information to infer evidence that any neurologic condition has been caused by a specific substance-induced illness or injury. This does not mean, of course, that these procedures have no clinical value or that we should not pursue the diagnostic meaningfulness of these measures within the context of clinical research. In many ways, both structural imaging and functional imaging are still in a process of development. Imaging reflects the promise, however, of providing detailed information on pathophysiology not before obtainable via non-invasive procedures. Many of the advances to be made will occur as a result of combining various techniques, such as imaging with non-imaging procedures (e.g., MRI and neuropsychological tests; Markowitsch, 1999), or one imaging approach with another (e.g., CT with PET; Novotny, *et al.*, 2003; Sack & Linden, 2003; Salek-Haddadi, Friston, Lemieux, & Fish, 2003; Matthews & Jezzard, 2004). In addition, the development of new methods for enhancing images from basic techniques such as MRI and PET will greatly increase the clinical value of these instruments (Goh & Ng, 2003). These multiple developments will allow for increased sensitivity of imaging approaches and, with that, the opportunity to establish diagnostic specificity for a greater number of disorders than is possible presently. Advances in both of these areas will be needed to use imaging procedures to diagnose neurotoxic disorders directly.

Neurophysiological tests

The material that follows reviews several types of neurodiagnostic tests that have been used to evaluate potential or suspected neurotoxic disorders. Tests commonly used to evaluate the nervous system in general are discussed in Chapter 6 and listed in Table 6.6. The table is separated into tests that evaluate different levels of the nervous system, and neurotoxicants exist that affect the nervous system at all of these different levels. Several of the tests listed are sensitive to neurologic dysfunction but are unable to localize the level of dysfunction. Others are capable of localizing abnormality to a greater degree than is clinically possible. Many of these tests have had sufficient clinical application to be considered extensions of the clinical examination by most clinicians.

The investigation of patients with suspected neurotoxic disorders frequently includes electrophysiological evaluation. Some electrophysiological tests are used primarily to assure the organic nature of a suspected disorder, whereas others are used to quantify the magnitude of impairment or to identify the underlying pathophysiology. Because neurotoxicants exist that affect the nervous system at different levels, the ability to localize the level of abnormality is an important feature of many electrophysiological tests. However, all electrophysiological tests have limitations. Whereas many electrophysiological measures are very sensitive and capable of detecting abnormality in the absence of clinical symptoms or signs, the electrophysiological abnormalities associated with most neurotoxic disorders are non-specific. In other words, few neurotoxicants display cardinal electrophysiological features that result in the diagnosis of a specific disorder. This lack of specificity limits the ability of the test to establish the cause of the neurologic impairment in most situations.

In general, the application and limitations of electrophysiological studies are well established with regard to the individual patient's diagnostic evaluation. The application to suspected neurotoxic disorders is less well established, particularly when used as a screening instrument to identify subclinical abnormalities or when used to establish the cause of a particular problem. The application and limitation of these studies vis-à-vis clinical neurotoxicology is reviewed in the material that follows. Whereas several electrophysiologic tests are available to evaluate the central nervous system in disorders such as encephalopathy, the most important neurotoxicological application involves those neurophysiology tests capable of evaluating the peripheral nervous system. The emphasis on peripheral nervous system testing in the following material reflects, at least in part, the primary impact electrophysiological tests have had on neurotoxicology evaluations. This emphasis also reflects the quantitative nature of the peripheral electrophysiology measures, and the relative ease of interpreting peripheral compared with central nervous system test results. With respect to each of the electrodiagnostic measures, the critique includes a brief description of the test plus comments on the strengths and weaknesses of each in terms of evaluation of a suspected neurotoxic disorder.

Electroencephalogram (EEG) (Aminoff & Albers, 1999; Albers, 2002)

The EEG waveforms are inspected visually and interpreted subjectively. The interpretation is based on a subjective evaluation of the waveform amplitude, frequency, coherence, symmetry, and responsiveness to external stimuli. Some of the criteria used to define abnormality are subjective and arbitrary, and minor interobserver differences exist in the determination of normal and abnormal. In addition, the EEG is influenced by numerous factors that may be difficult to control, including the subject's level of arousal. Electro-encephalography is a recognized subspecialty with established training and certification requirements. Within the specialty of Neurology, there is special recognition for those who have completed approved training programs and demonstrated appropriate proficiency in interpreting EEG and other electro-physiological studies (Added Qualifications in Clinical Electrophysiology).

The most important application of EEG to clinical neurotoxicology is related to the evaluation of encephalopathy. Many neurotoxic syndromes that produce central nervous system effects are characterized by an acute or chronic encephalopathy. The syndrome of 'encephalopathy' includes patients who manifest a wide spectrum of symptoms and signs. The presenting symptoms of acute encephalopathy are relatively independent of cause, depending primarily on the severity of the encephalopathy. When mild, non-specific headache and lightheadedness may be the only complaints, occurring with few or no neurological signs. As the severity of the acute encephalopathy increases, evidence of confusion, increased irritability, and altered levels of consciousness develop. The signs associated with acute encephalopathy are those of acute intoxication. They include altered judgment, impaired concentration, inappropriate behavior, nystagmus, and ataxia. At increasing levels of impairment, signs of restlessness and agitation, abnormal postural tremor, slowed motor performance, and impaired gait appear. These signs typically are associated with asterixis, dysarthria, akathisia, gross ataxia, and the appearance of primitive reflexes (snout, suck, and grasp). As delirium develops, reflexes become hyperactive, sometimes in association with myoclonus, and Babinski and Chaddock reflexes become evident. With further progression, the level of consciousness deteriorates, with diminished response to visual, auditory, and even painful stimuli. As the level of coma increases even further, decerebrate posturing develops. If the underlying cause of the encephalopathy is eliminated, almost all of the different stages of acute encephalopathy are reversible. Consider, for example, the remarkable resolution of the severe toxic encephalopathy associated with liver failure (hepatic encephalopathy) after successful liver transplant.

What is the role of the conventional EEG in the evaluation of a suspected neurotoxic disorder? In acute encephalopathy of any cause that has greater than mild severity, there is a good relationship between the EEG abnormalities and the level of encephalopathy (Markand, 1984; Aminoff & Albers, 1999). The EEG evaluation is therefore important in providing an objective measure of severity. At very mild levels of encephalopathy, the EEG provides objective evidence of an underlying electrophysiologic impairment. The EEG also has an important role in raising the suspicion for other problems that might occur, such as a seizure disorder.

The sensitivity of the EEG evaluation for detecting encephalopathy is modest, but most patients with clinically evident encephalopathy have an abnormal EEG. The EEG abnormality associated with encephalopathy is diffuse, intermittent or continuous, slowing of the background rhythm. This abnormality is symmetric, reflecting the symmetrical nature of all encephalopathies. Slowing first appears in the posterior rhythm, progressing from the low alpha into the high theta frequency range. As the degree of encephalopathy increases, so do the EEG abnormalities. In association with progressive slowing of the posterior rhythms, a dominant theta frequency becomes widespread. As the severity of encephalopathy increases even more, the EEG demonstrates poor reactivity to external stimuli, especially to visual stimuli, and intermittent delta frequency appears, most prominent over anterior regions. Severe encephalopathy is initially associated with large amplitude irregular delta activity, followed by progressive loss of amplitude and reactivity with further progression. Burst-suppression patterns precede loss of all electrical activity, coinciding with loss of cerebral function (Aminoff & Albers, 1999).

It might be assumed that the sequential EEG changes associated with progressive encephalopathy would make the EEG a powerful tool in the evaluation of suspected toxic encephalopathy. In this application, however, EEG has several limitations. First, it is relatively insensitive to very mild encephalopathy, the very situation where it could have its greatest utility. Second, and most importantly, the EEG has poor specificity, and slowing of the background rhythm is a non-specific finding that cannot distinguish between the many forms and causes of encephalopathy (Markand, 1984; Aminoff & Albers, 1999).

What EEG patterns, if any, suggest a specific type of encephalopathy? The appearance of triphasic waves suggests a diagnosis of hepatic encephalopathy to most clinicians, but triphasic waves also occur with other forms of encephalopathy, including those associated with water intoxication, hypercalcemia, thyroid disease, renal failure, and hypoxia (Aminoff & Albers, 1999). The presence of triphasic waves is best correlated with the level of consciousness, being most prominent in obtunded patients (Markand, 1984). Another limitation relates to the duration of cerebral impairment. The EEG is more likely to be abnormal in patients with an acute encephalopathy compared with patients who have the same level of impairment but a more chronic encephalopathy. Among patients with mild, chronic encephalopathy, the presence of any objective EEG evidence of cerebral dysfunction supports an organic aetiology. For example, in the encephalopathy that develops insidiously in association with chronic renal failure, the EEG typically is abnormal only in those patients who have clinical evidence of abnormal mental status.

The EEG findings are suggestive of a particular type of etiology in few other situations. For example, patients with acute barbiturate intoxication producing a form of drug-induced toxic encephalopathy have EEG abnormalities as described above, and the degree of abnormality correlates well with the degree of mental alteration and level of intoxication. In addition, the EEG demonstrates symmetrical beta activity in frontal head regions, a finding characteristic of a medication effect. Degenerative disorders associated with encephalopathy demonstrate reduced frequency and abnormal background rhythm regulation. Disorders characterized by cortical gray matter dysfunction produce primarily irregular slowing and reduced amplitude. Those disorders characterized by subcortical gray matter involvement, on the other hand, demonstrate bilateral synchronous, semirhythmic slow activity or spike-wave complexes (Markand, 1984).

Quantitative EEG (QEEG) and EEG brain mapping

QEEG refers to mathematical manipulation or processing of the EEG signal to highlight particular components of interest (e.g., epileptiform discharges) or to transform the signal to emphasize some particular information (e.g., slow-frequency activity). In the context of toxic encephalopathy, the one potential application might be frequency domain analyses to quantify the power of the signal, looking for excessive slow activity. Such quantification permits statistical comparisons between the individual patient and normative data, between groups of patients, or even between successive measurements of the same individual. Brain mapping refers to topographic display of the QEEG data in a variety of ways, including amplitude and frequency representations. Despite the potential advantages of QEEG and brain mapping, these research tools have had limited clinical application, and even less application in the evaluation of encephalopathy or dementia. As such, they have unknown sensitivity and specificity for this application.

An important difficulty encountered in interpreting the relevance of a small but significant difference in the QEEG identified between two groups of subjects is the possibility that the differences may simply reflect different levels of arousal that are too subtle to be visually detected in the conventional EEG. A recent assessment by the American Academy of Neurology and the American Clinical Neurophysiology Society concluded that these techniques are predisposed to false-positive errors, limiting their potential as clinical tools (Nuwer, 1997). The specific techniques used in QEEG were found to vary substantially between laboratories, and demonstration of clinical usefulness using one technique could not be generalized to other techniques. Further, artifacts easily identified on conventional EEG sometimes appeared on QEEG in unusual ways. These problems were in addition to the generation of new artifacts produced by the data-processing algorithms used in QEEG. An additional problem related to the use of multiple analyses, often involving hundreds of comparisons that produce multiple 'abnormalities', many occurring by chance alone. In the evaluation of dementia or encephalopathy, the finding of focal or generalized background slowing does support an organic disorder as opposed to an affective disorder such as depression. For such an application, QEEG likely parallels the role of conventional EEG. The American Psychiatric Association Task Force on Electrophysiological Assessment also concluded that QEEG can help detect excessive slow activity in organic disorders (American Psychiatry Association, 1991). However, group evaluations of QEEG techniques are often uncontrolled in that they are not random and are either not masked or are retrospective, making it difficult to evaluate the clinical utility of the specific test. Further, concern exists that many evaluations of individual techniques are conducted by investigators involved in the commercialization of the instrument, making it difficult to assess the objectivity of the results (Nuwer, 1997).

The assessment by the American Academy of Neurology and the American Clinical Neurophysiology Society on QEEG included a section on medical–legal abuse in relation to brain mapping and QEEG (Nuwer, 1997). The major problem with using QEEG in such context has been the occurrence of false-positive or false-negative results that are at odds with other clinical investigations. Concern was expressed by these professional organizations that results could be altered, sometimes dramatically, during the relatively subjective process of selecting portions of the EEG signal for evaluation and quantitative analyses. In spite of poor test–retest reproducibility, there are no objective safeguards to limit statistical or unintended errors of this type (Nuwer, 1997). The major concern in the application of studies of unproved sensitivity, specificity, and reliability is the resultant confusion caused by their misapplication. At present, the lack of general acceptance of EEG brain mapping has resulted in disallowance in recent state and federal court decisions under the older Frye rules and the newer Daubert rules (see the original report for discussion and references) (Nuwer, 1997).

Because prospective, controlled studies have not as of yet satisfactorily evaluated test specificity or sensitivity of these QEEG techniques, any conclusions about the particular advantages of these studies over conventional EEG studies are premature. The recommendation has been made that QEEG and brain mapping only be used by clinicians highly skilled in conventional EEG, and then only as an adjunct to interpretation of the traditional EEG. Use in any other context was classified as Class III quality (evidence provided by expert opinion, non-randomized historical controls, or case reports) (Nuwer, 1997).

Evoked potential studies

Evoked potential studies refer to the recording of electrical signals generated in the nervous system in response to a specific peripheral stimulus. The stimulus can be tactile, electrical, visual, or auditory. Recordings are made over a variety of locations including peripheral nerve, plexus, spine, or scalp. The resultant signals reflect some measure of the functional integrity of the afferent pathways.

Visual evoked potentials (VEPs) are recorded from the scalp in response to a visual stimulus, usually a shifting checkerboard pattern. These signals are sensitive to disorders of the optic nerve and anterior chiasm. Brainstem auditory evoked potentials (BAEPs) are used to evaluate the integrity of the auditory portion of cranial nerve VIII or the auditory pathways in the brain stem. Somatosensory evoked potentials (SSEPs) are analogous to sensory nerve conduction studies described in the following section, reflecting activity in large, myelinated peripheral axons and posterior and lateral afferent spinal cord pathways. Unlike peripheral sensory nerve recordings, the SSEP amplitude is substantially lower and varies considerably in response to variety of factors (e.g., averaging technique, electrode montage, muscle activity, and stimulation paradigm). This variability limits the usefulness of amplitude measures to detect abnormality, and amplitude abnormalities should be interpreted with caution (Arezzo, Simson, & Brennan, 1985; Albers, 1998). The most reliable abnormalities are identified as conduction slowing along the afferent pathway. Unfortunately, most neurotoxicants produce neuronal death and axonal loss, resulting in loss of response but little in the way of conduction slowing. For this reason, SSEPs have limited sensitivity in detecting neurotoxic injury. Further, selective lesions involving the smaller myelinated fibers typically do not produce SSEP abnormalities, although SSEPs recorded in response to thermal stimuli provide a possible mechanism to evaluate small fiber neuropathy. SSEP studies have may have potential application to identify subclinical involvement in central pathways in a variety of disorders (Aminoff & Albers, 1999), but the lack of specificity limits their application.

An initial application of evoked potential studies related to the search for a clinically silent second lesion in demyelinating disease such as multiple sclerosis. With the advent of MRI imaging and the increasing sensitivity allowed by this procedure to identify abnormalities of myelin, there has been a decrease in the demand for evoked potential studies because of their relative insensitivity and lack of specificity. Nevertheless, evoked potential studies occasionally detect unequivocal conduction slowing when other clinical and laboratory studies are normal, and there are scattered reports related to detection of neurotoxic disease using evoked potential techniques. For example, Rosenberg, Spitz, Filley, Davis, & Schaumburg (1988) reported abnormalities of BAERs in some toluene abusers at a time when no other clinical or electrophysiological abnormalities were identified, and they suggested a potential screening role for this test. Shortly after evoked response studies became clinically available, there was optimism expressed that they would have utility with other neurophysiological studies in the evaluation of workers with neurotoxic disorders. In that context, initial results suggested that demonstration of multiple lesions in the central and peripheral nervous systems should arouse consideration for a toxic etiology (Seppalainen, 1982). During the intervening decades, this idea has been modified somewhat. It is now recognized that widespread, not multifocal, neurological abnormalities characterize many neurotoxic disorders. The inability of evoked response studies to distinguish between the two represents a major limitation in their application. At present, the proposed occupational applications have yet to materialize or to be evaluated in a controlled environment.

Event-related potentials (e.g., P-300)

Event-related potentials are specialized EEG techniques developed to explore specific cortical processes, including those purportedly related to cognition and attention (Matsumoto, 1996). In these recordings, a specific event such as an auditory signal is time-locked to the EEG in order to explore temporally associated activity. An example of an event-related potential is the P-300. This potential is generated in response to a random auditory signal that the subject is instructed to count. This task requires active participation of the subject and encourages attention to the auditory stimuli. In part because of this active subject participation, the P-300 is sometimes referred to as a cognitive evoked potential. This label attributes some cognitive significance to the presence of the P-300 signal as opposed to a signal resulting from a purely physical stimulus. Nevertheless, the role of this signal in relation to cognition is controversial, and the P-300 may be an electrophysiological correlate of selected attention (Geisler & Polich, 1992; Polich, Moore, & Wiederhold, 1995; Matsumoto, 1996). Application of this technique is limited, and the sensitivity and specificity of the test is undefined. At best, this technique remains a research tool used by few investigators for a limited number of applications. It has not, as of yet, achieved any widespread application as a clinical neurodiagnostic test.

Electromyography (EMG)

The results of EMG studies are used to confirm clinical findings, localize specific abnormalities to a degree not clinically possible, and identify the underlying pathophysiology. The primary role is diagnostic. Recognition and formal consideration of factors that influence normal values, such as age, temperature, and body size increases the sensitivity and accuracy of these tests. Among the different components of the EMG examination, the nerve conduction studies are of greatest importance in terms of evaluation of potential neurotoxic disorders. This is because the peripheral nervous system is a common neurotoxic target. Most typically, the resultant syndrome is expressed in the form of a generalized peripheral neuropathy ('polyneuropathy').

Standard criteria exist for diagnosing subclincal, clinical, and confirmed polyneuropathy based on symptoms, signs, and electrodiagnostic results (American Diabetes Association, 1988; Dyck, Kratz, Lehman, Karnes, Melton, O'Brien, Litchy, Windebank, Smith & Low, 1991; Dyck, Karnes, O'Brien, Litchy, Low, & Melton, 1992; The Diabetes Control and Complications Trial Research Group, 1993).

The EMG examination is the most commonly requested and utilized study in the evaluation of patients with peripheral nervous system disorders. These studies are not without limitation, however.

Nerve conduction studies

Nerve conduction studies are considered specific for disorders of the peripheral nerve (Donofrio & Albers, 1990). Nerve conduction studies also are considered the 'gold standard' for evaluating suspected polyneuropathy, and they are objective, reproducible, and sensitive to detecting polyneuropathy. They are independent of patient cooperation or motivation (Simmons, 1992; Salerno, Franzblau, Werner, Bromberg, Armstrong, & Albers, 1998; Salerno, Werner, Albers, Becker, Armstrong, & Franzblau, 1999).

Nerve conduction techniques are well standardized, with only minor differences existing between laboratories. These differences relate to non-critical factors such as the use of fixed or anatomic distances, baseline-to-peak versus peak-to-peak amplitude measurements, and orthodromic versus antidromic stimulation. Variations in normal values used by different laboratories reflect these technical inconsistencies, as well as the use of different limb temperatures. Many normal values are age dependent and some vary according to patient size and possibly other factors, including occupation (Bolton & Carter, 1980; Rivner, Swift, Crout, & Rhodes, 1990; Stetson, Albers, Silverstein, & Wolfe, 1992; Trojaborg, Moon, Andersen, & Trojaborg, 1992; Salerno et al., 1998).

Improper recording or stimulating electrode placement, inaccurate surface measurements, failure to monitor and control limb temperature, and even the distance between stimulating and recording electrodes influence the electrodiagnostic results. For example, limb temperature is one source of variability particularly important in the evaluation of polyneuropathy. Within the physiologic temperature range, motor conduction velocity decreases by approximately 2 ms/°C, and distal latencies increase by approximately 0.2 ms/°C (Denys, 1991). The influence of temperature on nerve conduction times is substantial, reflecting the effect of temperature on the opening and closing rates of ionic channels, particularly sodium channels. The prolonged sodium channel opening time with decreased temperature not only reduces the conduction time of the nerve action potential, but also influences the amplitude of the action potential.

Consider, for example, the sensory responses shown in Figure 7.1, recorded from the same individual about 10 min apart. The only difference between the two recordings was hand temperature. The top tracing was recorded when the palm temperature was approximately 34°C, whereas the lower tracing was recorded after cooling the hand to about 26°C. This dramatic change in the configuration of the sensory nerve action potential is a physiologic change that reflects only local temperature of the nerve. Fortunately, cooling decreases conduction velocity and increases amplitude, a combination of findings atypical for any pathologic process. Limb temperature should be monitored and cool limbs warmed if necessary to approximately 32–36°C (surface temperature), and any clinical evaluation that does not report limb temperature should be viewed cautiously. Failure to consider limb temperature limits the importance of the resultant electrophysiologic information.

REPETITIVE MOTOR NERVE STIMULATION

Conventional techniques of repetitive motor nerve stimulation are well established and considered part of the nerve conduction study evaluation. Factors that adversely influence test results are similar to those described above and generally reflect poor technique, including inattention to limb temperature. In contrast to the effects of cool limb temperature, which sometimes mimic abnormal nerve conduction, cool temperature actually enhances neuromuscular transmission, thereby masking an underlying defect. In contrast, submaximal nerve stimulation, incorrect restraint of limbs, and loose recording electrodes produce variation in the response amplitude that may be misinterpreted as suggesting abnormal neuromuscular transmission.

BLINK REFLEX

Blink reflex studies are generally considered part of the nerve conduction evaluation. However, unlike conventional peripheral nerve conduction studies, blink reflexes represent responses resulting from a complex multisynaptic reflex with peripheral and central nervous system comments. Like other evoked response measures (VEP, BAEP, SSEP), the utility of blink reflexes has not been established in neurotoxic disease. Further, this complex polysynaptic reflex is sensitive to cueing, indicating that attention influences test results (Sanin, Kronenberg, & Stetkarova, 1993). It is likely that numerous other intervening factors also influence blink results. Like many other measures discussed in this chapter, the sensitivity and specificity are unknown, as are the numerous potentially intervening factors influencing results.

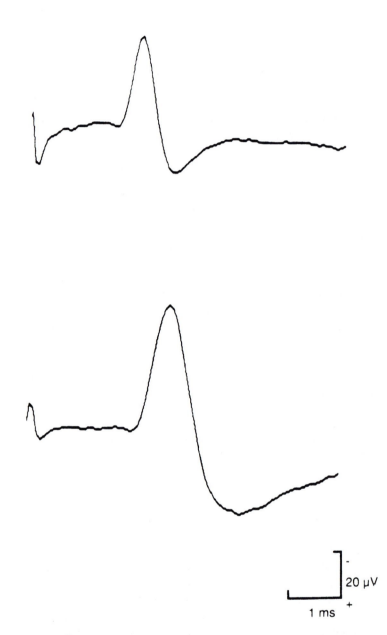

20 µV

1 ms

Figure 7.1 Median sensory responses recorded from the index finger in response to percutaneous supramaximal electrical stimulation of the median nerve at the wrist. The responses were recorded from the same individual approximately 10 min apart. Upper tracing, palm temperature = 34˚C; lower tracing, recorded after cooling the hand: palm temperature = 26˚C.

Needle electromyography

Whereas nerve conduction studies play a prominent role in the evaluation of potential neurotoxic disorders, the role of the needle EMG examination, while important, is somewhat more limited. This limitation reflects, at least in part, the lack of specificity of the needle EMG examination results. Although the needle EMG findings readily distinguish neuropathic from myopathic disorders, the primary utility of the needle EMG examination reflects its ability to identify muscle fiber necrosis of any cause, including all forms of axonal loss lesions and many forms of myopathy. Further, almost all forms of demyelinating neuroupathy have some degree of superimposed axonal loss, further limiting its influence in the diagnosis of disorders associated with conduction slowing. Therefore, the categories of neuropathy described in the preceding section, and the results most relevant to clinical neurobehavioral toxicology, rely almost exclusively on the information derived from the nerve conduction study evaluation. The needle EMG examination does provide ancillary information about the distribution and magnitude of axonal loss lesions or myopathy, and therefore it is useful establishing the diagnoses of neuropathy or myopathy from other disorders, and in establishing the chronicity, ongoing activity, and severity of the underlying neurological disorder.

The needle EMG examination includes subjective evaluation of several different forms of electrophysiologic potential. The evaluation includes an estimate of insertional activity, identification of any abnormal potentials not ordinarily present, and evaluation of MUAP recruitment, size, and configuration, as described in Chapter 6.

Correct identification of positive waves and fibrillation potentials provides a sensitive indication of ongoing or previous denervation. It frequently detects abnormalities that are neither clinically apparent nor symptomatic. It is also used to define the distribution of axonal lesions, identifying disorders sometimes confused with or superimposed upon a generalized polyneuropathy. The amplitude of positive waves or fibrillation potentials and the configuration of MUAPs are used to distinguish acute from chronic disorders and provide an estimate of the progression of axonal loss. This examination is almost totally dependent on the skill of the examining physician, as meaningful reproduction of the observed signals is neither available for later review nor relevant, even if the signal were available. This is in contrast to other forms of neurodiagnostic testing, such as imaging studies, which can be reviewed by others remote from the actual examination. The main reasons that the needle EMG signals cannot be practically reproduced for review is that they depend on the selection of muscle for examination, the location within the muscle, and the precision with which the EMG electrode is sequentially moved through the muscle tissue during the recording, to name a few.

SINGLE FIBER ELECTROMYOGRAPHY (SFEMG)

SFEMG is commonly used to evaluate neuromuscular transmission in patients with suspected myasthenia gravis, but it also has been used in a variety of physiologic and pathologic conditions of neuromuscular transmission and muscle fiber density, including those related to neurotoxicity (e.g., penicillamine-induced myasthenia gravis). SFEMG is an objective and extremely sensitive measurement of neuromuscular transmission. However, an abnormal SFEMG is not specific for any particular disorder of neuromuscular transmission, and false-positive studies occur in a variety of disorders associated with partial denervation and reinnervation (e.g., motor neuron disease, polymyositis, chronic neuropathy).

Application of nerve conduction studies and needle EMG in toxic neuropathy

Ignoring for a moment the limitations of the EMG examination as described above, how are the results applicable to the evaluation of peripheral nervous system disorders? Despite the limitations described above, nerve conduction study and needle EMG examination results are objective and reproducible measures of peripheral nerve function when performed by qualified individuals using standard techniques. Once a peripheral disorder is suspected on the basis of the clinical examination, the electrophysiologic tests are used to confirm the presence of neuropathy and refine the differential diagnosis. The most important of these is the electrodiagnostic examination, which is sensitive and specific for disorders of the lower motor neuron, the dorsal root ganglion, and its peripheral axon. Nerve conduction studies and the needle EMG examination are considered extensions of the clinical examination, and much of the resultant information is clinically relevant, with measures such as compound muscle action potential amplitude directly reflecting clinical examination findings.

Application of repetitive motor nerve stimulation technique in neurotoxic syndromes has limited application. Disorders known to demonstrate abnormal neuromuscular transmission in which these techniques are useful include acute organophosphorus intoxication, penicillamine-induced myasthenia gravis, and evaluation of iatrogenic neuromuscular blockage (Namba, Nolte, Jackrel, & Grob, 1971; Albers, Hodach, Kimmel, & Treacy, 1980; Kinnby, Konsberg, & Larsson, 1988). There are, however, numerous biological neurotoxins that interfere with neuromuscular transmission, including botulinum toxin, alpha-bungarotoxin, and curare (Cherington, 1998).

Blink reflex studies have had application in neurotoxic evaluations, however, especially those associated with solvent exposure (Feldman, Mayer, & Taub, 1970; Feldman, Chirico-Post, & Proctor, 1988). The use of blink reflex latencies to evaluate solvent neurotoxicity may have originated with the observation that trigeminal nerve and other cranial nerve dysfunction sometimes occurred after exposure to trichloroethylene (TCE) when used as a general anesthetic (Humphrey & McClelland, 1944). It has been proposed that blink reflex abnormalities could indicate subclinical solvent neurotoxicity (Feldman, Niles, Proctor, & Jabre, 1992; Feldman, 1994; Feldman, White, Eriator, Jabre, Feldman, & Niles, 1994). However, a recent review of blink reflex results recorded from railroad workers with long-term occupational exposure to solvents did not identify any workers with abnormal R1 and R2 blink reflex latencies (Albers, Wald, Garabrant, Trask, & Berent, 2000). The observation that R1 latencies correlated significantly with several nerve conduction measures suggests that some of the intersubject variability reflected intrinsic conduction properties, not isolated brainstem function.

Although individual latencies were all normal, the workers' average R1 latencies were prolonged compared with historical control groups, including gender-matched control subjects of similar mean age (11.2 versus 9.9 ms; p <0.0001). Stepwise multiple regression models demonstrated significant associations of R1 latency with age and use of CNS-active prescription medications ($p = 0.003$), but duration of occupational solvent exposure did not enter into the models. Paradoxically, workers using CNS-active medications had shorter, not longer, R1 latencies compared with workers not using such medications (10.9 versus 11.7 ms; $p = 0.01$). The overall results do not support a relationship between subclinical blink reflex abnormalities and occupational exposure to solvents. Small observed differences between exposed workers and control subjects were thought to be of no diagnostic importance and of uncertain physiologic importance that probably reflected unrecognized confounders and technical factors. (Lingle & Steinbach, 1988; Goetz & Cohen, 1990; Albers & Wald, 1997)

Electrophysiological tests of autonomic nervous system function

Sympathetic skin potentials (SSPs) can be recorded spontaneously or in response to a variety of stimuli, including percutaneous electrical stimulation, startle, cough, Valsalva maneuver, or by asking an emotionally charged question. Unlike standard nerve conduction studies, the purpose of the stimuli is not to depolarize the nerve directly, but to produce an autonomic response to startle or surprise. SSPs have been used to document autonomic impairment in disorders such as inflammatory or diabetic neuropathy, but they have limited application in neurotoxic disorders. In general, neither their sensitivity nor specificity is known. Other tests of ANS function exist, including evaluation of the cardiac R-R interval, orthostatic blood pressure response, and response to Valsalva maneuver or deep breathing. Postganglionic sympathetic function also can be measured using quantitative sudomotor axon reflex test (Q-SART); pre- and postganglionic sympathetic functions are measured by thermoregulatory sweat tests (Chelimsky, Low, Naessens, Wilson, Amadio, & O'Brien, 1995; Low, Opfer-Gehrking, & Low, 1999; Low, Vernino, & Suarez, 2003). Skin biopsies can be used to assess small unmyelinated nerve fibres or sweat glands. Tests of autonomic function are beyond the scope of this review. As far as is known, however, none of these techniques has had extensive application or study in the evaluation of neurotoxic disorders.

Other tests of neurologic function

A few additional tests of neurologic function have occasional use in neurotoxic evaluations. Most were developed as quantitative measures of some specific neurologic function measured subjectively with the clinical evaluation. Included, for example, are quantitative tests of vibratory sensation and body sway. All have had application for use in group comparisons, such as a masked cohort pharmaceutical evaluation of some medication purported to improve or protect neurological function. In pharmaceutical trials, the quantitative nature of these measures allows for use of parametric statistical comparisons. These tests differ, however, from the electrodiagnostic tests discussed above in that the subject can adversely influence test results. For this reason, application to individual subject evaluations is limited when masking of the subject and examiner is not possible and the results are subject to bias. Only quantitative sensory testing has had widespread application, and even these tests are available in many non-standardized forms (Moody, Arezzo, & Otto, 1986; Maurissen, 1988). The sensitivity and specificity of these tests have had limited evaluation to date.

Posturography

Static posturography is a quantitative measure of postural movement used to record minute swaying of the body during quiet stance. The subject stands on a platform, and pressure transducers or accelerometers monitor vertical and shear forces exerted by the feet. These measures can then be used to calculate the amplitude and rate of sway. In contrast, dynamic posturography applies the same techniques to record sway in response to some unexpected perturbation of the platform. This is sometimes combined with visual stimuli to isolate the vestibular and proprioceptive systems and to eliminate the effects of the visual system on posture. The most common application is in the evaluation of patients with suspected vestibular disorders. The American Academy of Neurology Therapeutics and Technology Assessment Subcommittee reviewed the clinical utility of posturography (American Academy of Neurology, 1992). In their report, members of the committee indicated that the specificity of this measure is poor and that the patterns of abnormality commonly associated with vestibular disorders do not exclude central or peripheral dysfunction. In spite of the quantitative nature of the measure, the implied stimulus–response output requires volitional cooperation of the subject in maintaining a stable upright posture. This is a limitation of the objectivity of the measure, and small volitional shifts in posture dramatically influence the test results. In a cooperative, motivated subject, the test results are repeatable. Posturography is not useful, however, in localizing lesions in the nervous system. Posturography also cannot be used to establish a specific diagnosis of vestibular or neurologic dysfunction (American Academy of Neurology, 1992). The subcommittee concluded that it is doubtful that this functional measure will become an efficacious diagnostic test. Additional information regarding test sensitivity remains limited.

Quantitative sensory testing (QST)

QST is used by many investigators in the assessment of toxic neuropathy, and these psychomotor tests have application in clinical, pharmacological, and neurotoxicology studies (Bleecker, 1985, 1986; Moody *et al.*, 1986; Maurissen, 1988). The validity of QST is established, and interexaminer comparisons are favorable, including comparison with paramedical personnel. (Maurissen, 1985; Maurissen & Chrzan, 1989; Gerr & Letz, 1994; Chaudhry, Eisenberger, Sinibaldi, Sheikh, Griffin, & Cornblath, 1996). Different sensory modalities such as vibration and thermal sensations can be evaluated, corresponding to different nerve fiber populations. The testing is non-invasive and well toler-ated, and the quantitative results allow parametric statistical analyses and detection of subtle group differences when used under controlled conditions. QST also is useful in monitoring longitudinal change over time. In some comparisons, such as the prospective study of pyridoxine neurotoxicity, thermal changes detected by QST occurred earlier and were more severe than changes in vibration sensation or changes in sural nerve action potential amplitude (Berger, Schaumburg, Schroeder, Apfel, & Reynolds, 1992). In contrast, others have compared QST and nerve conduction study results in the evaluation of diabetic polyneuropathy and found QST complementary but ancillary to nerve conduction studies, with the sural recording being the best single predictor of mild neuropathy (Redmond, McKenna, Feingold, & Ahmad, 1992). The application of QST to occupational evaluations has been proposed as a simple and reliable screening test to diagnosis polyneuropathy (Halonen, 1986). It is unclear whether or not such use has materialized. Independent of that application, however, there are several disadvantages to the use of QST as a diagnostic tool. The disadvantages include the time required to perform such studies; the need for patient cooperation; the sensi-tivity of the measures to subtle motivational factors, learning and age effects; and the inability to distinguish central from peripheral disorders.

Neuropathology

Tissue biopsy is commonly used in clinical neurodiagnostic evaluation and is occasionally used in neurotoxicology evaluations. The neurologist frequently uses results obtained from examination of biopsied tissue in arriving at a particular diagnosis. However, as discussed in Chapter 6, neuropathological information derived from selected tissues is more comparable with the information derived from other laboratory tests than to the results obtained from the clinical or electrodiagnostic examinations. In fact, neuropathological investigation is only pursued after the differential diagnosis has been focused on a relatively small number of possible diagnoses. That does not mean that the information is not useful in the context of neurotoxicology, because it is very helpful on occasion. Importantly, however, the clinician must know when pathological information can be used to establish a specific diagnosis. Unfortunately, there are a relatively small number of conditions that can be identified conclusively by the neuropathologist, and few of those conditions involve neurotoxicants.

In the context of clinical neurotoxicology, the neuropathological examination is used most often to evaluate peripheral nervous system disorders. An obvious limitation of the neuropathological investigation is the need to obtain nerve, muscle, blood vessel, or connective tissue for examination. This investigation is, by definition, invasive, and it usually is uncomfortable. In the case of peripheral nerve disorders, most pathological investigations are limited to examination of sensory nerves, such as the sural nerve at the ankle or a superficial sensory nerve in the forearm. Because of the length-dependent nature of most, but not all, toxic neuropathies, the region of greatest interest may not be assessable for biopsy. Conversely, if the patient's neuropathy is of more than modest severity, the available tissue may demonstrate only chronic changes associated with endstage involvement, providing limited diagnostic information about the underlying process. After a sensory nerve has been biopsied, it is unavailable for rebiopsy, as in the case of re-biopsy of the distal stump, for example, because of secondary changes associated with the nerve trauma. This means that the neuropathology examination cannot be repeated to monitor disease progression or to perform additional assessments (other than by biopsying the other side or another assessable nerve). Muscle tissue can be rebiopsied, but rebiopsy is performed rarely, usually involving needle biopsy, a technique that is less invasive than open biopsy but also provides less tissue for pathological investigation. One technique that can be performed repeatedly is skin biopsy. This technique, although relatively new, is applicable for evaluation of a small unmyelinated sensory nerve ending within the skin. Skin biopsy does not permit evaluation of large myelinated nerve fibers, the fibers involved most often in toxic neuropathies. At present, the specificity and sensitivity of this technique is not established. In the case of muscle disorders, involvement is sometimes patchy or multifocal within even a given muscle, and the biopsied material may not contain evidence of the underlying pathology. Similar problems exist for the evaluation of connective tissues, including blood vessels, where involvement in the form of vasculitis may be multifocal or segmental.

The role of neuropathology vis-à-vis toxic neuropathy has its greatest application at present in animal toxicology and research studies. Neuropathology is of particular importance in understanding the underlying changes associated with experimental animal models of specific neurotoxic disorders, including neuropathy and myopathy. Consider acrylamide neuropathy as an example. As discussed in Chapter 10 of Volume II, acrylamide is an extremely rare cause of toxic neuropathy among humans, but it is, nevertheless, an excellent example of a 'dying-back' axonal neuropathy. In this context, acrylamide has increased our understanding of several pathological mechanisms associated with toxic neuropathies, in particular, and axonal neuropathies, in general. Despite this important role, there have been no human post-mortem studies of acrylamide neuropathy, nor have there been credible reports of human nerve biopsies obtained during the active phase of acrylamide neuropathy. Further, the few nerve biopsies obtained from patients recovering from acrylamide neuropathy have shown only non-specific neuropathological findings of diminished numbers of large myelinated nerve fibers, the end-result of most neuropathies of any cause (Schaumburg & Berger, 1993).

A similar lack of neuropathological information, usually consisting of morphological evidence of only non-specific axonal loss, exists for most forms of toxic neuropathy. This includes the occupational neuropathies associated with carbon disulfide, ethylene oxide, methyl bromides, organophosphorus compounds, and organic solvents (Schaumburg & Berger, 1993). Among the numerous peripheral nervous system neurotoxicants, perhaps the hexacarbons produce the most distinctive neuropathological changes (see Chapter 10 of Volume II). Among patients with *n*-hexane-induced neuropathy, sural nerve biopsy shows characteristic focal axonal swellings consisting of neurofilament aggregates. Yet, evidence of unequivocal axonal swellings does not implicate any particular neurotoxicant, let alone a specific hexacarbon. It is not surprising that the neuropathological results, which are sensitive and specific for the diagnosis of 'neuropathy', only rarely permit the neuropathologist to identify a specific cause for the patient's neuropathy. There are exceptions, but even the exceptions usually fall in the category of findings 'consistent with' a specific neurotoxic disorder. For example, biopsy of skin, fascia, muscle, and nerve obtained from patients with eosinophilia-myalgia syndrome associated with l-tryptophan intoxication typically demonstrates perivascular inflammation with lymphocytes and rare eosinophils in connective tissue. In other neurotoxic disorders, tissue biopsy is rarely helpful or indicated, other than to document the presence of problems unrelated to toxic exposure. None of these measures is useful for screening purposes. As also discussed elsewhere in this volume, the most important role of nerve biopsy is to identify the few disorders for which findings are pathognomonic. These disorders include amyloidosis, hereditary neuropathy, sarcoidosis and other granulomatous neuropathies, and vasculitis. All of these disorders listed can be difficult to diagnose with certainty without pathological confirmation or other forms of laboratory testing.

Laboratory testing

This chapter is intended to critique relevant clinical tests, and a critique of standard laboratory testing is beyond the scope of this volume. Nevertheless, many limitations associated with laboratory results are self-apparent and well known to clinicians. Among the many limitations are the evaluation of substances that have a very short half-life, and that may be corrected, excreted, or metabolized before they can be evaluated. Consider, for example, measures of arterial blood gases, carboxyhemoglobin, or metabolic products of some common pesticides. Some biological measures are more amenable for investigation, such as serum concentrations of some medications, urinary excretion levels of some metals or metaloids (arsenic, mercury, or lead) or acetylcholinesterase activities associated with exposure to organophosphorus compounds. Yet, these measurements are obtained only after an appropriate differential diagnosis has been developed. Other substances, like lead or dioxin, are stored in tissue for many years, making it possible to predict even remote exposures of substantial magnitude and duration. Routine toxicologic examinations of blood and urine, such as routinely used in the emergency department, evaluate only the more common medications and substances of abuse. Other measures, such as determination of abnormal levels of particular chemicals in (or on) the hair, often cannot reliably distinguish endogenous exposure and surface contamination. Random samples for substances ubiquitous in our environment rarely provide information useful in establishing a diagnosis. Such difficulties are further complicated by insufficient understanding of normal values among normal subjects without known neurologic symptoms or disease.

The more typical use of laboratory testing in the context of clinical neurotoxicology is to monitor exposure to specific substances. This may involve measurement of medications or their metabolites in the serum, or measurement of liver, renal, or bone marrow function if these tissues represent target organs for adverse effects. Many industrial hygiene applications monitor exposure to a specific chemical or its metabolites in an occupational setting. Examples include measurement of urinary excretion of elemental mercury among exposed workers and monitoring of red blood cell acetylcholinesterase or plasma butyrylcholinesterase activities among workers exposed to organophosphorus compounds. Such biological measures provide information about internal exposure to the substance of interest.

By way of example, consider the numerous factors that must be taken into account in the seemingly straightforward laboratory evaluation for potential arsenic intoxication (Albers & Garabrant, 2004). Similar examples exist throughout volumes I and II related to specific investigations of substances appearing in the differential diagnosis. Arsenic is readily absorbed following ingestion and it is rapidly excreted in the urine, with a half-life in blood of about 60 h. Arsenic is rapidly cleared from the blood, and blood levels are clinically useful only if they are collected within several days of acute poisoning. Urinary excretion of arsenic better reflects the magnitude of exposure, and a 24-h collection is considered the most reliable method of establishing exposure. However, abnormal excretion levels indicate only that the potential for excess arsenic exposure exists. It does not establish intoxication, and transient increases are common after ingestion of some seafood. This is important because the organic form of arsenic contained in seafood is not neurotoxic (Albers & Garabrant, 2004). Because arsenic is bound to keratin, remote exposures can be documented by the amount of arsenic present in hair or nails, assuming contamination can be avoided. Like many neurotoxicants, there may be other non-specific laboratory findings that could reflect systemic involvement. In the case of arsenic, these abnormalities can include elevated liver function studies, pancytopenia, and basophilic stippling of red blood cells. Any one of the latter abnormal laboratory findings could prove a clue important in considering the possibility of a toxic exposure.

Summary

The neurologic and neuropsychologic examinations are the most fundamental form of standardized clinical testing that are capable of detecting subtle abnormalities potentially associated with neurotoxic exposure. The neurologist routinely interprets symptoms and signs in establishing the extent and clinical significance of a neurological impairment. The neurologist also is responsible for determining the cause of a specific problem before recommending treatment. These processes of establishing a diagnosis often include interpretation of results obtained from laboratory, electrodiagnostic, and imaging studies. In any application, it is important to know the limitations of individual tests, including information about their sensitivity and specificity.

There are numerous electrophysiologic tests that have been standardized and that have widespread application as part of the clinical neurological evaluation. The most frequently used in the neurotoxic evaluations are electrodiagnostic tests that evaluate peripheral nerve function. The peripheral nervous system is a common target of neurotoxic substances, and the conventional electromyography examination is used to evaluate patients with suspected peripheral neuropathy. These sensitivities and specificities of nerve conduction studies are established, and they are objective measures that are almost completely independent of patient cooperation or motivation. Other electrodiagnostic studies such as conventional EEG and evoked responses have extensive clinical application, although their application in potential neurotoxic evaluations is less well established.

References

Albers, J. W. (1990). Standardized neurological testing in neurotoxicology studies. In W. K. Anger, A. Durao, B. L. Johnson, & C. Xintarow (Ed.), *Proceedings of the*

Third International Symposium on Neurobehavioral Method in Occupational and Environmental Health (pp. 1–18), Chelsea: Levis.

Albers, J. W. (1998). Neurophysiologic tests: applications and limitations. In R. G. Feldman (Ed.), *Neurological toxicology: Diagnosis of occupational & environmental exposures* (pp 7PC.006-27 to 7PC.006-44). Minneapolis: American Academy of Neurology.

Albers, J. W. (2002). Neurological assessment: the role of the clinician in clinical neurotoxicology. In R. Masschelein (Ed.), *Neurotoxicology handbook* (pp. 507–549). Totowa: Humana.

Albers, J. W. & Garabrant, D. H. (2004). Arsenic poisoning. In D. J. Lynn and H. B. Newton (Eds.), *The 5-Minute Neurology Consult* (pp. 70–71). Philadelphia: Lippincott, Williams & Wilkins.

Albers, J. W., Hodach, R. J., Kimmel, D. W., & Treacy, W. L. (1980). Penicillamine-associated myasthenia gravis. *Neurology, 30*, 1246–1250.

Albers, J. W. & Wald, J. J. (1997). Neuroanesthesia and neuromuscular diseases. In M. S. Albin (Ed.), *Textbook of neuroanesthesia with neurosurgical and neuroscience perspectives* (pp. 453–499). New York: McGraw-Hill.

Albers, J. W., Wald, J. J., Garabrant, D. H., Trask, C. L., & Berent, S. (2000). Neurologic evaluation of workers previously diagnosed with solvent-induced toxic encephalopathy. *Journal of Occupational and Environmental Medicine, 42*, 410–423.

American Academy of Neurology (1991). Assessment: positron emission tomography. *Neurology, 41*, 163–167.

American Academy of Neurology (1993). *Assessment: posturography. Report of the therapeutics and technology assessment subcommittee. Neurology, 43*, 1261–1264.

American Academy of Neurology (2001). Clinical diagnostic guidelines (available at: http://www.aan.com).

American Diabetes Association (1988). Report and recommendations of the San Antonio Conference on diabetic neuropathy. *Muscle and Nerve, 11*, 661–667.

American Psychological Association (1985). *Standards for educational and psychological testing*. Washington, DC: APA.

American Psychiatry Association (1991). Quantitative electroencephalography: a report on the present state of computerized EEG technology. American Psychiatry Association Task Force on Quantitative Electrophysiological Assessment. *American Journal of Psychiatry, 148*, 961–964.

Aminoff, M. J. & Albers, J. W. (1999). Electrophysiologic techniques in the evaluation of patients with suspected neurotoxic disorders. In M. J. Aminoff (Ed.), *Electrodiagnosis in clinical neurology* (pp. 721–734). New York: Churchill Livingstone.

Arezzo, J. C., Simson, R., & Brennan, N. E. (1985). Evoked potentials in the assessment of neurotoxicity in humans. *Neurobehavioral Toxicology and Teratology, 7*, 299–304.

Bandettini, P. A., Wong, E. C., Hinks, R. S., Tikofsky, R. S., & Hyde, J. S. (1992). Time course EPI of human brain function during task activation. *Magnetic Resonance in Medicine, 25*, 390–397.

Berent, S. & Trask, C. L. (2000). Human neuropsychological testing and evaluation. In E. Massaro (Ed.), *Neurotoxicology handbook*, Vol. 2. Totowa, NJ: Humana.

Berger, A. R., Schaumburg, H. H., Schroeder, C., Apfel, S., & Reynolds, R. (1992). Dose response, coasting, and differential fiber vulnerability in human toxic neuropathy: a prospective study of pyridoxine neurotoxicity. *Neurology, 42*, 1367–1370.

Bigler, E. D. (1996a). *Neuroimaging I: Basic science*. New York: Plenum.

Bigler, E. D. (1996b). *Neuroimaging II: Clinical applications*. New York: Plenum.

Bleecker, M. L. (1985). Quantifying sensory loss in peripheral neuropathies. *Neurobehavioral Toxicology and Teratology*, *7*, 305–308.

Bleecker, M. L. (1986). Vibration perception thresholds in entrapment and toxic neuropathies. *Journal of Occupational Medicine*, *28*, 991–994.

Bloch, F., Hansen, W. W., & Packard, M. E. (1946). Nuclear induction. *Physical Review*, *69*, 127.

Boll, T. J. (2000). Measuring behavior. In J. W. Albers & S. Berent (Eds.), *Clinical neurobehavioral toxicology* (pp. 579–599). Philadelphia: W. B. Saunders.

Bolton, C. F. & Carter, K. M. (1980). Human sensory nerve compound action potential amplitudes: variation with sex and finger circumference. *Journal of Neurology, Neurosurgery and Psychiatry*, *43*, 925–928.

Bradley, W. G., Jr, Brant-Zawadzki, M., & Cambray-Forker, J. (2001). *MRI of the brain I* (2nd ed.). Philadelphia: Lippincott, Williams & Wilkins.

Budinger, T. F. & Lauterbur, P. C. (1984). Nuclear magnetic resonance technology for medical studies. *Science*, *226*, 288–298.

Buxton, R. B. (2002). *Introduction to functional magnetic resonance imaging: Principles and techniques*. Cambridge: Cambridge University Press.

Cakirer, S., Karaarslan, E., & Arslan, A. (2003). Spontaneously T1-hyperintense lesions of the brain on MRI: a pictorial review. *Current Problems in Diagnostic Radiology*, *32*, 194–217.

Calne, D. B., Eisen, A., & McGeer, E. (1986). Alzheimer's disease, Parkinson's disease, and motoneuron disease: abiotrophic interaction between aging and environment? *Lancet*, *ii*, 1067–1070.

Calne, D. B. & Snow, B. J. (1993). PET imaging in Parkinsonism. *Advances in Neurology*, *60*, 484–487.

Chaudhry, V., Eisenberger, M. A., Sinibaldi, V. J., Sheikh, K., Griffin, J. W., & Cornblath, D. R. (1996). A prospective study of suramin-induced peripheral neuropathy. *Brain*, *119*, 2039–2052.

Chelimsky, T. C., Low, P. A., Naessens, J. M., Wilson, P. R., Amadio, P. C., & O'Brien, P. C. (1995). Value of autonomic testing in reflex sympathetic dystrophy. *Mayo Clinic Proceedings*, *70*, 1029–1040.

Cherington, M. (1998). Clinical spectrum of botulism. *Muscle and Nerve*, *21*, 701–710.

D'Arceuil, H. E., De Crespigny, A. J., Rother, J., Seri, S., Moseley, M. E., Stevenson, D. K., & Rhihe, W. (1998). Diffusion and perfusion magnetic resonance imaging of the evolution of hypoxic ischemic encephalopathy in the neonatal rabbit. *Journal of Magnetic Resonance Imaging*, *8*, 820–828.

Denys, E. H. (1991). The influence of temperature in clinical electrophysiology. *Muscle and Nerve*, *14*, 795–811.

Division 40 Task Force on Education, A. a. C. (1989). Guidelines regarding the use of nondoctoral personnel in clinical neuropsychological assessment. *Clinical Neuropsychologist*, *3*, 23–24.

Donofrio, P. D. & Albers, J. W. (1990). Polyneuropathy: classification by nerve conduction studies and electromyography. *Muscle and Nerve*, *13*, 889–903.

Doyle, F. H., Gore, J. C., Pennock, J. M., Bydder, G. M., Orr, J. S., Steiner, R. E., Young, I. R., Burl, M., Clow, H., Gilderdale, D. J., Bailes, D. R., & Walters, P. E. (1981). Imaging of the brain by nuclear magnetic resonance. *Lancet*, *ii*, 53–57.

Dyck, P. J., Karnes, J. L., O'Brien, P. C., Litchy, W. J., Low, P. A., & Melton, L. J. (1992). The Rochester Diabetic Neuropathy Study: reassessment of tests and criteria for diagnosis and staged severity. *Neurology, 42*, 1164–1170.

Dyck, P. J., Kratz, K. M., Lehman, K. A., Karnes, J. L., Melton, L. J., O'Brien, P. C., Litchy, W. J., Windebank, A. J., Smith, B. E., & Low, P. A. (1991). The Rochester Diabetic Neuropathy Study: design, criteria for types of neuropathy, selection bias, and reproducibility of neuropathic tests. *Neurology, 41*, 799–807.

Eisenberg, H. M., Gary, H. E., Jr, Aldrich, E. F., Saydjari, C., Turner, B., Foulkes, M. A., Jane, J. A., Marmarou, A., Marshall, L. F., & Young, H. F. (1990). Initial CT findings in 753 patients with severe head injury. A report from the NIH Traumatic Coma Data Bank. *Journal of Neurosurgery, 73*, 688–698.

Eisenberg, R. L. (1992). Cathode rays and controversy. *American Journal of Roentgenology, 159*, 996.

Feldman, R. G. (1994). Occupational exposure to trichloroethylene: controversies concerning neurotoxicity. In M. A. Mehlman and A. Upton (Eds.), *The identification and control of environmental and occupational disease*. Princeton: Princeton Scientific Publ.

Feldman, R. G., Chirico-Post, J., & Proctor, S. P. (1988). Blink reflex latency after exposure to trichloroethylene in well water. *Archives of Environmental Health, 43*, 143–148.

Feldman, R. G., Mayer, R. M., & Taub, A. (1970). Evidence for peripheral neurotoxic effect of trichloroethylene. *Neurology, 20*, 599–606.

Feldman, R. G., Niles, C., Proctor, S. P., & Jabre, J. (1992). Blink reflex measurement of effects of trichloroethylene exposure on the trigeminal nerve. *Muscle and Nerve, 15*, 490–495.

Feldman, R. G., White, R. F., Eriator, I. I., Jabre, J. F., Feldman, E. S., & Niles, C. A. (1994). Neurotoxic effects of trichloroethylene in drinking water: approach to diagnosis. In R. L. Isaacson & R. F. Jensen (Eds.), *The vulnerable brain and environmental risks* (pp. 3–23). New York: Plenum.

Frackowiak, R. S. J. (1986). An introduction to positron emission tomography and its applications to clinical investigation. In M. R. Trimble (Ed.), *New brain imaging techniques and psychopharmacology* (pp. 25–34). Oxford: Oxford University Press.

Frackowiak, R. S. J., Lenzi, G. L., Jones, T., & Heather, J. D. (1980). Quantitative measurement of regional cerebral blood flow and oxygen metabolism in man using ^{15}O and positron emission tomography. *Journal of Computer Assisted Tomography, 4*, 727–736.

Freer, C. E. L. (1994). Imaging and the brain. In F. A. Huppert, C. Brayne, & D. W. O'Connor (Eds.), *Dementia and normal aging* (pp. 131–163). New York: Cambridge University Press.

Frey, K. A. (1999). Positron emission tomography. In G. J. Siegel, B. W. Agranoff, R. W. Albers, S. K. Fisher and M. D. Uhler (Eds.), *Basic neurochemistry: Molecular, cellular and medical aspects* (6th ed) (pp. 1109–1131). Philadelphia: Lippincott-Raven.

Frey, K. A. (2000). Neuroimaging in neurotoxicology. In J. W. Albers & S. Berent (Eds.), *Clinical neurobehavioral toxicology* (pp. 615–629). Philadelphia: W. B. Saunders.

Geisler, M. W. & Polich, J. (1992). P300 and individual differences: morning/evening activity preference, food, and time-of-day. *Psychophysiology, 29*, 86–94.

Gerr, F. & Letz, R. (1994). Covariates of human peripheral nerve function: II-vibrotactile and thermal thresholds. *Neurotoxicology and Teratology, 16*, 105–112.

Goetz, C. G. & Cohen, M. M. (1990). Neurotoxic agents. In A. B. Baker & L. H. Baker (Eds.), *Clinical neurology*, Vol.2 (p. 9). Philadelphia: J. B. Lippincott.

Goh, A. S. & Ng, D. C. (2003). Clinical positron emission tomography imaging – current applications. *Annals of the Academy of Medicine (Singapore)*, *32*, 507–517.

Halonen, P. (1986). Quantitative vibration perception thresholds in healthy subjects of working age. *European Journal of Applied physiology*, *54*, 647–655.

Housenfield, N. (1972). A method of and aparatus for examination of a body part by radiation such as X-ray or gamma radiation. British Patent #1283915.

Humphrey, J. H. & McClelland, M. (1944). Cranial-nerve palsies with herpes following general anaesthesia. *British Medical Journal*, *4*, 315–318.

Jacobs, A. H., Li, H., Winkeler, A., Hilker, R., Knoess, C., Ruger, A., Galldiks, N., Schaller, B., Sobesky, J., Kracht, L., Monfared, P., Klein, M., Vollmar, S., Bauer, B., Wagner, R., Graf, R., Wienhard, K., Herholz, K., & Heiss, W. D. (2003). PET-based molecular imaging in neuroscience. *European Journal of Nuclear Medicine and Molecular Imaging*, *30*, 1051–1065.

Junck, L. Albers, J. W., & Drury, I. J. (2000). Laboratory evaluation. In S. Gilman (Ed.), *Clinical examination of the nervous system* (pp. 269–303). New York: McGraw-Hill.

Kim, S. G. & Ugurbil, K. (1997). Functional magnetic resonance imaging of the human brain. *Journal of Neuroscience Methods*, *74*, 229–243.

Kinkel, W. R., Jacobs, L., & Kinkel, P. R. (1980). Gray matter enhancement: a computerized tomographic sign of cerebral hypoxia. *Neurology*, *30*, 810–819.

Kinnby, B., Konsberg, R., & Larsson, A. (1988). Immunogenic potential of some mercury compounds in experimental contact allergy of the rat oral mucosa. *Scandanavian Journal of Dental Research*, *96*, 60–68.

Latchaw, R. E. & Truwit, C. E. (1995). Imaging of perinatal hypoxic-ischemic brain injury. *Seminars in Pediatric Neurology*, *2*, 72–89.

Lee, S. H. & Rao, K. (1997). *Cranial computerized tomography and MRI* (2nd ed.). New York: McGraw-Hill.

Lezak, M. D. (1995). *Neuropsychological assessment.* (3rd ed.) New York: Oxford University Press.

Lingle, C. J. & Steinbach, J. H. (1988). Neuromuscular blocking agents. *International Anesthesiology Clinics*, *26*, 288–301.

Low, P. A., & Opfer-Gehrking, T. L. (1999). The autonomic laboratory. *American Journal of Electroneurodiagnostic Technology*, *39*, 65–76.

Low, P. A., Vernino, S., & Suarez, G. (2003). Autonomic dysfunction in peripheral nerve disease. *Muscle and Nerve*, *27*, 646–661.

Markand, O. N. (1984). Electroencephalography in diffuse encephalopathies. *Journal Clinical Neurophysiology*, *1*, 357–407.

Markowitsch, H. J. (1999). Functional neuroimaging correlates of functional amnesia. *Memory*, *7*, 561–583.

Matsumoto, J. Y. (1996). Movement-related potentials and event-related potentials. In J. R. Daube (Ed.), *Clinical neurophysiology* (pp. 141–144). Philadelphia: F. A. Davis.

Matthews, P. M. & Jezzard, P. (2004). Functional magnetic resonance imaging. *Journal of Neurology, Neurosurgery and Psychiatry*, *75*, 6–12.

Maurissen, J. P. J. (1985). Psychophysical testing in human populations exposed to neurotoxicants. *Neurobehavioral Toxicology Teratology*, *7*, 309–317.

Maurissen, J. P. J. (1988). Quantitative sensory assessment in toxicology and occupational medicine: applications, theory, and critical appraisal. *Toxicology Letters, 43*, 321–343.

Maurissen, J. P. J. & Chrzan, G. (1989). One-year reliability of vibration sensitivity thresholds in human beings. *Journal of Neurological Sciences, 90*, 325–334.

Moody, L., Arezzo, J. C., & Otto, D. (1986). Screening occupational populations for asymptomatic or early peripheral neuropathy. *Journal of Occupational Medicine, 28*, 975–986.

Namba, T., Nolte, C. T., Jackrel, J., & Grob, D. (1971). Poisoning due to organophosphate insecticides. Acute and chronic manifestations. *American Journal of Medicine, 50*, 475–492.

Novotny, E. J., Jr, Fulbright, R. K., Pearl, P. L., Gibson, K. M., & Rothman, D. L. (2003). Magnetic resonance spectroscopy of neurotransmitters in human brain. *Annals of Neurology, 54 (Suppl. 6)*, S25–S31.

Nuwer, M. (1997). Assessment of digital EEG, quantitative EEG, and EEG brain mapping: report of the American Academy of Neurology and the American Clinical Neurophysiology Society. *Neurology, 49*, 277–292.

Oldendorf, W. H. (1980). Some possible applications of computerized tomography in pathology. *Journal of Computer Assisted Tomography, 4*, 141–144.

Phelps, M. E., Mazziotta, J. C., & Schelbert, H. R. (1986). *Positron emission tomography and autoradiography. Principles and applications for the brain and heart.* New York: Raven.

Polich, J., Moore, A. P., & Wiederhold, M. D. (1995). P300 assessment of chronic fatigue syndrome. *Journal of Clinical Neurophysiology, 12*, 186–191.

Purcell, E. M., Taurry, H. C., & Pound, R. V. (1946). Resonance absorption by nuclear magnetic moments in a solid. *Physical Review, 69*, 37–41.

Redmond, J. M., McKenna, M. J., Feingold, M., & Ahmad, B. K. (1992). Sensory testing versus nerve conduction velocity in diabetic polyneuropathy. *Muscle and Nerve, 15*, 1334–1339.

Reitan, R. M. & Wolfson, D. (1993). *The Halstead–Reitan neuropsychological test battery: Theory and clinical interpretation.* Tucson: Neuropsychology Press.

Reivich, M., Kuhl, D., Wolf, A., Greenberg, J., Phelps, M., Ido, T., Casella, V., Fowler, J. Hoffman, E., Alavi, A., Sou, P., & Sokoloff, L. (1979). The [^{18}F]fluorodeoxyglucose method for the measurement of local cerebral glucose utilization in man. *Circulation Research, 44*, 127–137.

Rivner, M. H., Swift, T. R., Crout, B. O., & Rhodes, K. P. (1990). Toward more rational nerve conduction interpretations: the effect of height. *Muscle and Nerve, 13*, 232–239.

Rosenberg, N. L., Spitz, M. C., Filley, C. M., Davis, K. A., & Schaumburg, H. H. (1988). Central nervous system effects of chronic toluene abuse – clinical, brainstem evoked response and magnetic resonance imaging studies. *Neurotoxicology and Teratology, 10*, 489–495.

Sack, A. T. & Linden, D. E. (2003). Combining transcranial magnetic stimulation and functional imaging in cognitive brain research: possibilities and limitations. *Brain Research – Brain Research Reviews, 43*, 41–56.

Salek-Haddadi, A., Friston, K. J., Lemieux, L., & Fish, D. R. (2003). Studying spontaneous EEG activity with fMRI. *Brain Research – Brain Research Reviews, 43*, 110–133.

Salerno, D. F., Franzblau, A., Werner, R. A., Bromberg, M. B., Armstrong, T. J., &

Albers, J. W. (1998). Median and ulnar nerve conduction studies among workers: normative values. *Muscle and Nerve, 21*, 999–1005.

Salerno, D. F., Werner, R. A., Albers, J. W., Becker, M. P., Armstrong, T. J., & Franzblau, A. (1999). Reliability of nerve conduction studies among active workers. *Muscle and Nerve, 22*, 1372–1379.

Sanin, L. C., Kronenberg, M. F., & Stetkarova, I. (1993). Potentiation of the R component of blink reflex by anticipation [abstr.]. *Neurology, 43*, A289–A290.

Schaumburg, H. H. & Berger, A. R. (1993). Human toxic neuropathy due to inclusive agents. In *Peripheral neuropathy* (3rd ed.) (pp. 1533–1547). Philadelphia: W. B. Saunders.

Seppalainen, A. M. (1982). Neurophysiological findings among workers exposed to organic solvents. *Acta Neurologica Scandinavica, 92 (Suppl.)*, 109–116.

Simmons, Z. (1992). Nemaline myopathy; respiratory failure. Unpublished.

Society of Nuclear Brain Imaging Council (1996). Ethical clinical practice of functional brain imaging. *Journal of Nuclear Medicine, 37*, 1256–1259.

Sokoloff, L. (1983). Measurement of local glucose utilization and its use in localization of functional activity in the central nervous system of animals and man. *Recent Progress in Hormone Research, 39*, 75–126.

Sokoloff, L., Reivich, M., Kennedy, C., Des Rosiers, M. H., Patlak, C. S., Pettigrew, K. D., Sakurada, D. & Shirohara, M. (1977). The [14C]deoxyglucose method for the measurement of local cerebral glucose utilization: Theory, procedure and normal values in the conscious and anesthetized albino rat. *Journal of Neurochemistry, 28*, 897–916.

Sorenson, J. A. & Phelps, M. E. (1987). *Physics in nuclear medicine* (2nd ed.) Orlando: Grune & Stratton.

Stetson, D. S., Albers, J. W., Silverstein, B. A., & Wolfe, R. A. (1992). Effects of age, sex, and anthropometric factors on nerve conduction measures. *Muscle and Nerve, 15*, 1095–1104.

The Diabetes Control and Complications Trial Research Group (1993). The effect of intensive treatment of diabetes on the development and progression of long-term complications in insulin-dependent diabetes mellitus. *New England Journal of Medicine, 329*, 977–986.

Tippin, J., Adams, H. P., Jr, & Smoker, W. R. (1984). Early computed tomographic abnormalities following profound cerebral hypoxia. *Archives of Neurology, 41*, 1098–1100.

Trojaborg, W. T., Moon, A., Andersen, B. B., & Trojaborg, N. S. (1992). Sural nerve conduction parameters in normal subjects related to age, gender, temperature, and height: a reappraisal. *Muscle and Nerve, 15*, 666–671.

Ungerleider, L. G. (1995). Functional brain imaging studies of cortical mechanisms for memory. *Science, 270*, 769–775.

Van der Knaap, M. S., Jakobs, C., & Valk, J. (1996). Magnetic resonance imaging in lactic acidosis. *Journal of Inherited Metabolic Disease, 19*, 535–547.

Van Heertum, R. L. & Tikofsky, R. S. (2000). *Functional cerebral SPECT and PET imaging* (3rd ed.). Philadelphia: Lippincott, Williams & Wilkins.

Varnell, R. M., Stimac, G. K., & Fligner, C. L. (1987). CT diagnosis of toxic brain injury in cyanide poisoning: considerations for forensic medicine. *American Journal of Neuroradiology, 8*, 1063–1066.

Young, A. B., Penney, J. B., Starosta-Rubinstein, S., Markel, D. S., Berent, S., Giordani, B., Ehrenkaufer, R., Jewett, D., & Hichwa, R. (1986). PET scan investigations of Huntington's disease: cerebral metabolic correlates of neuro-logical features and functional decline. *Annals of Neurology*, *20*, 296–303.

Young, I. R., Hall, A. S., Pallis, C. A., Legg, N. J., Bydder, G. M., & Steiner, R. E. (1981). Nuclear magnetic resonance imaging of the brain in multiple sclerosis. *Lancet*, *ii*, 1063–1066.

Young, S. W. (1984). *Nuclear magnetic imaging: Basic principles*. New York: Raven.

8   Causality

Introduction

We do not know the cause for many of the clinical entities we deal with, and an accurate diagnosis, even an effective treatment plan, does not require causal determination in many clinical situations. Professionals are, nevertheless, often called upon to give an opinion regarding causality. The concept of causality is complex and not firmly defined. Even Webster's struggles when it comes to providing a succinct definition of the term. The definition of 'cause', according to Webster's (Merriam-Webster, 1993) is, 'something that brings about an effect or a result'. The concept of 'cause' has been viewed with scepticism by science. For one thing, the usefulness of the concept depends on the adequacy of the knowledge employed to render a causal explanation. This immediately leads to concerns about how such knowledge was obtained, as well as to questions about the accuracy, adequacy, and other aspects of that knowledge. While the concept of 'cause' on the surface appears to be simple, i.e., that which brings about an effect, the concept is difficult for science in that it is multidimensional, containing possibilities for serial as well as convergent and divergent explanations. Was more than one factor involved? Do we know all of the possible factors? Which factor came first? Which was the more influential? Stated simply, the challenge to science is to identify a causal relationship, or relationships, from amongst a myriad of potential spurious explanations. Awareness of these difficulties has been reflected in learned writings since ancient times (see Plato's *Dialogues* regarding the Sophists' challenges to Socrates; Hamilton & Cairns, 1961), and they have yet to be completely resolved.

Consider the following examples as illustrations of the complex issues that can arise in the determination of causation. Every year, dozens of pharmaceuticals enter clinical trials to evaluate their efficacy in modifying behavior or reducing neurological or psychological symptoms. Many of these agents have been available previously for other applications, but have been described in case reports to be effective in areas other than those initially established in controlled clinical trials. Without exception, many subjects in the new clinical studies will experience improvement, often dramatic, in their condition, regardless of whether or not the medication is ultimately found to be effective, and even regardless of whether the subject received the study drug or a placebo. This is, of course, the well-recognized, although not completely understood, *placebo effect*. Similarly, without debating the effectiveness of the numerous over-the-counter remedies available to improve memory, consider those who regularly experience increased cognitive and memory abilities after using such substances. How are these improvements to be explained? Perhaps the substance has an arousal effect associated with increased alertness. Maybe it reduces the person's anxiety, facilitating memory retrieval. Perhaps they unconsciously avoid challenging situations immediately after using the substance, or perhaps they just 'believe' that their memory and cognitive skills are improved. Such positive effects are not limited to cognition. Extend these considerations, for example, to a psychomotor activity, such as playing golf. The usually average golfer who makes an exceptionally good shot on one occasion may have numerous explanations for his or her success. If one thinks about the various factors, some known and some not, contained in the golf scenario just described, a host of possible causal explanations come to mind, some mentioned and some not. For instance, maybe it can be explained by new equipment, recent lessons, a particular wind or humidity conditions, better than usual concentration, a momentary distraction that left the golfer less self-conscious about form, or a lack of distraction resulting in a more efficient shot. Perhaps it had something to do with the person with whom he or she was playing, the absence or presence of another party on the hole, or the condition of the tee. It could have been a chance occurrence. Maybe it was a combination of factors, and perhaps one of these factors had more influence than did the others in the final result.

Viewed in this way, the determination of what caused someone's improved golf swing, or improved memory, seems to be an impossible task, even for someone who might be present to witness the event. Yet, many professionals appear to be quite willing to take on equally, or more, challenging problems of causal attribution, often with far less information than was available in the scenarios just described. Recognize that the difficulties associated with establishing that some medication or nutritional supplement 'caused' improvement are no different than those associated with establishing causation in terms of a purported adverse neurotoxicant effect. For instance, the person who believes that dental amalgams interfere with memory might experience a dramatic improvement in memory immediately after having his or her amalgams removed. It is scientifically unlikely, however, that amalgam removal, which results in increased exposure to elemental mercury immediately after removal, could so quickly produce improved memory. Nevertheless, there are those who have reported such an experience. It remains for the professional interested in clinical neurobehavioral toxicology to determine how such claims can be evaluated or explained. We hope to sensitize the reader to the complexities that are inherent in reaching explanatory conclusions for an event. At the same time, we wish to provide an orientation to the problem of causality that will allow one to address the issue effectively. In the end, however, the professional will be responsible for recognizing and communicating to others the limitations as well as the accuracy of her or his conclusions.

Patients will at times present to the clinician with some hypothesis about the cause of their complaint. In our experience, this appears to occur most often when the patient has vested some interest in a particular explanation – financial, intellectual, or personal. Sometimes the patient's suggestion of a cause is aimed simply to ensure that the clinician has 'all the facts'. A 79-year-old man with recent, mild but slowly progressive memory loss, for instance, reported that he was a retired electrician and that he had worked with solvent degreasers for many years before his retirement 14 years before.[1] He had read a newspaper article about the dangers of solvents in the workplace and wondered if this occupational background might be responsible for his symptoms of memory loss. The patient's spouse also reflected her concerns about her husband's past work with solvents. It is important to acknowledge the legitimacy of such concerns when the patient communicates them, and that was done in this case. It is important, also, to reassure the patient, and the patient's family when appropriate, that the clinical evaluation is designed to identify the problem and to determine further evaluation and treatment that may be indicated. In the process, all possible causes, including the concern presented by the patient, will be attended to within the context of a differential diagnosis. Unless it is blatantly clear that an expressed concern is unrelated to the presenting problem, e.g., a symptom that clearly represents some normal variation of physiological function, the initial phase of the evaluation is not the time to provide conclusions about the various diagnostic and etiological possibilities. First of all, the patient could be correct in his suspicion. Even when that is likely not to be the case, what can appear as a too casual dismissal of the patient's concerns could be interpreted as a lack of respect or negation of the legitimacy of the patient's thinking. Rapport between the clinician and patient could be damaged, and the patient and family members might become less likely than they were initially to share other important history with the clinician. Second, expressed concerns can have more than one meaning. When informed about a particular fact or occurrence, the clinician would do well to be curious about the reasons and alternative communications beyond the surface. In the present case, for example, the concerns about past work served to express the anxiety that was being experienced by the patient and his spouse. This was aside from what may have been the overt aim of ensuring that the clinician was aware of this history, perhaps in the hope that some treatable explanation for his complaints might be available. The test for a clinical proposition such as the one described above lies in its communication to the patient at the appropriate time in the clinical process; with an empathetic comment such as, 'I can see that you are very concerned about your symptoms and finding out why you are having them.' When the clinician's proposition is correct, its interpretation will affirm the legitimacy of the patient's concerns, allow the clinician to gauge more precisely the patient's mood by eliciting a more direct expression of the patient's feelings than may have been the case initially, and allow for helpful clinical intervention when appropriately indicated. When it is wrong, asking the question loses nothing. It is important, however, to state the proposition as a question, not as a conclusion.

The patient's final diagnosis in this particular example was 'probable Alzheimer disease' (American Academy of Neurology, 2001). The patient and his wife were informed in an *interpretive interview* (see Chapter 5) that, among other things, the temporal relationship between his work with solvents and the onset of his symptoms, as well as the subsequent symptom course, left it unlikely that his work history had anything to do with his memory loss. However, they were also told about the current state of our knowledge about progressive dementia and the fact that we do not yet know the exact cause of the disorder. The patient's dementia progressed over the course of the next 5 years in a pattern typical for Alzheimer disease. Until he was no longer able to communicate effectively with others, he never gave up his belief that his work with solvents was the cause of his illness. Among other things, this case illustrates the fact that, as mentioned above, we do not necessarily need to know the cause of something to arrive at a clinical diagnosis and treatment options. Cause may have multiple connotations and, for many, the clinical diagnosis itself is viewed as sufficient causal explanation.

Complex challenges inherent in the concept of causality led to active neglect of the concept by science for much of the 20th century. This reaction against causality was amply manifested by Karl Pearson who, building on the earlier work of Francis Galton, developed the contingency table and the mathematical concept of correlation (Pearl, 2000). Later developments, of course, brought back to science the legitimacy of considering cause and effect, but this did not minimize the complexities inherent in the concept or the concerns of science in reaching causal conclusions. To think in cause-and-effect terms is so ingrained in our thinking that anyone who has ever taken a statistics class will recall the emphasis placed by the instructor on cautioning that correlation does not imply causation. Of course, this lesson has been lost on some, and even scientists who should know better fall victim to the lure of cause by association. To think in terms of cause by association would appear to be adaptive to survival as it can manifest at an early age. On a trip to a national park years ago, one of the authors overheard a young child remark that the large number of black squirrels in the park must have resulted from the black birds that were also in great abundance in the park. 'The two must be related,' she remarked. In a young child, the fallacy of concluding causality from simple correlation can be cute, the reflection even of a bright mind. Further, knowledge of association may be as, or even more, valuable than knowing the true cause when it comes to the matter of immediate survival. A person who refuses to enter a jungle at night because he believes it to be haunted by evil spirits survives just as effectively as had he known about the eating practices of nocturnal predators. The implications of such parataxic thinking are far different when advanced by a professional who is seeking to establish an objective truth about a cause-and-effect relationship.

To provide an example from more formal research, recent analyses of some as yet unpublished data by the authors revealed statistically significant correlations between five of seven neurobehavioral summary outcome variables and the subjects' historical records of exposure to a pesticide (Berent, Albers, Garabrant, Giordani, Schweitzer, Garrison, Richardson, & Raz, n.d.). These relationships were not the result of extreme outliers as scatter plots revealed clear and continuous linear relationships between exposure and outcome for each neurobehavioral measure. The neurobehavioral outcome summary variables that showed a significant relationship to historical exposure included general intellect, problem-solving, verbal memory, visual memory, and psychomotor performance. The two of seven remaining measures were language and emotional functioning. While at first glance it might seem plausible based on these data to infer that the history of exposure must in some way be causally linked to neurobehavioral outcome, such a conclusion would be scientifically improper and, as it turns out, wrong. Returning to the example, we next performed a step-wise regression analysis in order to account for potential confounders. The first factor to be included in this analysis was age, and this variable was found to explain the seeming relationship between psychomotor functioning and historical exposure. Age represented a true confounder since it was related to both historical exposure and to psychomotor slowing (Lezak, 1995). The next factor entered was education level, and this factor was found to explain the remaining four outcome measures that initially appeared to be significantly related to historical exposure. The final conclusion to be drawn from these scientifically proper analyses is that neurobehavioral outcome was explained by a simple regression model that contained a combination of historical exposure, age, and education. A combination of age and education was explanatory, while historical exposure was not explanatory. Unfortunately, it is fairly easy to find published examples of conclusions based on correlations similar to those we observed initially but without consideration of potential confounders.

Causality as invention

The concept of causality is a human invention.[2] Despite its seemingly evolutionary characteristics, the concept may not be inherent to the human mind universally, and there is at least one culture in which the practice of causal attribution appears to be absent. The Shokleng people of the Amazon in South America were found to be empirical in their observations of the world, with no apparent need to explain the 'why' behind their observations (O'Barr, 2001). Even in those cultures that do employ the concept of causation, there is no universal agreement on the parameters used to explain an event. O'Barr, for instance, described the Azande people of the Eastern Sudan in contrasting the ways in which two cultures, the Azande and the Western World, might differ when explaining the same occurrence in terms of cause and effect. While each of these cultures has the capacity to deal with the observable facts involved in an occurrence, either might invoke superstition or other paranormal occurrence to explain the event as well. In the West, an accident might be explained on the basis of faulty tires, speeding, or some other observable or deducible event or series of events, but fate or divine intervention might also be offered as an explanation. The Azande, too, might recognize the physical factors involved in an accident, but, for the Azande, there is always a sorcerer or witch (an evil person) at work in the explanation for any accident (O'Barr, 2001).

How the individual sees the world influences their view of cause even within a given culture. A patient suffering from acute schizophrenia appeared to be in terrible personal agony until he 'realized' that the reason for his confused thinking was the result of a clandestine 'CIA experiment'. This type of realization is sometimes referred to as 'psychotic insight' and may mark the change from the acute to the chronic form of this disorder (Berent, 1986). Once such a realization has been made by the patient, his demeanor appears to be calmer than in the acute phase, perhaps underscoring the importance placed in our society on the need for, and perhaps the functional significance of, an explanation. One might ask how such a disorder would manifest itself in the Shokleng culture discussed above, where causal explanation appears to be absent. The truth or falsity of the explanation is not of paramount importance. Nor is the content, and one sees the function of anxiety reduction in normal individuals as well as patients who do not evidence psychopathology. In the case example of the patient with Alzheimer disease who wondered about the causal relationship between his symptoms and his historical work with solvents, for instance, the idea of having some explanation for his plight appeared to provide him with some comfort. He was resistant to discarding this explanation, even when presented with contradictory evidence. The content of proposed causal events can be more or less plausible and could include anything from 'the boss has it in for me' to the effects of a 60 cycle current from overhead electrical wires or toxicants in the environment. Sometimes the individual has intractably adopted the explanation. At other times, it appears to be a proposition under consideration. Clinicians are familiar with the patient who asks whether a particular symptom might be due to this or to that cause. Of course, such questions demand that the clinician deal with issues of causality and have the knowledge to explain why the patient's query is not likely or to present a plan about how the suspicion will be further investigated. The bottom line is that most of us think in terms of cause and effect, and we appear to be comforted by having a causal explanation for events we experience. Interestingly, this comfort may occur even at those times when the explanation provides nothing to change the situation. We have observed patients express relief when they had just been given a terminal diagnosis. When asked about this seemingly paradoxical reaction, one patient said, 'Well, now I have a real explanation for my symptoms. At least, I know I am not just crazy.' It may be that similar reasoning applies to the patient with a diagnosis of schizophrenia as discussed above. While most of us would rather not become the target of a secret government experiment, 'discovering' that to be the case might help alleviate the panic that accompanies feeling that one is losing self-control.

Science as a belief system

Why does the patient bring personal concerns, and questions regarding possible causes, to the clinician? Similarly, why does the legal system look to scientists for help in determining causality in the courtroom? The answer is simply that science, or more precisely the scientific method (see Chapter 3), has come to be accepted as a systematic and objective way best to determine the relative importance of potentially causative factors amongst an almost unlimited myriad of possible explanatory variables. The clinician looks to science in order to bring objectivity to her or his practice. The patient looks to the clinical institution for answers because he or she has been taught that this institution has the objective (i.e., scientifically derived) knowledge to 'know' the explanation for the complaint. In this way of thinking, science reflects a belief system, one that has been consensually agreed upon as the best way to escape the quagmire of our subjectivity. While belief in a particular institution like science may be the best we can do at the moment, it is important to note that the expectations placed on science, and its spokespersons, as a result of this esteemed role will far exceed the realities of the method's limitations ability to solve personal and societal problems. For one thing, science proceeds in small and cautious steps, each advance in knowledge building upon what has been learned before and indicating new questions that remain to be answered. While objectivity does lead to the value of learning something that we did not know, there is still the reality that there is much more to learn than is known. In the area of toxicology, for instance, it has been estimated that there are about 100,000 substances that have been registered for commercial use and that most of these have not been well studied in terms of their possible health effects (Conley, 2001).

One should not confuse 'belief' in a system with the idea of 'belief' with regard to the knowledge that is generated by that system. One of the authors was once asked while giving testimony in a discovery deposition whether or not he 'believed' that low-level, chronic exposure to solvents such as trichloroethylene could produce the symptoms that were complained about by the plaintiff in question. While such a question might on the surface appear innocuous, in actuality it is fraught with complexity, and it challenges an important aspect of the conceptual foundation of the scientific approach. To address such a question required that the expert first clarify for the questioner the nature of science as a method for enquiry and the nature of the knowledge that is generated by this method. To paraphrase, the expert responded to the question by saying that it was not a matter of what the expert believed, but, rather, it was a matter of what the expert viewed as the current state of the scientifically derived knowledge about this topic.

One's beliefs are a matter of personal opinion, and there is a difference between one's personal and professional opinions. Professional opinions derive from the status of current, objectively derived data, which may or may not be compatible with our personal wishes or beliefs. Beyond contributing to the generation of testable hypotheses, the personal opinions held by an individual are of little importance in the deposition situation described above. A better question by the attorney in the example given, from the expert's viewpoint, would have been the following: 'What in your opinion is the current state of our knowledge with regard to the effects of low-level, chronic exposure to solvents such as trichloroethylene on the nervous system and behavior?' Questions asked in depositions, however, are not likely to be phrased as the expert would wish, and one has to respond carefully to what is asked. In this instance, the attorney's question as originally posed was a compound of multiple inferred questions in addition to its surface meaning. Some of these questions included what the expert believes about the effects of such exposure, whether or not the expert believes the plaintiff's symptoms were the result of such exposure, is the expert biased, and would the expert accept the existence of such a causal relationship under any circumstances. Also, as originally presented, the question invited the expert to accept certain implied assumptions in rendering an answer, e.g., that all solvents might represent a class of agents with effects similar to trichloroethylene and that the plaintiff did indeed manifest certain symptoms, to name two of these implied assumptions. Whether intentional or not, compound questions such as described are commonly asked in legal proceedings. The expert would do well to listen carefully to what is asked, and request that ambiguous questions be clarified and that a compound question be simplified so that each component can be addressed in turn. When the question is posed in a clear and simple form that can be answered, the expert can respond. In so doing, the expert may, as in the present example, need to provide very briefly some education about the nature of her or his work. To provide an accurate answer, of course, the expert must have the discipline required to distinguish professional knowledge from personal belief. Aside from personal gain and satisfaction and the value of making a contribution to the legal system that might derive from acting as an expert witness, the demand on the professional to remain current in knowledge and disciplined in the communication of that knowledge represent professional benefits that come from such involvement. It should not be forgotten, however, that one needs to be cautious and disciplined in all aspects of professional work and that serving in the capacity of expert should never take precedence over those activities that make one an expert to begin with.

On the nature of scientific knowledge

This might be a good place to remind the reader that clarifying what is not known can be as important as is recounting what is known about a given topic. Distinctions can be drawn between personally not knowing something, knowing what is not known, and recognizing what cannot be known. It is important to make these distinctions clear in responding to questions, whether responding to patients, attorneys, colleagues, or one's own thinking. The answer 'I don't know' can be ambiguous if it does not convey the correct connotation of what is meant by that response. If speaking to methodological limitations, a clear answer would be something like, 'The methods of science are not suited to address that particular question.' In another instance, a clear answer might be, 'Science has not yet addressed (or concluded its work) on that problem.' Of course, when it is a matter of personal lack of knowledge, it is important to state, 'I do not know the answer to that question.' Although it occurs, personal ignorance is fortunately rare when a professional has correctly held him- or herself out to others as an expert in a given topic. One is more likely to have to say that he or she will need to consult a reference work before giving an answer to a given question. It is not reasonable to expect that even an expert will know by rote fashion every fact that might be requested. Also, it is likely that there will be times when the question will be about something that is outside of the person's area of expertise. Knowing what is, and is not, within one's professional purview is important, and when asked, the expert makes the questioner aware of that. Professionals have become highly specialized, and the true expert recognizes his or her own areas and levels of competence. One might qualify as an expert in one or more areas but not in another, even though it might lie within one's own professional discipline. A clear notion of areas of specialty expertise is especially important in a field like neurobehavioral toxicology because of the multidisciplinary nature of this endeavor. This requirement is not limited to the legal setting.

Science and the legal system

Recognizing its limitations, while reflecting a continuing belief in the scientific approach, the legal system in recent years has become increasingly stringent in validating science in its courts. This increased vigilance has not been without criticism, but is perhaps best reflected in the movement from the *Frye* test of the admissibility of an expert's testimony to the *Daubert* criteria. Frye and Daubert both derived from key court decisions that are beyond the scope of this work to detail. Briefly, however, under Frye, a court would allow testimony based on the determination that the opinions to be offered by the expert were within the mainstream of scientific opinion (Sanders & Machal-Fulks, 2001). Following Daubert, however, the court is invited to decide on the reliability of the evidence to be offered, that is, to examine the methodology and reasoning that forms the basis for the expert's opinion (Sanders & Machal-Fulks, 2001). In other words, how sound is the science that underlies the expert's opinion? Both Frye and Daubert are most likely imperfect in deciding on the admissibility of an expert's testimony. Science is not fixed, either in terms of its knowledge base or in its methodology. Science continually scrutinizes its own methods and philosophical underpinnings. The business of science is to generate new knowledge, and this leads to a continually changing knowledge base and, therefore, changes in consensus. The courts are faced with a tremendous task in developing a lasting formula for determining the admissibility of a given expert's opinion. Having said that, one might ask, what should the expert do when presenting testimony in court? The simple answer to this question is the following: do what you always do. That is, reflect professional opinions that are consistent with your training, experience, and usual practices.

In response to a question about career objectives, a student once confided in her supervisor that she wanted to be an 'expert witness'. Aside from the observation that one needs to examine the communication of professional priorities to elicit such a response from a trainee, the response by the professor was, 'If that is your wish, then the first thing you must do is become an expert.' It is a serious mistake to change what one does in everyday practice in order to fit perceived legal expectations. Sherman (1994), for instance, called attention to the fact that there is a complex distinction between scientific and legal proof. Sherman stated, 'Scientists, accustomed to the laboratory are often hesitant to attempt an opinion concerning a medical–legal matter, erroneously believing that 100% certainty is required.' She went on to contrast her observation about scientific certainty to the requirement by most courts dealing with toxic tort cases that there be a *more likely than not* cause-and-effect relationship or contribution to the person's injury. As a basis for determining these more likely than not relationships, Sherman indicated that most courts require that the probability of correctness must be greater than 50%. The reader should be cautioned not to interpret Sherman's remarks to mean that scientific findings can be considered 'factual' if they are based on studies that report significance at $p < 0.50$. In using this greater than chance rule in the court, the judicial system can employ a wide range of information in arriving at its own conclusion, as well as to give one side or the other the 'benefit of the doubt' in the decision process. An important part of the information available to the court in the decision-making process is represented by the data, reasoning, and opinions provided by the expert witness. These should be based on the customary professional practices of the expert, not modified to meet a different set of criteria, i.e., those of the court. The court can do that for itself. As the student mentioned above was advised, it is the person's expertise in a given field that qualifies him or her to give testimony. For the individual giving testimony to modify what is customarily done in their discipline is to move from being an expert in one's own area to become a novice in another person's field. Such a change affects both methodology and the fund of knowledge and, therefore, fits neither the Frye nor the Daubert criteria for determining acceptable testimony.

The logical (rational) and the empirical

In science

It is important to discuss logical–empirical distinctions to some extent since they are foundationally involved in scientific method and also influence the nature of clinical practice. A statement can be logically true or false, and the rules that are applied to document the validity of this have been developed over thousands of years. The validity of these propositions is determined through *deductive logic* and assumes the truth of specified underlying axioms. For instance, if A = B and B = C, then A = C is a logically true statement. Such a proposition becomes much more complex, however, when the idea of cause and effect comes into the picture. For example, if 'A' causes 'B' and 'C' causes 'B,' then 'A' causes 'C' is not a valid conclusion. Why? The explanation is simply that both 'A' and 'C' may be causally related to 'B,' but for totally different reasons. In the example given above about the relationship between historical exposure to pesticide and neurobehavioral outcomes, for instance, an apparent relationship was initially observed between exposure and psychomotor performance. Following analyses that properly considered the effects of confounding, however, it was revealed that age, and not historical exposure, was the significant factor affecting psychomotor function. In that situation, exposure was associated with outcome because of its association with age, the latter being the significant factor affecting psychomotor function. Outcome (A) was related to age (B), and exposure (C) was related to 'B,' but 'C' was not directly related to 'A'. As one ages, psychomotor function may decline. Also, with the passage of time, i.e., aging, cumulative measures of exposure increase. The apparent relationship between exposure and performance was spurious, a by-product of the cumulative nature of the exposure measure.

The application of deductive reasoning to answer professionally relevant questions is more complex than the simple models would suggest. In actuality, few variables are unitary, and the terms 'A', 'B', and 'C' used above are more precisely defined by a series of conditions under which these relationships occur. Most of us will have observed misuses of these formulas, based either on oversimplification of one or more terms in the formulas, failure scientifically or otherwise objectively to document the premised functional relationships between variables, or by commission of invalid reasoning in stating 'logical' conclusions. Consider, for example, the professional, who in giving expert testimony in a toxic tort matter states the following. 'The plaintiff worked with organophosphorus pesticides. Such pesticides are known to produce the symptoms evidenced by the plaintiff. Therefore, the most likely explanation for his symptoms is exposure to pesticides at work.' Often, in our experience, such causal attribution is accompanied by a phrase such as, 'I am not aware of anything else it could be' or 'There is no other substance that produces this constellation of symptoms.' While, depending on the source, the first of these two statements may be believable, the second is almost never correct. Symptoms, even constellations of symptoms, are seldom this specific with regard to an underlying cause.

In this example of the worker presumably exposed to pesticide, the rules of deductive logic are violated in several ways. First, there is an oversimplification of the many factors involved in that the conditions associated with A, B, and C were not specified. Translating the expert's reasoning into a deductive model, it appears that 'A' = exposure to pesticide, 'B' = the fact that exposure can give rise to a specified collection of symptoms, and 'C' = the plaintiff's symptoms. Even if we were able to document that the conditions of this exposure were capable of producing a specified set of symptoms (A = B) and, further, that the plaintiff evidenced the symptoms described in 'B' (C = B), the rules of logic given above would preclude our being able to conclude that exposure caused the plaintiff's symptoms (i.e., that A = C). Put another way, the plaintiff's symptoms might be due to something else entirely. In this example, the expert's reasoning is a case of pseudo-logic in that it achieves only a semblance of the logical model. It sounds logical when, in fact, it is not. Neither association nor commonality alone is capable of establishing causality. By commonality, we mean that a cause cannot be inferred by effect alone. This important fact is a reason for scientific method in general as well as the basis for differential diagnosis in clinical practice. Many of the symptoms of disease, including the adverse effects of chemicals, are non-specific. Usually, there are many possible explanations for the patient's complaints, including misinterpretation of normal variations in physical and psychological functions. Concluding the 'obvious' when determining causation is more the stuff of superstition than of science. Take, for example, an elderly patient who has been diagnosed with Parkinson disease (PD) and who develops dementia over the course of several months in treatment. Since dementia is known to occur in PD (Vander, Minoshima, Giordani, Foster, Frey, Berent, Albin, Koeppe, & Kuhl, 1997), the 'obvious' conclusion would be that this is a product of disease progression and the patient's diagnosis would be changed from simple PD to PD with dementia. A proper differential diagnostic process, however, might reveal that the patient's new symptoms are the result of adverse side-effect to a medication, an independently treatable and reversible condition.

Deductive reasoning is an important part of Mathematics. It also has a place in science and clinical practice, e.g., as a method for hypothesis generation, in reaching conclusions in the process of differential diagnosis, in the interpretation of findings from empirical research, and in reaching reasoned conclusions more generally. However, it is also a method that is easily abused to sound scientific when that might not be the case or even to fall victim ourselves to the seeming logic of our deductions when those deductions are, in fact, illogical. In many ways, deductive reasoning is limited by its assumptions. To be accurate, these assumptions need to be based on factual knowledge.

In the example about the pesticide worker in a tort case given above, for instance, one would need to know, at the least, that exposure to pesticides can in fact lead to certain symptoms or to a specified set of symptoms before making an attempt to deduce a causal link. Thinking in terms of those variables that are known to be associated with the terms 'A', 'B', and 'C' in the model, one would need to identify and objectively verify as many of these as possible. For example, what kind of pesticide was the person exposed to? Often, these are organophosphorus compounds that have the capacity to inhibit acetylcholinesterase (AChE). Not all of these compounds are equally toxic to humans, and Feldman (1998) described four major categories that, among other things, reflect the relative toxicity of the specific compound to humans. These categories, according to Feldman, include phosphorylcholines (highly toxic, e.g., phospholine), fluorophophorus compounds (next most toxic, e.g., sarin), cyanophosphorus and halophosphorus compounds (e.g., tabun), and the relatively least toxic alkylphosphorus and arylphosphorus compounds (e.g., dichlorvos). It is this last category of chemicals that has the lowest impact on AChE that is generally used for commercial pesticides. To complicate matters, the final pesticide product is at times a combination of primary compounds and other substances, the latter having at times themselves the potential for toxicity. The presence of these compounds in the exposed person can be determined through laboratory tests, although often such test results are unavailable. When they are available, they may be difficult to interpret, and it is likely that it is only the acutely and severely exposed person who has been tested. When these test results are not forthcoming, the clinician must use some analog in an attempt to approximate the exposure. Such analogs range from a description of the physical environment from which the person is known to have come (e.g., occupation as an insecticide applicator), to actions or experiences the person may have had (e.g., a home owner whose house was recently treated for termites), to responses to treatment attempts (e.g., improvement following treatment with atropine). The further removed one becomes from objective evidence for exposure to a specified substance, the greater is the chance for an erroneous assumption regarding exposure.

When exposure is considered to be well documented, there is the need to know the consequences of such exposure. What can occur as a result of exposure, as well as what are the consequences of such factors as amount and duration and route of exposure (dermal, pulmonary, ingestion). Biological sensibility here becomes an important consideration. That is, the signs and symptoms that might result from overexposure to organophosphorus (OP) pesticides should reflect inhibition of AChE and the resultant increase in acetylcholine (ACh) at receptor sites. This might include muscle fasciculations, muscle weakness, slowed heart rate and lowered blood pressure, excessive salivation, visual changes, and in more severe cases lethargy, ataxia, seizures, coma, and death. While not manifest in all cases, three stages of symptom progression have been described. These include the initial 'acute cholinergic crisis', an 'intermediate syndrome', and 'delayed peripheral neuropathy' (Feldman, 1998). Of course, what is biologically sensible depends on how well we understand the biology of the systems that underlie clinical manifestations, in general and specifically in this instance with regard to OP exposure. This understanding, in turn, derives from scientific inquiry. While much is known about the toxic effects of OP exposure, we are forever limited by the need to remain within the confines of reasonable limits to research generalization. Over-generalization can make for excellent hypothesis generation but can be erroneous in the determination of causality. To a considerable extent, our conclusions using the deductive model will be as valid as the knowledge upon which our assumptions are based.

Consider for a moment the case of long-term, low-level exposure to toxic substances. As just briefly reviewed above, we know a considerable amount about the acute effects of OP overexposure. It is compelling to generalize from that knowledge to hypothesize that similar events, if to a lesser extent of severity, will occur when an individual is exposed to lower amounts of the same compounds. If so, such a finding might have meaningfulness beyond the effects of OP alone and help to explain a host of illnesses for which we do not yet have a complete etiological understanding, e.g., Alzheimer disease and Parkinson disease, to mention two examples. Such reasoning makes for excellent science in that it has the capacity to lead to creative research, which in turn could produce findings of enormous theoretical and applied importance. Too often, however, individuals confuse the asking of a good question with having the answer. Studies may be cited that appear to support one side of the issue or another, although the research may be flawed or otherwise inconclusive or only partially relevant to the original question. This type of activity might be driven by 'dissonance reduction' (the tendency to select, and even perceive, information that supports our declared viewpoint while giving less respect to opposing views or facts; Festinger, 1957, 1962) or by some other human motivation. While such non-scientific reasoning sometimes finds its way into clinical treatment applications, it is more likely to appear in legislative lobbying, in the context of litigation, or in casual conversation. This is the stuff of pseudo-science in that the work of science has not yet provided an understanding of the proposed phenomena, sufficient to espouse its validity. Is the proposed relationship between toxin and pathology possible in such scenarios? The answer to this question, of course, is that anything is possible. In fact, such hypotheses are often quite plausible. When talked about enough, they may become labeled as 'controversial' (Albers & Berent, 2000) or even accepted as fact by the public. The designation 'controversial' itself may become used by proponents of such propositions as if to impart some truth to the concept.

The scientist speaks to what is probable when drawing conclusions, however, and the possible is left to empirical test. When these empirical tests are not yet complete, the answer can only be, 'it is unknown'. As discussed above, it must be stated clearly when making such an assertion, perhaps especially in the context of giving legal testimony, that no one knows, not you alone. While this does not prohibit one from addressing the issue in an individual case, it does mean that it would be wrong to label it as fact under the assumptions required by the deductive model. The clinical methods described in this volume are used to provide the 'facts' needed to address the variables associated with the individual. Always, however, the findings from clinical examination must be filtered through the scientifically derived database in reaching final decisions about what can be included in our reasoning. While deduction is important to the process of reaching conclusions based upon what is known, the generation of new factual knowledge requires inductive logic.

Inductive logic can be contrasted with deductive reasoning, the former referring often to a combination of empirical inquiry and logic (Burks, 1977). The logic of empirical enquiry follows certain rules that, for the present purpose, can be thought of as scientific method (see Chapter 3). At the risk of oversimplification, one of these rules is to formulate a question and then to test its truth or falsity through systematic observation. Through observation, we discover new truths, some of which might contradict underlying premises we held to be true and some that might go beyond the then present state of knowledge. That is, we might need to change the way in which we previously thought about a given topic, or we might discover a fact that is without causal explanation. Consider for a moment the proposition 'if $A = B$ and $B = C$, then $A = C$'. In keeping with our earlier illustration, let 'A' represent exposure to OP pesticides, 'B' the symptoms of such exposure, and 'C' a person known to have been exposed to an OP compound. As was done by the 'expert' in our earlier example, it might appear that one could reasonably deduce from this proposition that person 'C' will evidence the symptoms represented by 'B' in our model; however, actual observation might reveal that 'C' is symptom free. Further, even if person in 'C' were found to have such symptoms, we would still not be able to conclude that these were caused by 'A', since the dysfunction might be due to something else entirely. This scenario underscores the importance of empirical observation and the need to consider observable phenomena in making logical conclusions. It is rendered inductive through the inclusion of a conditional proposition (a hypothesis, see Chapter 3). If 'C' is (or has been) exposed to 'A', then 'C' will evidence the symptoms described in 'B'. As will be readily apparent, the hypothesis as described is necessary to conclude objectively an association between 'A' and 'C', but it is not likely sufficient in itself to conclude a causal relationship. Depending on the nature of the results from observation (e.g., the outcome of a clinical evaluation), the findings may either support or fail to support a positive connection between 'A' and 'C'. Through a series of such propositions and tests, however, evidence can be accumulated that will allow for a properly reasoned, if probabilistic, conclusion about the proposed relationship.

An important note to make about the results of inductive argument is that these results are always probable, never absolute, since something could always occur by chance (Burks, 1977). Also, there could be causal factors at work that were not considered in the parameters of the observation, e.g., confounders. Again, Burks provided an effective example of such a situation. A symmetrical coin would be expected to land heads 50% of the time following multiple tosses. Therefore, a reasonable proposition would be that if a coin were tossed 50 times, it would land heads 25 times and tails 25 times. Suppose, though, that a given coin is tossed repeatedly and found to land heads 70% of the time? Provided that this experiment were repeated enough times to ensure a difference from the expected greater than chance (traditionally a level of $p < 0.05$), we might conclude that our knowledge about the behavior of a symmetrical coin does not necessarily generalize to all coins. With further investigation, we could probably discover the peculiar aspects of the irregular coin, e.g., it could be disproportionately weighted on one side. Also, there is the problem of negative results, not confirming a proposed relationship does not prove it does not exist. The negative result indicates only that under the conditions of our observation, it was not found. This last comment is no small point in that it underscores the importance of systematization in science, e.g., careful recording of the procedures and methods employed as well as other aspects of the observation or experiment. Perhaps the coin that showed the unanticipated proportion of heads versus tails in our example was not asymmetrical at all. It could be that the conditions under which the coin was tossed differed between the two experiments. In fact, both propositions could be true (i.e., that a coin will land heads 50% of the time and that it will land heads 70% of the time), the difference being explainable by some interaction between two or more factors. To distinguish between the two different outcomes in a given condition, however, is something that is done regularly in science and, in so doing, one or the other may be found to be empirically true or false (Burks, 1977). Although establishing cause and effect may not be necessary to the process, through the step-wise approach in science, and building upon both negative and positive findings, we can at some point approximate causal relationships. At the least, we may be able to state that something is more probable than not.

In clinical practice

Newton (2001: p. 299) defined 'rationalism' in the field of medicine as, 'the search for and emphasis on basic mechanisms of disease'. 'Empiricism', Newton defined as, 'the emphasis on the outcomes of individual patients and groups of patients'. Newton viewed the modern clinical setting as one of tension between these two theoretical orientations. In terms of causality, the rational approach looks to underlying mechanisms that lead to disease manifestation. The empiricist is likely to view disease as multiply determined and conditional on a variety of intervening factors. Following publication of the Flexner (1960) report, the model for medical education changed dramatically, according to Newton. This change, he believes, was in large part a move away from the empirical approach in medicine at the time to a model that emphasized the investigation of underlying mechanisms of disease and of relating fact to theory. As such, Newton wrote, it 'was a triumph of rationalism over empiricism'. While the physician needed to care for patients, the Flexner model essentially based medical practice in laboratory science. In the specialty of Clinical Psychology, the 'Boulder', 'Scientist–Practitioner' model (Baker & Benjamin, 2000) called for the clinician to be trained as a scientist as well as a practitioner, and in actuality, the Boulder model may be more in the empirical than in the analytic tradition. The Boulder model calls for a scientific orientation in the sense of systematic approaches to treatment. This seems to be in the empirical tradition. While one can identify clinical techniques in Psychology that derived from theory (e.g., analytically oriented psychotherapy, measurement of memory function), many others have proven to be empirical (e.g., the Minnesota Multiphasic Personality Inventory). At the least, there is a mixture of theory as well as empiricism in these applied clinical approaches.

For Newton (2001), the advent of clinical epidemiology in the mid to late 1900s strengthened the empirical approach in medicine and set the stage for critical appraisals of clinical knowledge. This shift in emphasis, again according to Newton, led to the development of such activities as 'outcomes research', 'practice guidelines', and 'evidence-based medicine'.

Evidence-based medicine (EBM)

EBM is mentioned and discussed in a number of places in the present work. Also, the general principles contained in this approach to understanding clinical problems permeate the treatment of clinical case material we present in various sections of the present work. 'EBM' is the term used to describe an approach to clinical care that underlies a series of papers published in the *Journal of the American Medical Association* (Guyatt & Rennie, 1993). While these writings were aimed at the medical profession, they are equally applicable to other disciplines that rely on scientific research and literature for their work, e.g., Psychology. Also, the strategies reported in the series of papers were designed originally for medical disorders, but they apply to all healthcare conditions. The approach consists of a sequence of guidelines that permit the clinician to integrate information derived from published research into the care of individual patients. Although the term 'EBM' is well established, the rubric 'evidence-based healthcare' is equally appropriate (Guyatt, Haynes, Jaeschke, Cook, Green, Naylor, Wilson & Richardson, 2000a; Guyatt, Meade, Jaeschke, Cook, & Haynes, 2000b).

Several aspects of EBM are directly applicable to the concepts established herein for neurobehavioral toxicology. Clinicians appropriately rely on knowledge obtained from clinical research, independent of the intended use of the information. For example, strategies that evaluate the validity of published research apply equally well to diagnostic or treatment decisions. Inherent in the acquisition of new knowledge derived from the literature is information about clinical manifestations of a given disease. EBM has as its foundation the scientific method. A fundamental premise of EBM is that clinical intuition, unsystematic clinical experience, and authoritative statements based on unscientific rationale are inadequate methodologies for deriving clinical decisions about diagnoses or treatment (Guyatt *et al.*, 2000b). An important aspect of EBM involves a methodology to determine whether available evidence fulfills certain basic standards involving validity, results, and applicability. The methodology of EBM emphasizes a set of defined hypothesis-generating and -testing rules that emulate the scientific method and are complementary to professional training and common sense. Particularly relevant to our purposes are the EBM criteria used to verify a patient's diagnosis and critically evaluate published papers on disease manifestation (Richardson, Wilson, Williams, Moyer, & Naylor, 2000, and Chapters 3 and 4).

Conclusions

Near the beginning of this chapter, reference was made to Plato's challenge to Socrates. Plato asked Socrates how he could enquire about something he knew nothing about or, for that matter, about something he did know something about. Briefly, Plato repeated the Sophists' paradox, stating that to inquire about something one knows is unnecessary while to inquire about something one does not know is impossible (Hamilton & Cairns, 1961). For Plato, the solution to this apparent dilemma was to postulate a theory of innate knowledge, knowledge that could be accessed by asking the correct questions and, perhaps, by asking the right person. To this, the Sophists asked, does one learn what they already know, or do they learn what they do not yet know? Burks (1977) provided an excellent discussion of these dilemmas, ancient concerns that still challenge us today. For Burks, the solution to these dilemmas lay in the scientific approach to problem solving. Knowledge comes from enquiry, and proper enquiry is guided by questions. It is not possible, however, to ask some questions until others have been answered, often until many others have been answered. Burks sees scientific knowledge as highly complex, with a hierarchy of interconnecting parts. Scientific learning and enquiry proceed in successive approximations. With these considerations in mind, Burks' answer to the Sophists' paradoxes is that one learns what is already partially known.

In this chapter, we discussed and contrasted two types of logic, deductive and inductive. In the practice of science, the two are not simple to disentangle. The deductive allows for logically true or false statements, whereas the inductive leads to empirically true or false statements. However, deductive arguments also might be used to derive one empirical statement from another (Burks, 1977). According to Burks, science seeks truth through empirically true or false statements using observation and experiment, but it must also use reasoning and reflection. The body of knowledge generated by science is interconnected in its various parts by deductive as well as inductive arguments. Since inductive arguments lead to probability statements and not absolute truth, there is always an element of uncertainty in scientific conclusions (Burks, 1977; Pearl, 2000). The solution for science to this apparent dilemma is to follow sets of rules that allow for the best approximation of truth that can be achieved at a given time and based upon the then state of all else that is known about the problem. Three such rules that are particularly relevant here can be termed simplicity, probability criteria, and parsimony. With regard to the first of these concepts, the scientist attempts to ask the simplest question when making a scientific enquiry. Through addressing a series of simple questions, one can develop answers to more complex issues. The second rule reflects the recognition that scientific truth is not absolute. In any observation or experiment, or clinical evaluation for that matter, there may be unseen factors that have (causally) influenced the findings (Pearl, 2000), or the results might have occurred by chance. By defining a priori the probability level that will be considered to be significant, an operational definition has been made for what result will be considered to be more likely than not, i.e., significant. Non-scientists have often criticized the final consideration, parsimony, as being arbitrary since the simplest explanation for a finding might not be the 'true' explanation. History has shown, however, that this is the best way to advance knowledge. Sometimes referred to as 'Occam's razor', the principle directs one to rule out any theory (or explanation) for which a simpler explanation is equally consistent with the data (Pearl, 2000). The scientist accepts this principle as a basis for concluding the most likely objective truth at a given time and as a step in the direction of more advanced explanations.

Notes

1   Details of the history have been modified to preserve the anonymity of the patient and his family.
2   It is true that this statement reflects considerable philosophical debate among scholars (e.g., Pearl, 2000). Since the present work emphasizes a statistical and probabilistic approach to the topic, the chosen wording appears to be appropriate and practical. If the concept of causality is innate, it is still true that we are struggling with how to define and apply it to everyday problems. In this sense, if no other, the concept is still a human invention.

References

Albers, J. W., & Berent, S. (2000). Controversies in neurotoxicology: current status. *Neurologic Clinics, 18*, 741–764.

American Academy of Neurology (2001). Clinical diagnostic guidelines (available at: http://www.aan.con/professionals/practice/index.cfn).

Baker, D. B., & Benjamin, L. T., Jr (2000). The affirmation of the scientist-practitioner. A look back at Boulder. *American Psychologist, 55*, 241–247.

Berent, S. (1986). Psychopathology and other behavioral considerations for the clinical neuropsychologist. In S. Filskov and T. J. Boll (Eds.), *Handbook of clinical neuropsychology*, Vol. 2. New York: Wiley.

Berent, S., Albers, J. W., Garabrant, D. H., Giordani, B., Schweitzer, S., Garrison, R., Richardson, R., & Raz, J. (n.d.) *Historical exposure to chlorpyrifos and neurobehavioral outcome in a group of chemical workers.* Unpublished research report.

Burks, A. W. (1977). *Chance, cause, reason: An inquiry into the nature of scientific evidence.* Chicago: University of Chicago Press.

Conley, J. M. (2001). Law and contemporary problems: Forward. *Law and Contemporary Problems, 64*, 1–4.

Feldman, R. G. (1998). *Occupational and environmental neurotoxicology.* Philadelphia: Lippincott–Raven.

Festinger, L. (1957). *A theory of cognitive dissonance.* Stanford: Stanford University Press.

Festinger, L. (1962). Cognitive dissonance. *Scientific American, 207*, 93–98.

Flexner, A. (1960). *Medical education in the United States and Canada: A report to the Carnegie Foundation for the Advancement of Teaching.* Independent report.

Guyatt, G. H., Haynes, R. B., Jaeschke, R. Z., Cook, D. J., Green, L., Naylor, C. D., Wilson, M. C., & Richardson, W. S. (2000a). Users' Guides to the Medical Literature: XXV. Evidence-based medicine: principles for applying the Users' Guides to patient care. Evidence-Based Medicine Working Group. *Journal of the American Medical Association, 284*, 1290–1296.

Guyatt, G. H., Meade, M. O., Jaeschke, R. Z., Cook, D. J., & Haynes, R. B. (2000b). Practitioners of evidence based care. Not all clinicians need to appraise evidence from scratch but all need some skills. *British Medical Journal, 320*, 954–955.

Guyatt, G. H., & Rennie, D. (1993). Users' guides to the medical literature. *Journal American Medical Association, 270*, 2096–2097.

Hamilton, E. & Cairns, H. (1961). *The collected dialogues of Plato.* Princeton: Princeton University Press.

Lezak, M. D. (1995). *Neuropsychological assessment* (3rd ed.). New York: Oxford University Press.

Merriam-Webster, A. (1993). *Marriam-Webster's collegiate dictionary* (10th ed.). Springfield: G. & C. Merriam.

Newton, W. (2001). Rationalism and empiricism in modern medicine. *Law and Contemporary Problems, 64*, 299–316.

O'Barr, W. M. (2001). Culture and causality: non-Western systems of explanation. *Law and Contemporary Problems, 64*, 317–323.

Pearl, J. (2000). *Causality: Models, reasoning, and inference.* Cambridge: Cambridge University Press.

Richardson, W. S., Wilson, M. C., Williams, J. W., Jr., Moyer, V. A., & Naylor, C. D. (2000). Users' guides to the medical literature: XXIV. How to use an article on the clinical manifestations of disease. Evidence-Based Medicine Working Group. *Journal of the American Medical Association, 284*, 869–875.

Sanders, J., & Machal-Fulks, J. (2001). The admissibility of differential diagnosis testimony to prove causation in toxic tort cases: the interplay of adjective and substantive law. *Law and Contemporary Problems, 64,* 107–138.

Sherman, J. D. (1994). *Chemical exposure and disease: Diagnostic and investigative techniques.* Princeton: Princeton Scientific Publ.

Vander, B. T., Minoshima, S., Giordani, B., Foster, N. L., Frey, K. A., Berent, S., Albin, R. L., Koeppe, R. A., & Kuhl, D. E. (1997). Cerebral metabolic differences in Parkinson's and Alzheimer's diseases matched for dementia severity. *Journal of Nuclear Medicine, 38,* 797–802.

Postscript

We have tried to reflect in the various chapters in this volume the idea that the solutions to problems in neurobehavioral toxicology depend on a variety of factors. These factors include an understanding of the knowledge base relevant to the specialized problems addressed. Since this knowledge base is vast and often specialized within different disciplines, we have encouraged a multidisciplinary approach to the subject-matter. We focused on the two fields of Neurology and Neuropsychology to illustrate their complementary nature and underscored this by discussing clinical and clinical research principles common to both. Also, we identified the need for systematic and accurate collection and organization of data in both research and clinical practice, and emphasized the application of traditional methods to the specialized problems of toxicant-induced disorders. Importantly, the clinical approach in both disciplines occurs within an evidence-based approach to the process of developing a differential diagnosis and establishing a final diagnosis. Finally, we discussed the complex issues associated with establishing causality. While, as we indicated, clinical diagnoses and treatments are frequently concluded independently of establishing the cause of the particular disorder, there is often the need to identify or exclude a toxic etiology in the field of neurobehavioral toxicology. To accomplish these objectives, the field depends on the methods of science and the knowledge derived from scientific method. From a philosophical viewpoint, science may not provide certainty with respect to cause, but we conclude that the probability statements that result from these methods are the best available approximations to such truths.

Our intention here has been to describe the field of clinical neurobehavioral toxicology. We emphasized basic concepts and methods. These basic ideas can serve as a foundation for the presentation of specific behavioral and physiological phenomena, normal and disordered, that we view as relevant to this area of specialized professional practice.

The principles outlined in this volume are reflected in the case materials and discussions that follow in the next two volumes. Volume II focuses on the peripheral nervous system, while Volume III deals with disorders primarily involving the central nervous system. Specific case presentations have been chosen because they provide a particularly good illustration of one or more of the principles or dilemmas discussed in Volume I. In other instances, we have chosen a case based on an actual or suspected exposure to a particular toxicant because it represents a class of cases seen frequently in clinical practice. At other times, the choice is based on the rarity of the exposure and because its rarity makes it interesting. Since we emphasize through these examples the development of a complete differential diagnosis as critical to the clinical process, many cases will have an ultimate explanation not related to the exposure in question. Such is the nature of clinical neurobehavioral toxicology.

The emphasis in the following two volumes is on clinical application. As stated repeatedly, such application is based in science, but it is not in itself science. That is, clinical applications are ideally limited by the scientifically generated knowledge base that exists at any given time. The evidence-based clinician employs a systematic approach, inductive and deductive logic, and other principles we have discussed in reaching his or her conclusions in a given case and seeks to verify these conclusions with reference to a scientifically derived knowledge base. In practice, some of these elements may be implied and not immediately obvious. In addition, the limits set by the current level of knowledge may leave the clinician unable to address certain questions or to provide answers that are greater than possible in other cases. A basic rule that the authors attempt to follow in this work, and one that may be as important as any other advice we might offer, is never to go beyond the limits of available knowledge and methodologies in stating conclusions.

Index

Page numbers in *italic* indicate tables and figures.